# Communications in Computer and Information Science     1632

More information about this series at https://link.springer.com/bookseries/7899

Matthes Elstermann · Stefanie Betz ·
Matthias Lederer (Eds.)

# Subject-Oriented Business Process Management

## Dynamic Digital Design of Everything – Designing or Being Designed?

13th International Conference on Subject-Oriented Business
Process Management, S-BPM ONE 2022
Karlsruhe, Germany, June 29 – July 1, 2022
Proceedings

*Editors*
Matthes Elstermann
Karlsruhe Institute of Technology
Karlsruhe, Germany

Stefanie Betz
University of Applied Science
Furtwangen, Germany

Matthias Lederer
Technical University of Applied Sciences
Weiden, Germany

ISSN 1865-0929          ISSN 1865-0937 (electronic)
Communications in Computer and Information Science
ISBN 978-3-031-19703-1          ISBN 978-3-031-19704-8 (eBook)
https://doi.org/10.1007/978-3-031-19704-8

This Springer imprint is published by the registered company Springer Nature Switzerland AG
The registered company address is: Gewerbestrasse 11, 6330 Cham, Switzerland

# Preface

The 13th International S-BPM ONE Conference (S-BPM ONE 2022) was held at Karl-sruhe Institute of Technology from June 29 to July 1, 2022. After a pandemic-related break of two years, with one conference being held online, the conference was held in person under the main theme "Dynamic Digital Design of Everything – Shaping or Being Shaped?". We think, with this conference, we were able to resume the innovative thread of subject orientation as a method, modeling approach, path, and goal of innovation in process management.

The progressive and, above all, increasingly rapid digitalization of companies and societies poses fundamental questions about modelability and the use of technology. Business processes are central to this because they encapsulate the behavior of people and things (i.e., everything). So, they are key to the design of workflows and situations we experience in everyday life. Their representation(s) form the basis for the exchange, exploration, and ultimately the implementation of new developments or dynamic adaptations. Therefore, the conference posed the question of the value of digitalization and models with the overall theme "Dynamic Digital Design of Everything – Shaping or Being Shaped?".

The conference provided an open discussion forum for the fundamental issues of modeling of processes. Researchers and practitioners addressed innovative approaches on how organizations and societies can support their stakeholders to design processes and thus participate more in the value creation framed by digital technologies.

The call for papers covered the full spectrum of innovative process management topics from both the business and research worlds:

- (Everything-to-Everything) X2X communication
- X-value streams
- X-modeling, transformation, and execution
- Speculative X-design
- Internet of Everything
- Intelligent X process design
- X2X intelligence
- X design systems
- Continuous design integrating X
- Digital X twins
- Design is everything (You are in total control)
- Organizational design with X
- Sense-making through X design
- X design principles for Industry 4.0, smart cities, healthcare, smart logistics, and hyper automation CPS
- X's business
- Modelling dynamic X behavior
- Process change and transformation

- Autonomous digital workplace design
- Explainable and transparent process design
- Accountable process engineering
- Multi-/Interdisciplinary perspectives on process engineering
- Examples and cases of (subject-oriented-) BPM research and practice

All submitted 15 papers were reviewed by at least two members of the international Program Committee. As a result, after double-blind peer review, seven papers were accepted as research contributions in this conference volume (acceptance rate of 47%). Additionally four contributions were originally submitted or accepted as short paper contributions.

On another note, a successful conference is always based on the interaction of many contributors, whom we would like to thank at this point:

- All presenters and contributors of research reports, all of whom have advanced the knowledge of innovation in and with business processes.
- All reviewers, who have checked the academic quality of the contributions with their many hints increasing it further.
- All participants on site in Karlsruhe for the constructive discussions at a high scientific level.
- The two keynote speakers, who offered highly topical and exciting insights into the world of real subject orientation.
- All sponsors, who made a valuable contribution to S-BPM ONE with their financial support.
- And finally, all readers of this conference series, who strengthen the value of the discipline with their interest in questions of (subject-oriented) business process management.

Lastly, we would also like to thank the Karlsruhe Institute of Technology and the many helping hands who created a pleasant environment for the conference. Likewise, our thanks go to the Institute for Innovative Process Management, which provides the framework for the conference.

July 2022

Matthes Elstermann
Stefanie Betz
Matthias Lederer

# Organization

## General Chairs

Matthes Elstermann     Karlsruhe Institute of Technology, Germany
Stefanie Betz     University of Applied Science Furtwangen, Germany
Matthias Lederer     Technical University of Applied Sciences Amberg-Weiden, Germany

## Steering Committee

Albert Fleischmann     InterAktiv Unternehmensberatung, Germany
Werner Schmidt     Technische Hochschule Ingolstadt, Germany
Christian Stary     Johannes Kepler University, Linz, Austria

## Program Committee

Antunes, Pedro     Victoria University of Wellington, New Zealand
Becker, Jörg     Universität Münster, Germany
Betz, Stefanie     Hochschule Furtwangen, Germany
Dittmar, Anke     University of Rostock, Germany
Elstermann, Matthes     Karlsruhe Institute of Technology, Germany
Fischer, Herbert     TH Deggendorf, Germany
Fleischmann, Albert     InterAktiv Unternehmungsberatung, Germany
Gadatsch, Andreas     Hochschule Bonn-Rhein-Sieg, Germany
Helferich, Andreas     International School of Management, Germany
Hoppenbrouwers, Stijn     HAN University of Applied Sciences, Germany
Hvannberg, Ebba     University of Iceland, Iceland
Kannengiesser, Udo     Johannes Kepler University Linz, Austria
Koch, Stefan     Johannes Kepler University Linz, Austria
Komarov, Mikhail     HSE University, Russia
Kurz, Matthias     Germany
Lamersdorf, Winfried     University of Hamburg, Germany
Lederer, Matthias     Technische Hochschule Amberg-Weiden, Germany
Lawall, Alexander     IU Internationale Hochschule, Germany
Märtin, Christian     Hochschule Augsburg, Germany
Matzner, Martin     Universität Erlangen-Nürnberg, Germany

| Neubauer, Matthias | University of Applied Sciences Upper Austria, Austria |
| Oppl, Stefan | Danube University Krems, Austria |
| Proper, Henderik | Public Research Centre Henri Tudor, Luxembourg |
| Rossi, Gustavo | UNLP, Argentina |
| Schaller, Thomas | Hof University, Germany |
| Schieder, Christian | Technische Hochschule Amberg-Weiden, Germany |
| Schmidt, Werner | Technische Hochschule Ingolstadt, Germany |
| Singer, Robert | FH JOANNEUM, Austria |
| Stary, Chris | Johannes Kepler University Linz, Austria |
| Strecker, Florian | actnconnect, Germany |
| Turetken, Oktay | Eindhoven University of Technology, The Netherlands |
| Vidakis, Nikolas | TEI of Crete, Greece |
| Wachholder, Dominik | flink, Austria |
| Weichhart, Georg | Johannes Kepler University Linz, Austria |
| Winckler, Marco | Paul Sabatier University, France |
| Wirtz, Guido | University of Bamberg, Germany |
| Zehbold, Cornelia | Technische Hochschule Ingolstadt, Germany |
| Zemaitaitiene, Gintare | Mykolas Romeris University, Lithuania |

## Sponsoring Institutions and Individuals

**SEAL Systems AG**, Röttenbach, Germany
**InterAktiv Unternehmensberatung**, Wardenburg, Germany
**Hagen Buchwald**, Karlsruhe, Germany

# Contents

# Technology

# Privacy by Sharing Autonomy – A Design-Integrating Engineering Approach

Christian Stary⬡ and Richard Heininger(✉)⬡

Institute of Business Informatics, Johannes Kepler University Linz,
Altenberger Straße 69, 4040 Linz, Austria
{christian.stary,richard.heininger}@jku.at

**Abstract.** The more Cyber-Physical Systems (CPS) propagate to everyday life and business activities, the more privacy concerns move to the center of development and operation. Both require meeting individual privacy requirements and thus, privacy protection that can be customized. We introduce a synchronized Digital Twin (DT) approach suggesting that sharing autonomy of heterogeneous and dynamically evolving system components helps to increase transparency and ultimately user control of privacy concerns. The proposed architecture is based on behavior models for integrated design and engineering of CPS. The executable and federated nature of the DT approach enables a user-centered system validation of privacy management capabilities, both for organizations, and individuals. The resulting reduction of complexity is exemplified for an Internet-of-Things-based application in the logistics domain. We explore some implications of the presented approach for future research, practice, and development.

**Keywords:** Shared autonomy · Cyber-Physical Systems · Digital Twin · System-of-Systems · Subject orientation

## 1 Introduction

Cyber-Physical Systems (CPS) increasingly propagate to various industrial and private sectors, including energy, transportation, construction, production, and healthcare. The physical parts are often based on Internet-of-Things (IoT) components, whereas the digital parts provide computational algorithms to implement intelligent systems. CPS are engineered in a way that they seamlessly integrate physical and digital components, integrating sensing, computation, control and networking into physical objects and infrastructure, connecting them to the Internet and to each other [28]. The integration task increases the development and operational complexity, as typical examples reveal, such as smart home applications with sensor components that can be controlled remotely by mobile devices.

© The Author(s), under exclusive license to Springer Nature Switzerland AG 2022
M. Elstermann et al. (Eds.): S-BPM ONE 2022, CCIS 1632, pp. 3–22, 2022.
https://doi.org/10.1007/978-3-031-19704-8_1

Once information affecting privacy is accessed or processed concerning either individuals or organizations, privacy management issues pop up. They include the collection of personal data and the protection of intellectual property. In particular, the granularity and diversity of sensors of CPS could compromise privacy [16]. Endangering privacy is connected with loss of control, which persons or technologies have access in which way and how [29] (cf. the management of cookies with respect to web applications). Although privacy attacks are mostly passive, stakeholders need to control the access to privacy-relevant data. In the context of this work stakeholders are all private or organization-relevant users that require transparent collection, storage, processing, and distribution of data concerning privacy. Even when requirements can be met automatically, e.g., through rule-based systems, their implementation requires user control, such as for cookie use.

Privacy as an expression of the rights of self-determination and human dignity is considered a core value in democratic societies and is recognized either explicitly or implicitly as a fundamental human right by most constitutions of democratic societies [10,31]. Most important, security and privacy management capabilities influence in how far users trust digital systems [24], and finally, keep them 'in-the-loop' [25]. Moreover, organizations increasingly protect their intangible assets through governance schemes for reasons of intellectual property and privacy [32].

Research and development in the field of privacy management technologies have been motivated by the vision to provide technical means allowing individuals to retain control over their personal spheres [15]. Facing increasing development dynamics and unprecedented breaches of acceptable ethical conduct by organizations and individuals, human-centered privacy management suggests that the sharing of data facilitates taking care of sensitive stakeholder information and its exchange (cf. [9]). Consequently, the research question addressed in this paper is: How can privacy requirements of individual stakeholders or organizations be met in a human-centric way?

We propose to consider CPS as networks of autonomous nodes that can share their autonomy to handle cross-cutting concerns, such as privacy management - forming a federated system (cf. [11,20,40]). Our notion of sharing is grounded in the emerging concept of shared autonomy [34]. Stemming from the field of human-robot interaction, in the context of this work it denotes interactive stakeholder design and control processes for privacy management. This research aims to reach the goals individuals or organizations pursue to protect their privacy. With shared autonomy, external influence factors, such as the General Data Protection Regulation (https://gdpr.eu), can be integrated with personal and/ or organization-specific privacy needs in a transparent and customized form. It is specified by mutual interactions and data exchanges between humans and digital systems (cf. [17]).

Research examining human-centered customization of CPS with respect to privacy concerns including a technological or organizational perspective is relatively rare [8,23,37]. To the current knowledge no research to date has examined shared autonomy facilitating CPS privacy management. This research aims to fill this gap by examining shared autonomy concepts for privacy management. It aims to empower stakeholders when (i) they express privacy concerns in terms of CPS requirements, and (ii) they meet these requirements by specifying the respective operational CPS behavior. Given these objectives, the paper extends the current understanding of shared autonomy by using it as concept for structuring user-centric privacy management. Its focus is deploying a model-based representation scheme and architecture to inform privacy management practice through intelligible implementation.

In the following we introduce the user-centered development and adaptation scheme and architecture to demonstrate how sharing autonomy can work for human-centric privacy management. The federated system approach is based on behavior specifications representing a Digital Twin (DT) model of a CPS, as each physical CPS component and its relations are also captured in digital form. Thereby, subject-oriented modeling supports the integration of design with engineering activities, since it allows for automated execution of behavior models. We detail how the validation of run time behavior of the DT model facilitates privacy management, given transparent sharing of autonomy of concerned CPS components.

Our work is structured as follows: Sect. 2 contains related work on shared autonomy and privacy management in the context of CPS development and operation, acknowledging its origin and major application domain. It also provides details on the methodological approach taken to meet the objectives of the paper. Section 3 introduces the behavior-centered integrated design and engineering approach to generate and operate DT models. Section 4 provides an exemplary case on privacy management for adaptable IoT-container-based transportation. It demonstrates user-centered privacy requirements specification and implementation support. Section 5 concludes the paper recapturing the objectives and achievements of the work and providing an outlook of further research.

## 2   Related Work

In this section related work is reviewed to provide relevant inputs to sharing autonomy for privacy protection when humans are kept 'in-the-loop'. Both, findings from shared autonomy, and privacy management are detailed. The final consolidation section refers to user control, transparent development, and required capabilities of autonomous components. According to the applied Design Science methodology (cf. [33]), requirements have been derived from existing work for triggering design cycles towards sharing autonomy for human-centered privacy management.

### 2.1   Shared Autonomy

The concept of shared autonomy has been introduced and elaborated in the context of human-robot interaction. Thereby, shared autonomy has its focus on interaction patterns and the way these can be adapted. Latest research addressed higher level tasks comprising low level or immediate activities as well as collaboration between groups and robots [34]. Driven by complex planning and multiple agent interaction, run time adaptation has moved to the center of research interest. Thereby, each component is assigned to a certain task. Control with respect to autonomy is considered on different levels of abstraction - see Fig. 1. Sharing autonomy is driven either by establishing common ground, transparency and shared beliefs, or aligning goals and communication to build trust. Each of these issues can require to adjust the degree of mutually recognized autonomy.

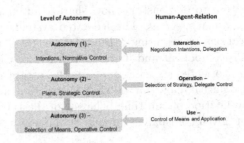

**Fig. 1.** Autonomy layers according to [35]

The different layers of autonomy on the left side of Fig. 1 concern decision making from several intertwined perspectives and levels of abstraction [35]. Shared autonomy denotes the capability to analyze and design corresponding types of interaction patterns between human users and/or system elements (see right side of the figure).

According to this framework, the bottom level deals with selecting means to achieve goals that can be reached without further processing and thus, decision making. The intermediate level enables implementing strategies that can meet more abstract or composed goals. Consequently, the top level relates to intentional actions requiring more complex decision making and implementation effort - higher-level activities depend on lower action levels.

As reported in [34] the layered framework has been applied on how cooperation can be organized between multiple agents in a collaborative assembly process. On a high level, activities have been put into a sequence through sharing autonomy while generating proposals for actions through incremental reinforcement learning. They can be selected depending on information about user capabilities and the current operational context (background knowledge). The intermediate level could be tested for aligning individual plans and planning processes of autonomous agents and human users. Thereby, human expert knowledge has to be used for adjustments. The corresponding abstraction so far concerned details about robot behavior, such as collision avoidance. Hence, autonomy was shared with respect to routes that could be taken rather than how a route needs to be handled by the robot.

Ajmera et al. [2] balanced the task load between a robot and a human user by implementing shared autonomy through a web interface. Shared autonomy has been tested by selecting work-relevant information to be presented to users, and by integrating user inputs with the autonomous capabilities of the robot in order to increase the overall performance of the robot. Abstracting from robot activities helped reducing the cognitive user workload. The user got presented only performance-relevant information on the web interface. The setting has been extended to group settings, employing human-robot mutual adaptation to increase the effectiveness of team collaboration.

From these findings it can be concluded that sharing of autonomy (i) can be applied to networked system architectures, and (ii) affect different levels of development and operation, allowing for human control of task allocation and adaptations supported by abstract representations.

## 2.2   Privacy Management and CPS

For privacy management Privacy-Enhancing Technologies (PETs) have been introduced, in particular to establish and enforce privacy principles [5]. Targeting privacy protection, PETs focus on data objects containing personal data of individuals rather than on behavior models and business logic. Privacy enhancing mechanisms feature anonymity, pseudonymity, and unobservability with respect to users, their identity, and the affected data subjects [6]. Hence, they can be used for privacy protection mechanisms of CPS. Since neither cyber- nor physical-privacy concepts alone can protect CPS - crossover effects can introduce unexpected vulnerabilities - security and privacy have become key concerns for CPS design, development, and operation [38].

Privacy considered as primary security requirement in CPS has led to intense research on privacy preservation, however, in a domain-specific way [1]. A first generic attempt has led to an integrative framework consisting of separate privacy protection mechanisms on different levels of a CPS architecture. It targets different kinds of privacy, referring to content, location, identity, date, time and the like [1]. Structural alignment enables coordinating these items and control of privacy constraints, to ensure CPS robustness albeit non-linear system behavior [7].

Barhamgi et al. [4] have put user privacy to the center of design when developing smart CPS. Privacy requirements are collected using CPS management features. Effective privacy protection for users is achieved by data sharing. Privacy risks are reflected with user potential benefits. User support includes decision making for effective privacy management. Several key challenges turned out, among them meaningful data degradation strategies, pricing strategies, and contextual modeling.

The first challenge concerns the variety of generated data that require different forms of degradation, such as anonymization. The second challenge addresses pricing for privacy-sensitive data which might require different forms of benefits, such as financial or social ones, as well as user assistance to help users assessing the sensitivity of data concerning their privacy.

The third challenge concerns capturing the CPS context and respective monitoring of CPS behavior to trigger decision making on privacy issues. Modeling is required for representing and controlling behavior, in particular when context changes and behavior needs to be adapted. Thereby, several constellations of system components may evolve over time [17]. When identifying and representing relevant events, complex event processing techniques and systems can be used to track behavior and to structure decision making [4].

In summary, privacy management (i) addresses several cross-cutting concerns of CPS development and operation, such as identity management of networked actors; it (ii) has been investigated with respect to fundamental design issues that require dedicated engineering activities, such as contextual modeling for user interventions, and finally, (iii) a variety of mechanism to protect privacy has been developed and tested in the field.

### 2.3  Structuring the Findings

In Table 1, we structure the findings of the analyzed related work with respect to contributions to the privacy management approach. The table header contains the fields we have addressed in each of the subsections. We analyze the contributions of each field with respect to human-centeredness, transparency and addressed development capabilities for adapting CPS according to privacy needs. Although it becomes evident from the entries that each field represents a certain perspective on privacy management, several commonalities can be identified. They are related to layers of abstraction, and context representation.

Layering enables different levels of abstraction which helps not only to differentiate various flavors and categories of privacy but also structuring assignments of functionality to achieve privacy objectives. It has to be complemented with privacy requirements specification features. Controlling their implementation requires context models. These models have to capture data object and behavior to be validated and adopted to privacy needs.

## 3  Sharing Autonomy for CPS Privacy Protection

In this section we detail privacy management by sharing autonomy starting with the Digital Twin (DT) representation of CPS for contextual modeling. We proceed with the federated system architecture, and provide basics on the modeling notation enabling executable CPS models to validate the implementation of privacy requirements.

### 3.1  Digital CPS Representation

Digital Twins (DT) models enable representing CPS. Figure 2 shows sample candidates for DT representations. The grey copies of the CPS (component) symbols for CPS represent the DTs, and thus the networked CPS architecture

**Table 1.** Contributions from existing work cited in the previous subsections relevant for privacy customization

| Domain target | Shared autonomy | CPS privacy management | Privacy enhancement techniques & technologies |
|---|---|---|---|
| Human Centeredness | Layered abstraction enabling task (load) visibility<br>Expertise for planning adjustment | (Domain-specific) privacy requirement collection<br>Decision support for risk assessment<br>Data degradation<br>Sensitivity assessment | Privacy principles and their enforcement<br>Informed consent on use of personal data |
| Transparency | System tasks presented to users for decision support | Different types of privacy<br>Structural alignment of data<br>Tracing of requirements implementation | Features to prohibit collecting personal data and their exchange<br>Feature for making personal data not visible |
| Development and Operation Capabilities | Interactive control of means & applications<br>Abstraction of tasks<br>Collaboration support<br>Analysis & design of interaction patterns<br>Runtime adaptation | Structural alignment of different types of privacy<br>Contextual behavior modeling and tracking including data sharing<br>Privacy assessment method implementation | Data object analysis<br>Data minimization<br>Information hiding |

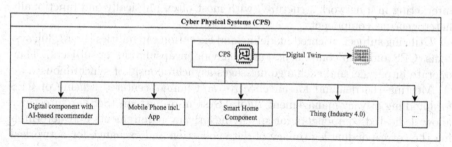

**Fig. 2.** Digital twin representation of CPS

(see Fig. 3). In this figure the right part shows the conceptual mappings to the proposed integrated design and engineering explained in Sect. 3.2.

When considering a CPS as a set of networked nodes representing physical or digital components, or a combination of both, each node can be represented as a system through a model of its behavior. The System-of-Systems (SoS) perspective helps to implement dedicated features on the set of nodes, such as privacy

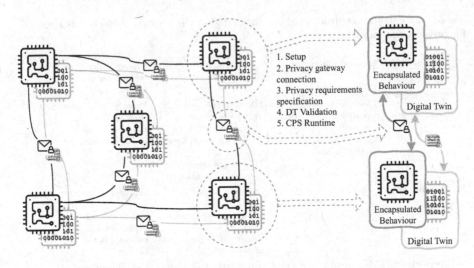

**Fig. 3.** Digital twins as digital behavior model of CPS (components)

management [19] - see the interactive access point for privacy management in Fig. 4. SoS have as essential properties, namely 'autonomy, coherence, permanence, and organization' [19, p. 1] and are constituted 'by many components interacting in a network structure', with most often physically and functionally heterogeneous components.

Utilizing subject-oriented modeling and execution capabilities [12, 13, 30], systems (CPS and their components) are behavior encapsulation (or subjects). They operate in parallel and exchange messages asynchronously or synchronously.

Meeting the demand for an effective and human-centered scheme of CPS for handling privacy management, digital System-of-Systems (SoS) architectures allow dedicated components for specifying privacy requirements and determining the corresponding legitimacy of data collection and exchange for networked resources from any device and component at any time.

Human-centered adaptable privacy management requires a stakeholder to connect to a dedicated node - see also network node 'Privacy Gateway' marked in red in Fig. 4. The privacy gateway is the primary CPS component for privacy management. All affected sensor or digital components need to connect to the privacy gateway, which ensures they can be managed with respect to privacy needs.

In principle, the privacy gateway not only provides access to other CPS components, it also lets them communicate with each other. Since each component may use different (connectivity) technology, some abstract representation helps addressing various aspects of privacy, e.g., securing intellectual property in (service) production, and ensuring anonymity of users when requesting specific services or performing specific quality checks.

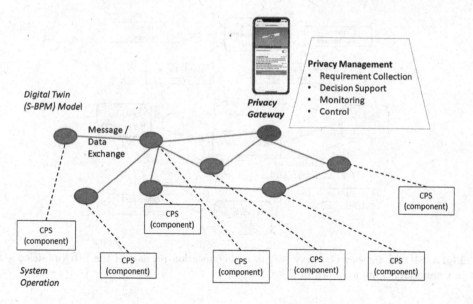

**Fig. 4.** SoS for privacy management

Privacy concerns are checked and requirements are implemented in behavior models (i.e. Digital Twin (DT) models) representing services connecting CPS components and exchanging messages. The latter carry data in business objects, thus allowing transparency with respect to internal data collection and processing, and interfaces to other components in terms of receiving and transmitting data.

According to the SoS perspective, CPS operate as autonomous, concurrent behaviors of distributed components. These components or subjects are behavioral roles assumed by some entity that is capable of performing actions. The entity can be a human, a piece of software, a machine (e.g., a robot), a device (e.g., a sensor), or a combination of these, such as intelligent sensor systems.

For the specification of the DT models two types of diagrams conjointly represent a CPS: Subject Interaction Diagrams (SIDs) and Subject Behavior Diagrams (SBDs). SIDs provide an integrated view of all components or CPS subjects involved in privacy management and the messages/data objects they exchange (see also Fig. 5). SBDs for each subject of an SID detail the behavior in terms of sequences of states representing component-specific actions, including sending and receiving messages/data objects.

Once the components and services have been captured by an SID and detailed by SBDs, business objects can be specified [41]. They structure the data that are exchanged between the subjects (CPS components or services). Consequently, only those data need to be specified that are either are processed internally by a subject (as specified in an SBD), or shared with another subject (as specified by the SID of representing the DT of a CPS).

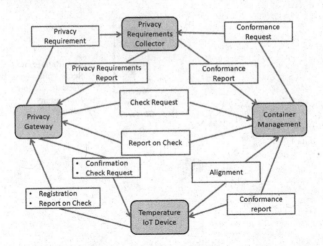

**Fig. 5.** SID for Privacy Gateway (Setup and connection); a part of the SBD modeled in Compunity Suite is shown in Fig. 6

Subject-oriented DTs can be validated interactively, and executed without further model transformation. Keeping humans in the loop, stakeholders can specify and implement by design, as well as adapt CPS behavior by re-design, replacing behavior specifications during runtime. Subject-oriented run-time engines, such as the Compunity Suite (https://compunity.eu) or Ueber-Flow using the Akka framework (http://akka.io) [22], or the Metasonic Suite (https://www.metasonic.de/en) execute actions or tasks in the sequence as defined through SBDs and SIDs. Digital Twin models representing CPS nodes are connected to their physical counterparts in the course of implementation to finally operate a CPS. Since the subject-oriented runtime support enables to synchronize the twin interaction, privacy management activities become effective once being captured by the DT model.

## 3.2   Design-Integrating Engineering of Privacy Concerns

In the following we introduce the management of the digital representation scheme to set up a CPS architecture that can handle privacy concerns. Since CPS components are capable of either human-to-machine or machine-to-machine communication, once they get access to the Internet, accessible data can be privacy-relevant information. So, it is essential to construct an authorization scheme for both machines and human users to secure these data from any privacy-corrupting access. In order to avoid unintended disclosure of privacy-sensitive data and misuse, an appropriate logic for sharing autonomy must be defined at an abstract level (cf. [14,39]) at design time for each CPS component that is to be controlled by users.

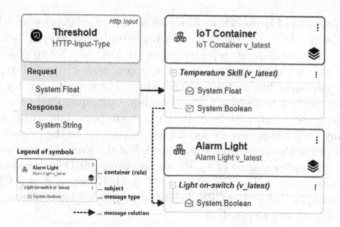

**Fig. 6.** SID in Compunity Suite; two containers, each with a subject and a message relation between them; additionally an external HTTP input

The proposed adaptable privacy management approach utilizes the previously presented behavior modeling and process execution technology. It is designed to check the implementation of privacy requirements prior to operation. It is structured in a DT representation according to several phases: setup, privacy gateway connection, privacy requirements specification, DT validation, and CPS runtime.

**Setup:** The configurator/administrator of the CPS generates a digital behavior model (DT): Each concerned service and CPS component including physical (Internet-of-Things) devices is represented by a behavior model (Subject Behavior Diagram SBD). In this way (i) the messages including the data that can be processed by the component, (ii) the functions (actions) it can perform, and (iii) the messages it sends, thus, the data it shares with other components or services, are specified. The control flow is also encapsulated in the SBD.

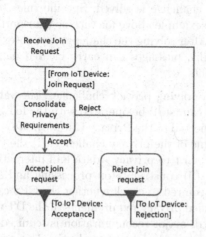

**Fig. 7.** Consolidation during setup

**Privacy Gateway Connection:** Since each concerned service or CPS component (including IoT devices) is in principle capable to receive, process, and send privacy-relevant data, as represented by its SBD (see Setup phase above), it needs to be connected to the 'caretaker' component of the DT representation. This component has a clearing function with respect to privacy and acts as a gateway to privacy-conform CPS operation. Correspondingly, we termed it privacy management gateway. In order to perform according to its functional behavior, any CPS component or service has to connect to the privacy gateway to check for privacy requirements compliance. For the sake of uniformity and to execute the DT representation of a CPS we also use an SBD for the specification of the gateway (part of the SBD shown in Fig. 7). However, it is a CPS node, as it represents the SoS of the CPS dedicated to privacy management (see also node *Privacy Gateway* in Fig. 4).

**Privacy Requirements Specification:** In order to check whether privacy requirements are met when operating a CPS, privacy-relevant data need to be identified. Privacy requirements can either stem from the environment representing the context of a CPS, or set up by the stakeholders running the CPS. An example for the first case is organizationally binding privacy regulations stemming from authorities or (inter)national bodies, as it is the case of GDPR (https://gdpr.eu). An example for the latter is restricting access to address information for sensitive deliveries in an IoT-based supply chain, as specific stakeholders need to make this information available only for others in a certain context, such as it is done in vaccine logistics ordered by governments, ensuring privacy in public interest.

Privacy requirements can be captured through push or pull from other CPS components and services. Each component or service either sends a message for clearance of privacy-related data to the privacy management gateway, or privacy-relevant items are collected interactively from the privacy management role taker (stakeholder). If the privacy management gateway authorizes the utilization of that data, the privacy challenge is solved. Specific rules (e.g., stemming from GDPR) may apply (see example above for vaccine transportation) and provide a specific context of use. After solving the challenge for contextual and component-related items successfully, messages can carry cleared data along interactions between CPS components.

**DT Validation:** After solving privacy challenges, the validation can start to check whether the CPS can (still) be operated with the IoT devices, CPS components, and services connected to the Privacy Gateway. We consider several cases, according to the outcome of the privacy challenge: (i) the CPS can be operated without any constraint w.r.t to privacy - data and interactions are not relevant for preserving privacy; (ii) constraints on processing and sharing data apply - DT re-specification is required to check whether the CPS can be operated when implementing the specified privacy requirements in the DT representation. If the CPS cannot be operated, major reconfiguration is required, affecting the entire architecture. Thereby, currently known mechanisms to protect privacy [26, 36] can be applied. However, since the CPS has not been operated in real time so far due to the model checking throughout validation, no harm has occurred and no further technological effort has to be spent.

**CPS Runtime:** It denotes the operation of the CPS, once privacy requirements have been implemented successfully (see phases described above). However, due to highly dynamic nature of CPS, adaptation on-the-fly must be enabled. During runtime (based on executable behavior models of the DT), additional IoT devices and services can send a registration message to the Privacy Gateway to check in, get challenged with respect to privacy requirements and in this way share their autonomy through the privacy management gateway. Once the evaluation is complete, the CPS operation can either continue or some reconfiguration has to start.

According to the concept and aforementioned phases privacy management concerns data processed within a subject (in-depth) which requires export of meta-data to identify privacy-relevant actions. Privacy management also concerns interactions when referring to messages or data received and exchanged with other subjects. They are exemplified in the following use case.

# 4   Transportation Use Case

Most recently, smart transportation has become a research topic. For instance, Mohanty [27] consider intelligent CPS making transportation smart when meeting the need of high urban population density in terms of services, such as traffic management and ridesharing. Most of them also have become an issue in the course of Covid-19 restrictions [18, 21].

For transparent and traceable CPS development in transportation, a structured approach has been proposed by Karthik et al. [21]. It comprises a data layer dealing with data streams, a batch layer for storing and processing massive amounts of data, analysis layer to perform analytics, and a service layer to specify various services for implementing requirements. These layers are expected to handle the variety of CPS data stemming from real-time developments, autonomous behavior of communication, and inter-component information exchange including real-item decision making.

These functionalities can also be arranged in a choreographic setting utilizing the behavior-centered subject-oriented representation scheme [17, 40]. Transportation applications need to take into account IoT components and logistic services, which both need to be adaptable on-the-fly in case of changing operational conditions, such as change of modality.

In our current case study, we target vaccine transportation in intelligent container boxes. They are enriched with IoT elements, such as a temperature sensor and actuator, allowing to adapt ongoing transportation operation to changing conditions. The operation requires the provision of details on the vaccine and conditions that are accessible for selected stakeholder groups. For instance, the current temperature data of the vaccine is only accessible to the vaccine producer and currently operating transportation provider.

We develop an autonomy-sharing DT solution for a transportation provider for packaging and temperature-controlled thermal shippers. They need to maintain a storage condition of $-70°C$ for the transported good (i.e., vaccines). Each container box contains GPS-enabled IoT heat sensors combined with location tracking to prevent disruptions during operation.

Privacy requirements exist with respect to the type, amount, and condition of vaccine that needs to be delivered to a vaccine center. In addition, the location of the vaccine center needs to be kept private between sender and receiver of the vaccine due to shielding the transport from the public. In the following we exemplify the use of the developed adaptable privacy management scheme according to the phases described in Sect. 3, utilizing the subject-oriented SoS representation scheme for the autonomy-sharing DT.

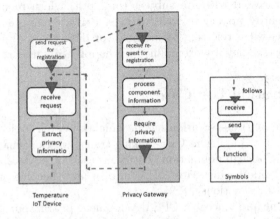

**Fig. 8.** SBD for Privacy Gateway

**Setup:** The digital behavior model (DT) of the CPS comprises the CPS components. It includes the IoT devices as well as the dedicated privacy management services in grey shapes and their exchange of data (rectangles along the edges between the components and services). Figure 8 exemplifies a relevant part of the use case by an SID. The fundamental SoS is the Privacy Gateway that is connected to all other CPS components or services. The Privacy Requirements Collector supplements the gateway and is also a consolidator to automatically check whether certain requirements have already been checked in, so that privacy constraints can be handled in a consistent way (see Fig. 5 for the respective SBD part). The Container Management handles the vaccine containers and is connected with all IoT components required for vaccine transportation. In the figure, the most important one is included, namely the Temperature IoT Device. Another important one is the location tracker (not part of the figure).

**Privacy Gateway Connection:** The Privacy Gateway coordinates privacy management activities, and manages the sharing of autonomy of CPS components. It enables (interactive) access for stakeholder groups as well as the CPS components and services when joining the CPS (see also Fig. 5). When privacy requirements have to be met, it triggers the (re-)specification of behavior of a CPS component or service, represented by a Subject Behavior Diagram. It is supported by the Privacy Requirements Collector consolidating not only the reported meta data of each application component, such as the Container Management, but also external regulations, such as GDPR requirements. It sets up and maintains a catalog of privacy relevant data and their relations.

**Privacy Requirements.** Specification: Privacy-relevant data are identified for vaccine container management and processed by the gateway. Each relevant item is checked and needs to be cleared for further processing. In terms of choreographic DT, each component sends a clearance challenge of privacy-related data to the privacy management gateway, and may require interactive decisions from a stakeholder affecting the autonomy of involved components, in the sample case the vaccine transport organizer.

Figure 9 shows a macro representing a pattern that can be used for first-time implementation of privacy requirements and during operation when privacy requirements change and the autonomy of CPS components and thus, their behavior needs to be adapted.

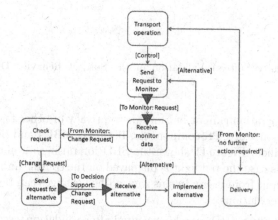

**Fig. 9.** Adaptation pattern (SBD) for monitoring

**DT Validation:** Once a certain item is blocked due to privacy concerns, a validation flag is raised. It has to be checked whether the CPS can still achieve the original objectives. For instance, it needs to be specified what data about the temperature need to be revealed to which stakeholder when running the CPS-based transportation process. As long as the temperature remains within certain tolerance, the authorities do not have to be informed about these deviations - the vaccine can be delivered as planned.

Figure 10 exemplifies a validation part when running the specified transportation behavior on the actor-based suite Compunity (http://compunity.eu).

It reveals that in case the temperature is below a certain threshold an alarm is set and becomes visible. However, error transitions have not been set so far. It is exactly the same mechanism that can be used for privacy protection. An alarm event needs to be raised in case of violating a privacy requirement and a proper action needs to be taken, e.g., stopping further execution of privacy-relevant data. Given this type of architecture, behavior models representing the accomplishment of functional tasks, such as controlling the temperature along a logistic chain, can be used to share autonomy when implementing privacy requirements.

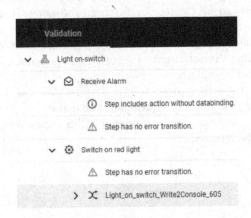

**Fig. 10.** (Compunity Suite's) Validation of the Subject Behavior Diagram (SBD) shown in Fig. 11

In case, an operation cannot be run due to privacy or other restrictions, and affects the autonomy of CPS components, both, the SBDs and SID of the DT have to be modified. Figure 11 shows the SBD for raising an alarm in case of violations. In this case red light is displayed on the console and the system is waiting for an input from users. In this way, ad-hoc changes can be implemented through user interventions.

**CPS Runtime:** Since SBDs can be executed after validation - see Fig. 10 - any DT can be run as specified and adapted dynamically as long as the interactions, i.e., the exchange of messages or data, between CPS components are not affected. Hence, the benefit of an encapsulated behavior specification for DTs lies in the opportunity to adapt CPS component or actor behavior during runtime as long as the interaction to other components or actors does not have to be changed. This capability means that modifying privacy requirements, and thus the sharing of autonomy can be put to operation dynamically. However, changes may not only affect internal behavior, but also the data that are passed on to other CPS components. These cases require checking the compatibility with the behavior of the affected components, in particular to process them for privacy protection. The SID representing the CPS, i.e. the overall system architecture might have to be adapted accordingly.

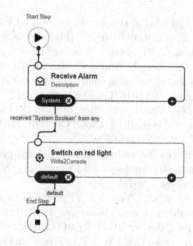

**Fig. 11.** SBD in Compunity Suite

## 5   Conclusion

Privacy management of CPS based on sharing autonomy is an adaption approach based on human-centered customization of Digital Twin representations. Each component shares autonomy by making transparent privacy-relevant data through message exchange with other components, and allowing a dedicated component to decide whether restrictions on exchange and internal processing apply. Enablers of the federated system architecture is a behavior-centered specification scheme. It integrates design and engineering of CPS, as the DT model can be automatically processed for validation and dynamic adaptation of autonomy sharing. By handling the DT, users remain in control throughout development.

The approach scales due to its openness for CPS components and choreographic nature. Future work will include industrial or smart factory applications. It also needs to consider additional phases, in particular the connection for status of work for each physical device, critical component identification, and optimization (cf. [3]). Sharing autonomy for this purpose will affect the interaction patterns to be handled by the designated management component as well as the business logic for each CPS component.

## References

1. Agarwal, R., Hussain, M.: Generic framework for privacy preservation in cyber-physical systems. In: Panigrahi, C.R., Pati, B., Mohapatra, P., Buyya, R., Li, K.-C. (eds.) Progress in Advanced Computing and Intelligent Engineering. AISC, vol. 1198, pp. 257–266. Springer, Singapore (2021). https://doi.org/10.1007/978-981-15-6584-7_25

2. Ajmera, Y., Javed, A.: Shared autonomy in web-based human robot interaction. In: Arai, K., Kapoor, S., Bhatia, R. (eds.) IntelliSys 2020. AISC, vol. 1252, pp. 696–702. Springer, Cham (2021). https://doi.org/10.1007/978-3-030-55190-2_55

3. Bagheri, B., Rezapoor, M., Lee, J.: A unified data security framework for federated prognostics and health management in smart manufacturing. Manuf. Lett. **24**, 136–139 (2020). https://doi.org/10.1016/j.mfglet.2020.04.011

4. Barhamgi, M., Perera, C., Ghedira, C., Benslimane, D.: User-centric privacy engineering for the internet of things. IEEE Cloud Comput. **5**(5), 47–57 (2018). https://doi.org/10.1109/MCC.2018.053711666

5. Burkert, H.: Privacy-enhancing technologies: typology, critique, vision. In: Agre, P.E., Rotenberg, M. (eds.) Technology and Privacy: The New Landscape, pp. 125–142. MIT Press, Cambridge (1997)

6. Cha, S.C., Hsu, T.Y., Xiang, Y., Yeh, K.H.: Privacy enhancing technologies in the internet of things: perspectives and challenges. IEEE Internet of Things J. **6**(2), 2159–2187 (2019). https://doi.org/10.1109/JIOT.2018.2878658

7. Chen, J., Gupta, V., Quevedo, D.E., Tesi, P.: Privacy and security of cyberphysical systems. Int. J. Robust Nonlinear Control **30**(11), 4165–4167 (2020). https://doi.org/10.1002/rnc.5051

8. Damjanovic-Behrendt, V.: A digital twin-based privacy enhancement mechanism for the automotive industry. In: Jardim-Gonçalves, R., Mendonça, J.P., Jotsov, V., Marques, M., Martins, J., Bierwolf, R. (eds.) 2018 International Conference on Intelligent Systems (IS), Funchal, Portugal, pp. 272–279. IEEE (2018). https://doi.org/10.1109/IS.2018.8710526

9. Elahi, H., Castiglione, A., Wang, G., Geman, O.: A human-centered artificial intelligence approach for privacy protection of elderly App users in smart cities. Neurocomputing **444**, 189–202 (2021). https://doi.org/10.1016/j.neucom.2020.06.149

10. Fischer-Hübner, S.: Privacy-enhancing technologies. In: Liu, L., Özsu, M.T. (eds.) Encyclopedia of Database Systems, pp. 2142–2147. Springer, Boston (2009). https://doi.org/10.1007/978-0-387-39940-9_271

11. Fleischmann, A., Schmidt, W., Stary, C.: Subject-oriented development of federated systems - a methodological approach. In: Rabiser, R., Torkar, R. (eds.) 2014 40th EUROMICRO Conference on Software Engineering and Advanced Applications, Verona, Italy, pp. 199–206. IEEE (2014). https://doi.org/10.1109/SEAA.2014.24

12. Fleischmann, A., Schmidt, W., Stary, C. (eds.): S-BPM in the Wild. Springer, Cham (2015). https://doi.org/10.1007/978-3-319-17542-3

13. Fleischmann, A., Schmidt, W., Stary, C., Obermeier, S., Börger, E.: Subject-Oriented Business Process Management. Springer, Heidelberg (2012). https://doi.org/10.1007/978-3-642-32392-8

14. Friedow, C., Völker, M., Hewelt, M.: Integrating IoT devices into business processes. In: Matulevičius, R., Dijkman, R. (eds.) CAiSE 2018. LNBIP, vol. 316, pp. 265–277. Springer, Cham (2018). https://doi.org/10.1007/978-3-319-92898-2_22

15. Gao, F., Zhu, L., Shen, M., Sharif, K., Wan, Z., Ren, K.: A blockchain-based privacy-preserving payment mechanism for vehicle-to-grid networks. IEEE Netw. **32**(6), 184–192 (2018). https://doi.org/10.1109/MNET.2018.1700269

16. Giraldo, J., Sarkar, E., Cardenas, A.A., Maniatakos, M., Kantarcioglu, M.: Security and privacy in cyber-physical systems: a survey of surveys. IEEE Des. Test **34**(4), 7–17 (2017). https://doi.org/10.1109/MDAT.2017.2709310

17. Heininger, R., Stary, C.: Capturing autonomy in its multiple facets: a digital twin approach. In: Proceedings of the 2021 ACM Workshop on Secure and Trustworthy Cyber-Physical Systems, pp. 3–12. ACM, New York (2021). https://doi.org/10.1145/3445969.3450422

18. IATA: IATA - Vaccine Transportation. https://www.iata.org/en/programs/cargo/pharma/vaccine-transport/

19. Jamshidi, M. (ed.): System of Systems Engineering. Wiley Series in Systems Engineering and Management, vol. 58. Wiley, Hoboken (2008). https://doi.org/10.1002/9780470403501

20. Jost, T.E., Stary, C.: A single point of contact for privacy management in cyber-physical systems. In: Elstermann, M., et al. (eds.) S-BPM ONE 2022. CCIS, pp. xx–yy. Springer, Cham (2022)

21. Karthik, K., et al.: Biosafety concerns during the collection, transportation, and processing of COVID-19 samples for diagnosis. Arch. Med. Res. **51**(7), 623–630 (2020). https://doi.org/10.1016/j.arcmed.2020.08.007

22. Krenn, F., Stary, C., Wachholder, D.: Stakeholder-centered process implementation: assessing S-BPM tool support. In: Mühlhäuser, M., Zehbold, C. (eds.) Proceedings of the 9th Conference on Subject-oriented Business Process Management, pp. 1–11. ACM, New York (2017). https://doi.org/10.1145/3040565.3040571

23. Kuehn, W.: Simulation in digital enterprises. In: Proceedings of the 11th International Conference on Computer Modeling and Simulation, ICCMS 2019, pp. 55–59. ACM Press, New York (2019). https://doi.org/10.1145/3307363.3307370

24. Li, K.C., Gupta, B.B., Agrawal, D.P. (eds.): Recent Advances in Security, Privacy, and Trust for Internet of Things (IoT) and Cyber-Physical Systems (CPS). CRC Press, Boca Raton (2020)

25. de Mello, R.C., Jimenez, M.F., Ribeiro, M.R.N., Laiola Guimarães, R., Frizera-Neto, A.: On human-in-the-loop CPS in healthcare: a cloud-enabled mobility assistance service. Robotica **37**(9), 1477–1493 (2019). https://doi.org/10.1017/S0263574719000079

26. Mendez Mena, D., Papapanagiotou, I., Yang, B.: Internet of things: survey on security. Inf. Secur. J. Glob. Perspect. **27**(3), 162–182 (2018). https://doi.org/10.1080/19393555.2018.1458258

27. Mohanty, S.P.: Advances in transportation cyber-physical system (T-CPS). IEEE Consum. Electron. Mag. **9**(4), 4–6 (2020). https://doi.org/10.1109/MCE.2020.2986517

28. Monostori, L.: Cyber-physical systems. In: Chatti, S., Laperrière, L., Reinhart, G., Tolio, T. (eds.) CIRP Encyclopedia of Production Engineering, pp. 460–467. Springer, Heidelberg (2019). https://doi.org/10.1007/978-3-662-53120-4_16790

29. Mourey, J.A., Waldman, A.E.: Past the privacy paradox: the importance of privacy changes as a function of control and complexity. J. Assoc. Consum. Res. **5**(2), 162–180 (2020). https://doi.org/10.1086/708034

30. Neubauer, M., Stary, C. (eds.): S-BPM in the Production Industry. Springer, Cham (2017). https://doi.org/10.1007/978-3-319-48466-2

31. Nissenbaum, H.: Privacy in Context. Stanford University Press, Stanford (2009). https://doi.org/10.1515/9780804772891

32. Owman, L.: The ungoverned space of cyber: protecting your intangibles. In: Matos, F., Vairinhos, V., Salavisa, I., Edvinsson, L., Massaro, M. (eds.) Knowledge, People, and Digital Transformation. CMS, pp. 235–244. Springer, Cham (2020). https://doi.org/10.1007/978-3-030-40390-4_15

33. Peffers, K., Tuunanen, T., Rothenberger, M.A., Chatterjee, S.: A design science research methodology for information systems research. J. Manag. Inf. Syst. **24**(3), 45–77 (2007). https://doi.org/10.2753/MIS0742-1222240302

34. Schilling, M., Burgard, W., Muelling, K., Wrede, B., Ritter, H.: Shared autonomy - learning of joint action and human-robot collaboration. Front. Neurorobot. **13**, 16 (2019). https://doi.org/10.3389/fnbot.2019.00016

35. Schilling, M., et al.: Towards a multidimensional perspective on shared autonomy. In: Proceedings of the AAAI Fall Symposium Series 2016, Stanford (USA), pp. 1–7. AAAI Press, Palo Alto (2016)

36. Seliem, M., Elgazzar, K., Khalil, K.: Towards privacy preserving IoT environments: a survey. Wirel. Commun. Mob. Comput. **2018**, 1–15 (2018). https://doi.org/10.1155/2018/1032761

37. Sharpe, R., van Lopik, K., Neal, A., Goodall, P., Conway, P.P., West, A.A.: An industrial evaluation of an Industry 4.0 reference architecture demonstrating the need for the inclusion of security and human components. Comput. Ind. **108**, 37–44 (2019). https://doi.org/10.1016/j.compind.2019.02.007

38. Song, L., Shokri, R., Mittal, P.: Privacy risks of securing machine learning models against adversarial examples. In: Proceedings of the 2019 ACM SIGSAC Conference on Computer and Communications Security, pp. 241–257. ACM, New York (2019). https://doi.org/10.1145/3319535.3354211

39. Stary, C., Wachholder, D.: System-of-systems support - a bigraph approach to interoperability and emergent behavior. Data Knowl. Eng. **105**, 155–172 (2016). https://doi.org/10.1016/j.datak.2015.12.001

40. Stary, C.: The internet-of-behavior as organizational transformation space with choreographic intelligence. In: Freitag, M., Kinra, A., Kotzab, H., Kreowski, H.-J., Thoben, K.-D. (eds.) S-BPM ONE 2020. CCIS, vol. 1278, pp. 113–132. Springer, Cham (2020). https://doi.org/10.1007/978-3-030-64351-5_8

41. Stary, C., Elstermann, M., Fleischmann, A., Schmidt, W.: Behavior-centered digital-twin design for dynamic cyber-physical system development. Complex Syst. Inform. Model. Q. (CSIMQ) **30**, 31–52 (2022). https://doi.org/10.7250/CSIMQ.2022-30.02

# An Im- and Export Library for the Subject-Oriented Exchange Standard

Matthes Elstermann[✉] and Lukas Gnad

Institute for Information Management in Engineering, Karlsruhe Institute of
Technology, 76131 Karlsruhe, Germany
matthes.elstermann@kit.edu

**Abstract.** In this work we present a summary and analysis of the
requirements, structure, and development of an open-source application programming interface (API) library written in C# for .Net, that
enables the creation, im- and export, as well as in-memory manipulation
of subject-oriented process models. The alps.net.api was created to
enable the simple and comfortable handling of process models using the
OWL exchange standard for the standard version of the PASS modeling
language, as well as the Abstract Layered PASS (ALPS) extension of
PASS.

Thereby, next to deriving and discussing the general requirements for
such a library, the created API functions as a proof of concept for the
extensibility of the PASS exchange standard while at the same time being
extensible and adaptable itself. It is explicitly designed to be used and
extended in individual software project that require its functionalities.

**Keywords:** PASS · ALPS · Exchange standard · OWL · alps.net.api

## 1 Introduction

In [7] the semantic exchange standard for the subject-oriented process modeling
language *Parallel Activity Specification Schema (PASS)*[1] was proposed and subsequently adopted into a community driven standardization effort [11,12]. The
standardization now covers formal definitions for model structure using the Web
Ontology Language (OWL) [14] as well as a definition for the execution of such
models using the Abstract State Machine (ASM) formalism [6].

---

[1] In principle, this work requires the reader to have at least fundamental knowledge
of PASS. However, to give the minimal background: PASS was originally created by
[8] and further elaborated in [10]. It is a subject-oriented process modeling language
consisting of two separate diagrams types: Subject Interaction Diagrams (SID) that
define active entities—the subjects—in a process, as well as Subject Behavior Diagrams (SBD) that can be used to describe the individual behavior of a subject within
the process.

M. Elstermann et al. (Eds.): S-BPM ONE 2022, CCIS 1632, pp. 23–40, 2022.
https://doi.org/10.1007/978-3-031-19704-8_2

However, beyond a referential implementation for the run-time [15] and one MS Visio based modeling tool that can export its models into the exchange standard format, there are no software tools yet that practically work with the standard [9].

Next to the novelty of the approach itself, it can be supposed that an important factor in the lack of tools is the general uncommonness and challenge of handling OWL based documents. Handling OWL documents and adhering to the semantic web-standards efficiently and correctly usually requires knowledge the extensive domain that is the semantic web technologies [1] and even with that knowledge it can be 'fiddly'.

As a consequence and to allow for easier usage of the exchange standard, we have created the `alps.net.api`-Library, an open-source (MIT licensed) C# based implementation of general in-memory model handling for .NET (core[2]) that allows easy import (parsing), model modification, and export, from, with and to standard conform PASS OWL documents.

The great benefit of such a library is that any programmer wanting to create a software solution using PASS models—be it workflow engines, editors, or AI analyzing of business processes—will be able to import the implementation into his or her C# project and use or extend it. All without the need to in-depth learn the peculiarities of RDF/OWL or the PASS exchange standard and without the need to implement a robust import or export function themselves.

In this work we discuss and analyze the general requirements, challenges, and subsequent design decision that where necessary to implement a solution that fulfills the initially stated goal—especially in the regard that the library should as easily as possible be adoptable by third parties for their software projects.

Therefore this contribution does not only serve a proof-of-concept for the exchange standard, but at the same time it derives the conceptual foundation for programmers that might to implement similar libraries in other programming languages.

## 2 Requirements and Basic Concepts

### 2.1 General Concept and Technical Background

The main idea was to realize the general concept for using the exchange standard described in [4] and [7]. As shown in Fig. 1, a Tool Y that wants to use process models stored in the OWL exchange standard would, ideally, consist of two aspects. First a generic OWL import library as well as the actual parsing engine, that is able to *translate* OWL concepts into an in-memory model that can be modified via API commands and does not require knowledge about OWL and its peculiarities.

The use of an separate triple-store entity is not necessary but advisable since OWL itself is a conceptual language and can be encoded itself in a multitude of formats such as XML, JSON, or turtle script. A triple store should already be

---

[2] See Sects. 2.2 for details on .NET versioning.

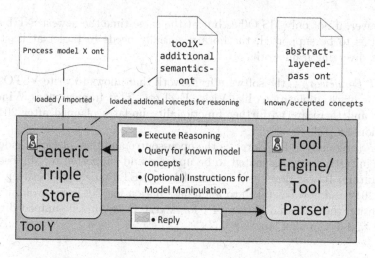

**Fig. 1.** Conceptual Import Process (SID) (from [7]).

able to handle these various different serialization formats without the need of the programmer to support them all by writing an individual importing codes base on character inputs.

A triple store can import any kind of process models files[3] plus additional semantic concepts. It can also be used to check the consistency of the loaded definitions if running general logic engines, so called *reasoners*. On the other hand, a tool-specific parser naturally, can only retrieve or handle concepts from the triple stores that are known to it and are relevant for the program it was created. For PASS, obviously, the concept a too-specific parser should understand must include the *standard-pass-ont* itself. In our case, this additionally also includes *ALPS concepts* itself (see Sect. 2.3) that are stored in the `abstract-layered-pass-ont`.

## 2.2 Programming Language and Runtime Support

To support a variety of projects with PASS functionality, the overall goal must be to have multiple libraries for most of the common programming languages. However, a single project can more or less support only one single language and/or technical framework.

In this case, the decision for the first language fell on C#, mainly influenced by the fact that the library's initial purpose is to be the base for projects integrated into Microsoft Office applications that are build on the .NET-Framework. More specifically, the target is MS Visio, an application that has been used before as the basis to create PASS and ALPS models and now also requires an import functionality [9].

---

[3] Or theoretically also connect to other remote data repositories/semantic stores.

However, if not only MS Office but at the same time the newest .NET environment is to be supported, the library actually needs to target at least two different diverging frameworks:

- *.NET Framework* is the software framework that allows to write VSTO add-ins for office applications like Visio, Exel etc. This framework is Windows only, and there are no further functionality updates planned after 2019 or Version 4.8 [13].
- *.NET* (originally .NET Core), is the open-source and free, platform independent infrastructure designated to be updated and supported by Microsoft in the future. It was developed in parallel to .NET-Framework between 2015 and 2019 and now has taken to main designation for .NET. To avoid naming confusion there was no Version 4.x for ".NET Core" and it jumped directly from ".NET Core 3.x" to ".NET 5.x".

## 2.3   Requirements

The analysis of the initially set goals and boundary conditions lead to the derivation of the following requirements for such an API. Most of them are logical consequences from the purpose of the PASS exchange standard itself. This includes the target of increasing the accessibility, availability, and ease of use of tools for Subject-Oriented (Business) process management (S-BPM) and is based on experiences with several prior tries ourselves as well as exchanges with other projects such as [15] that have implemented or tried to implement similar importer or exporters but fell short of being usable for the overall goal. From that experience and exchange several possible usage-scenarios for the library were derived that also impacted the following listing.

**Import and Export.** The library should first and foremost offer the functionality of importing and exporting PASS models from and into the exchange standard. It should support any file in OWL/RDF format as input and should be able to export a model to this type of file as well, no matter the actual serialization format.

If two different (or at least one) parties have different extensions, the library should still be able to import up to the known concepts, making use of the full flexibility of OWL.

**In-Memory Model.** The subsequent question is, what should be a target or origin of the im- or export function? Import from and export to the PASS OWL export standard is given. But what is the counterpart? Logically, there must be an in-memory PASS model that can be edited. Therefore, the library should provide a user the full functionality of creating and working with in-memory PASS models. It should be easy, comfortable, and intuitive to work with existing, imported models or to simply create new models from scratch.

**Connectivity.** The original concept from [4] mainly focuses on the idea of using a local triple store to im- and export serialized OWL-elements from and to various formatted text files. However, that is not necessarily the only way PASS/OWL models can be stored or exchanged with RDF/OWL. Besides working with local files directly, the library should ideally work as a connector to/from remote triple stores that allow continuous updating of the models, especially in exchange with other modelers.

**Extensibility.** The library is meant to give an implementation for each model element in a way that users can interact with it easily and generate basic models. However, since the standard itself was created to be extensible, the architecture of the library should be created in a way where users that want to add more functionality, can use the library as a foundation without the need of having to implement everything again for their specific use case. Naturally following from that, even with user-created model element classes, the importing and exporting functionality should not be impaired. Further more, the library should even be able to adapt to new classes and offer the possibility to directly parse model class instances to instances of the new C# classes. To achieve this, a dynamic parser that finds and uses model-element-implementation-classes at runtime is needed.

**Support All of Standard PASS.** As a general purpose library not intended for a specific use-case, it must support *all* elements and concepts defined for PASS in the standard, including complex aspects such as choice segments, multiple behaviors, or all variants of time-transitions.

**Support for ALPS.** As an internal requirement, the library should not only allow for handling the PASS standard, but at the same time also support the extension of the standard known as the *Abstract Layered PASS* (ALPS) concept, as drafted in [5].

This intrinsic requirement derived from our own goal to further develop and support the ALPS concept as a general research direction. At the same time it is also a proof of concept for the extensibility of the OWL based PASS exchange standard [4,7] and the according requirement. Successfully implementing it would demonstrate that the standard can, indeed, be extended without hindering the backwards or sideways compatibility for tools.

While the ALPS concept itself is fully backwards compatible, to support it, the library is required to follow the fundamental conceptual difference of ALPS to the standard which comes into play when creating models with multiple behaviors like guards, macros, or extensions.

As shown in Fig. 2, the standard envisions only one SID per model and a subject containing multiple SBDs. In contrast, ALPS follows the line of *One behavior (SBD) per subject per SID*. Therefore, if multiple behaviors are needed, a new model *"layer"* is introduced, that basically is a separate SID containing so-called *"subject-extensions"* that, in turn, each posses their own behavior[4]. This especially needs to be considered when importing models that are only standard PASS and not ALPS models, as well when exporting ALPS models to the standard, so that even multi-layer/behavior models can still be understood by non-ALPS-based tools.

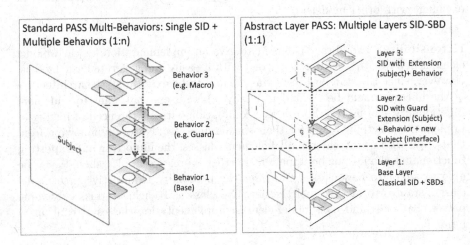

**Fig. 2.** Visualization of the Difference in Multi-Behavior Concepts in Standard PASS (left) and ALPS (right)

# 3    Implementation

This section describes the structure and inner workings of the finished alps.net.api. The actual implementation occurred iteratively in agile, scrum based approach over several years—including a complete rewrite after an initial prototype that was found lacking in several areas in regards to the pre-set requirements.

## 3.1    Supported Framework and Used Libraries

As discussed in Sect. 2.2, the library multi-targets two different runtime environments, namely .NET Framework 4.8 and .NET Core 3.1. As the .NET Runtime Environment is backwards compatible with .NET Core 3.1, the library thereby can also be imported to projects targeting a later version of the .NET runtime

---

[4] The advantage of this approach is that other subjects being relevant only for, e.g., the communication with a guard behavior can (not must!) be modeled only on the particular layer. Thus the *"base"* layer is kept relatively free and modeling focuses on fundamental process aspects.

environment. The library is hosted mainly at Github[5], but it can as well simply be integrated into any C# project by downloading it via the NuGet package manager system.

To deal with OWL/RDF formatted files, this library makes use of the *DotNetRDF* library. DotNetRDF offers the functionality to parse such files into a triple store graph and vice-versa, and allows to work with triples, OWL classes, and class instances [2, 3].

## 3.2   Brief Definition

In the following sections, a distinction is made between OWL classes and C# classes. To emphasis this distinction and help the reader see the difference, the according concepts are color coded.

- OWL classes mean the classes contained inside OWL/RDF formatted files (like the standard_PASS_ont_v_1.1.0.owl). These are the classes describing the PASS standard, an example would be the FullySpecifiedSubject class.
- C# classes refer to the classes contained inside the library. These classes are implementations in C#, and each of these classes should represent a previously mentioned OWL class.

Note that the possibility of naming confusion does not imply that every name exists both in the context of OWL classes and C# classes. There are OWL classes that have no direct class counterpart in C#. Read more about it in Sect. 3.3.

## 3.3   Model and Components

Following standard practice for Object-Oriented programming to allow for later extensibility and the handling of multiple-inheritance, every component existing in the standard or ALPS context is firstly represented by an *interface*. However, the library also provides to (almost) every interface a standard implementation for the component, that contains the actual functionality[6].

Due to the fact that multiple inheritance is possible for ontology classes, but not allowed for C#-classes, some of the functionality is merged together in single classes in the library. I.e. there might be an instance in an ontology that is both a DoState and an Abstract State at the same time. In the library, this is modeled as DoState with an attribute set stating that it is also an abstract State.

---

[5] https://github.com/I2PM/alps.net.api.

[6] Using interfaces in addition to actual classes is, to our knowledge, a standard practice in object-oriented programming of larger complex system as it give a larger degree of flexibility especially if later changes or extensions need to be incorporated. Because of that, we require the reader to at least have a basic familiarity with the concept to acknowledge this design decision. .

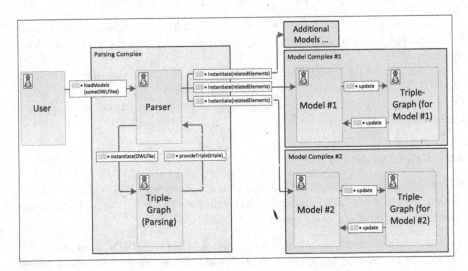

**Fig. 3.** A simple overview over the structure of the importer and in memory models.

## 3.4  Trouble with Triple Stores

There are multiple parts of the library that make use of the triple store graph functionality provided by DotNetRdf. These parts can be seen in Fig. 3.

*Import.* On import, the library reads given OWL/RDF formatted input files. The input of these files is parsed as a list of triples that is stored inside a triple store graph, which is then used for instantiating the C# classes. In the following sections, this graph is referred to as the *parsing triple store graph* The graph does not only contain triple information, but information about the defined owl classes (from PASS standard and ALPS) and class instances (the modeled elements) as well. All owl classes are found inside this graph, and every new C# class instance receives information in the form of triples belonging to itself from this graph (Read more in Sect. 3.5).

*Model.* Every in memory instance of a PASS model holds or is connected to a triple store graph wrapper (See Fig. 5). This wrapper referred to as the *model triple store graph* It contains a real triple store graph provided by the Dot-NetRDF library, which may be replaced by own implementations or a remote triple store graph.

Every bit of information that cannot be parsed correctly[7] is still written into the model triple store graph of the created model. This ensures that no data is lost on import, and all data that was imported will as well written to the files on export.

---

[7] I.e. because there have been modifications to the standard that are unknown to the library.

*Remote Model Triple Store Graph.* All the information about class instances in models is stored twice:

1. Every instance stores its data in the form of class attributes
2. All the data is stored in form of triples in the model triple store graph

This leads to a synchronization overhead: All the data must be kept up to date to not lead to inconsistencies.

One reason for the design choice of storing data twice and wrapping the underlying graph with the model triple store graph wrapper is to allow a bidirectional communication with the graph, see Sect. 3.7.

Another reason is to use the export functionality the DotNetRDF library offers, which can be easily done once all data is available in the form of a triple store graph (See Sect. 3.6).

## 3.5  Import

The import functionality is capable of importing a model given as OWL/RDF formatted file into an in-memory model. The process of importing can be split up into 3 standalone steps of which the first two are analysis steps necessary to prepare for step three, the actual import:

1. Generating class extension trees
2. Generating a parsing dictionary by mapping the trees
3. Parsing an ontology model to C#-instances by using the dictionary

**General Idea.** The general idea for the exporter is to create two class extension trees once the parser is initialized, one tree for `OWL classes` and one for `C# classes`. These two trees contain the structural information about how classes are ordered, meaning their inheritance structure. Afterwards, a dictionary should be created that maps a C#-class as a valid representation to an OWL class. The parser then should be able to parse models defined in OWL/RDF-formatted files by using this dictionary.

**Generating Class Extension Trees:** There are two different trees that will be created.

1. An **ontology class extension tree:** The ontology tree is created from the hierarchical order of the ontology classes contained in the standard- and abstract layered PASS ontology, as well as, potentially, any other extension used for a given model. All those formal model taxonomies must be available to the parser (must be loaded inside the triple store). This can be done by loading the e.g. the abstract-layered-pass-ont as a separate OWL file. Alternatively all extensions can, naturally be included in a single OWL file containing model as well as information regarding an extension. This way, the PASS ontologies can be easily replaced with newer versions and ad-hoc extensions

are a possibility. Files containing the model taxonomies (either the separate files or the ones containing all information) must be loaded once on parser initialization to create the tree. The tree can later be re-created on each parsing call if necessary.

2. **A C#-class extension tree.** The C#-class tree is also created at runtime and contains a hierarchical structure of all classes that extend the standard `PASSProcessModelElement` class. By default, only classes inside the library are found. To support extensions from outside the assembly, it is however possible to register other assemblies to the library. This way, all classes in the new assembly (meaning extensions to alps.net.api by third parties) are searched as well, without the need to override the source code inside the library.

The parser expects that for the ontology tree the root node is `PASSProcessModelElement`, as well as for the C#-tree the root node is asserted being the `PASSProcessModelElement` class. It begins creating the tree by using these base classes.

**Generating a Parsing Dictionary by Mapping the Trees.** Once both trees are created, a dictionary will be filled with class mappings. To achieve the mapping, the parser goes through both trees respectively, mapping C#-classes to ontology classes. To understand the mapping, the definition *"valid representation"* is introduced. A C# class defines a method `canParse(string name)` that takes the name of an OWL class. It returns if this C# class is a valid representation for the OWL class, alas if an OWL class instance can be parsed to an instance of this C# class.

There are several conditions for classes to be mapped:

– A C#-class will only be mapped to an ontology class if it is a valid representation for the ontology class. To be a valid representation for an ontology class, the `canParse(string name)` method must return **true** when given the name of the ontology class as input.
– Classes will only be mapped if they share mapped parents. If at some node both trees diverge, none of the children of this node will be mapped.
– Classes are mapped if they are on the same height in the trees. There are two exceptions:
  1. There is no C#-class that is a valid representation for the current ontology class. The current ontology class and its children are then mapped with the valid representation of the parent ontology class.
  I.e. a `FullySpecifiedSubject` that could not be mapped is then instantiated as `Subject`, as this is mapped with the owl parent class `Subject`.
  2. A child C#-class of the currently mapped class is also a valid representation for the current ontology class. The importance of this rule will be discussed in the next section.

**Keeping the Parser Extensible.** As described in the previous section, there might be scenarios were multiple C# classes are valid representations for one owl class. This would be the case, e.g., if a user created his/her own implementation for an ontology class, extending the standard implementation of the library. To keep the parser as extensible as possible, it does not store a single C# class as possible instantiation for a owl class, but a list of possible classes. In case a standard implementation is extended by a new child class, this child C#-class is mapped with the current ontology class as well. This can be seen in Fig. 4, where the FullySpecifiedSubject is extended by a new class called *"VisioFullySpecifiedSubject"*. This new class is also mapped with the FullySpecifiedSubject as it states that it is also a valid representation for this owl class. A detailed conceptual description of the depicted scenario can be found in Sect. 4.

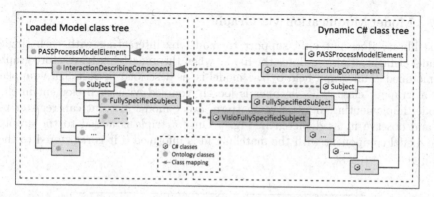

**Fig. 4.** The mapping of the loaded ontology class structure and the dynamically created C# class tree. Note that the VisioFullySpecifiedSubject is not part of the library but plays a role in Sect. 4.

**Parsing an Ontology Model to C#-Instances.** With the loaded parsing dictionary, a given OWL/RDF formatted file containing one or more model(s) can be imported. The parser uses a factory class[8] to parse the instances of ontology classes to C# instances.

As described in Sect. 3.3, ontology class instances might inherit from multiple classes. The factory decides which of the **OWL** classes it wants to use for instantiation and chooses afterwards one of the valid C# representations.

If a user extends the library with an own class and wants to ensure this class is chosen from the pool of valid representations, the standard factory should be replaced with an own factory by the user.

---

[8] A class implementing IPASSProcessModelElementFactory, the standard is to use BasicPASSProcessModelElementFactory.

## 3.6   Export

`alps.net.api` uses the functionality of the DotNetRDF library to export models to RDF/OWL formatted files. DotNetRDF supports to export a given triple store graph into a RDF/OWL formatted file. As all the model data is stored inside the model triple store graph (Fig. 5), this graph may be used directly for export.

If a user wants to extend the library with an own class that should be exportable, it must be assured that the class writes its data to the model's triple store, e.g. by using the functionality of its parent class. If the new class is not only a programming extension, but also a conceptional extension to the PASS standard, for that extension a corresponding OWL should be created and published or written into the export file.

## 3.7   Model Modification via Graph

The library does not only support to model by interacting with each single model element, it also updates the model when the underlying triple store graph is modified. This graph held by the model is, as described in Sect. 3.4, wrapped by a wrapper class. The wrapper is loosely coupled with each element in the model implementing an observer pattern, every model element can register to it and observe it, as depicted in Fig. 5. Once a triple is added to the graph, the model component with the matching id is informed if it is registered to the wrapper.

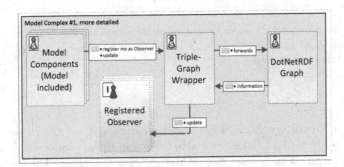

**Fig. 5.** A wrapper wraps the functionality of the real triple store graph and implements an observer pattern to inform model components on triple change.

This way, the model element instances will be updated on a graph update. To handle the update inside each element instance, the same parsing methods as during the import are called (exploiting the fact that graph updates are encoded as triples), requiring no further code to be written.

The implementation of the bidirectional communication between model triple store graph and model element instances enables the use of a remote triple store graph as underlying graph to the model triple store graph wrapper, which could trigger an update of the data in the class instances once its own stored triples change.

However, the functionality of the model triple store graph is restricted, as it is currently not possible to instantiate new model classes. It is limited to update the class attributes of existing class instances. More about this in Sect. 5.

## 3.8  Layered vs. Non-layered Models

A special case when importing are standard (non-ALPS) PASS models that do not contain layers, but possibly multiple behaviors.

In order to keep navigation and manipulation consistent, non-ALPS models are basically converted. If no layers exist, at least one base layer is always added to each model. Furthermore, if a model does not contain layers but does contain multiple behaviors for a single subject (which must be on the base layer), additional layers and an according subject-extension are added, in order to have entities to which to attach the according behaviors.

Due to the library explicitly following the ALPS concept the model navigation must also be done this way. Namely, e.g., an extension behavior of a base behavior is navigate to via its "extension layer" and the therein contained "extension" of the according subject on that extension layer.

When exporting a model this difference is rather unproblematic. Due to the graph (and not tree based) nature of OWL, simply both concept are exported at the same time. On one hand, an exported model will always contain layers. However on the other, all elements on a layer that also exist in Standard PASS will be linked accordingly. E.g., a guard behavior belonging to a guard extension on a guard layer, will also be linked to the according subject on the base layer. Consequently, importing programs that follow only the standard PASS set will only see subjects belonging to the model (no matter the layer) and find multiple behaviors linked to the subject on the base layer. It simply must ignore all unknown concept such as the layers.

## 4  Proof of Concept

As initially stated, `alps.net.api`, while explicitly being a stand alone library for general use, was created as the basis for the the import functionality of a Plug-In for Microsoft Office Visio. This Plug-In is used to supplement the functionality of the VBA-based PASS modeling stencils presented in [9].

Goal of the new import functionality is to load a model from a file in RDF/OWL format, generate a Visio-model from it and visualize it in Visio by using the PASS stencils.

As every model component is visualized by a specific *shape*-type that all behave somewhat differently in how they are placed and what data fields they posses, it is useful to store a reference to the given shape in each component instance. This way the interactions with Visio visualizations in C# code becomes much easier. However, since this a specific use-case, the according code that interacts with MS Visio and its API obviously, must not be written in the general `alps.net.api`. Storing the shape reference and manipulation code to each component is rather done in extended (inherited) classes that are only relevant for the plug-in project.

This example describes the case for adding the shape reference to a `FullySpecifiedSubject`. The `FullySpecifiedSubject` is extended by a new class called `VisioFullySpecifiedSubject` (Fig. 6).

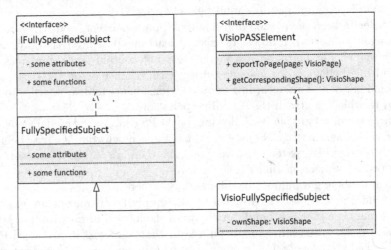

**Fig. 6.** The UML class diagram for the new `VisioFullySpecifiedSubject` class

To make use of the functionality the new class contains, it must be achieved that every model component of type `FullySpecifiedSubject` is parsed as a `VisioFullySpecifiedSubject` rather than a `FullySpecifiedSubject` within this extension project. As described in Sect. 3.5, the current assembly must be known to the `ReflectiveEnumerator` class to find the `VisioFullySpecified-Subject` class. Once it is known two parsing values will be created for the key "FullySpecifiedSubject":

- The standard implementation contained in the library, the `FullySpecified-Subject` class
- The new created implementation extending the standard class, the `Visio-FullySpecifiedSubject` class

The tree created by the parser is partly visualized in Fig. 4.

The parser is now able to parse `FullySpecifiedSubject` components as `VisioFullySpecifiedSubject` instances, but it is not guaranteed that it will prefer this implementation over the standard `FullySpecifiedSubject` implementation inside the library. Therefor, the factory class of the parser needs to be replaced by a new implementation defined by the user. In this case, the new

`VisioClassFactory` extends the `BasicPASSProcessModelElementFactory` and makes use of its functionality (Fig. 7).

```
class VisioClassFactory : BasicPASSProcessModelElementFactory
    {
        Pair<Element, String> decideForElement(IDictionary<Element, String> possibleElements)
        {
            // Search if one of the possible values is of type IVisioExportable
            foreach (Pair<Element, String> pair in possibleElements)
            {
                if (pair.Key is IVisioExportable) return pair;
            }
            // If not, pass the decision of the base implementation
            return base.decideForElement(possibleElements);
        }
    }
```

**Fig. 7.** A (simplified) representation of the implementation for a factory prioritizing new Visio classes over standard library classes.

The method `decideForElement(...)` provided by the `BasicPASSProcess-ModelElementFactory` class follows the *"template method"* design pattern. Extending child classes receive a dictionary of possible instantiations mapped with ontology class names these instantiations would represent once the template method has been called. The child can then decide for one instantiation and return it. The `IVisioPASSElement` interface that was introduced earlier is used in this example to easily differentiate between new classes intended for the Visio-Plugin extension and standard implementations of `alps.net.api` (Fig. 8).

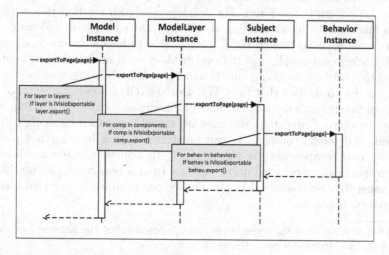

**Fig. 8.** Writing an in-memory model to Visio recursively in a hierarchical way.

In principle, the prior described mechanism will lead to the creation of an in-memory model that consist of the new classes. Once the classes have been parsed to the new Visio implementations and the in-memory model has been created, the new extended functionality can be used to write all model elements hierarchically into a Visio file. This writing functionality is realized with every class implementing the `IVisioExportable` interface containing the `exportToPage(Page page)` method to drop a shape representation of itself onto a Visio page. It then iterates through its child instances[9], filtering for those implementing `IVisioExportable`. Afterwards, the export function is called on these recursively.

Consequently, to export a model to Visio, it is sufficient to call the export method only once on the model itself.

## 5   Summary and Outlook

In this contribution the requirements for and as well as the subsequent structure of the `alps.net.api` open-source software library were presented. The library is now available and can be included in any .net/C# software project that wishes to handle subject-oriented PASS or ALPS process models. We also have created an importer project for MS Visio as a proof-of-concept for the approach that uses and extends the `alps.net.api` and thereby shows how that and how the initially set goal of applicability and extensibility can be achieved. Other Programmers can now easily make use of PASS process models in their own project with a greatly reduced workload and knowledge overhead.

However, to be truly useful and not only bound to the .NET/C# world, similar libraries or at least bindings would be needed for other popular programming environment and languages such as, a.o., JAVA, Python, C++, or Angular/TypeScript/JavaScript. For developers of such solution this work provides a fundamental understanding of how to approach such an endeavor.

Furthermore, even though the library is able to handle model modification via the background graph that is being held by each model, it is not entirely possible to model by accessing only the owl-graph in the triple store.

This is due to the fact that the OWL/DotNetRDF graph-instance is not able to initiate the instantiation of new model elements on its own. It is a completely passive structure. Currently, only existing model components can be edited/-modified, and model components can be removed. It is however not possible to create new components via the graph[10]. To achieve a scenario where the OWL-graph might receive addition updates from a remote graph, the library graph must first be connected to the library parser in some way that element instantiation is possible.

---

[9] Child instances not in the sense of the inheritance tree but the internal model hierarchy tree of Model-> Layer->Subject ->Behavior.

[10] To clarify: an addition of the in-memory model can always be written into the OWL graph in the triple store to keep both models "in sync". But additions to the model in the triple store, e.g. via a remote call or update synchronization with another triple store are not written back to the in-memory model.

Another concept, not implemented so far is the direct use of a reasoner—a general purpose logic inference engine—for the parsing engine. In general RDF or OWL stores can be worked on by such an logic engine with the goal of uncovering logical fallacies, contradictions, syntactical errors, as well as to add additional connections and rules based on the definitions of the various ontologies. In principle this should be simple as the DotNetRDF API possess the according features to apply a suitable reasoners. However, this has not been tested. Instead, for now, the according reasoning step, if required, needs to be done with an external program before the actual import. Having this functionality built in would be a considerable improvement and ease of use.

Finally, as stated, the long time goal of such a library is to be used by other projects. There is no point in it as a stand alone program otherwise. Consequently, next to improving the library itself and bring it from its current 0.8.0 to a 1.0.0 version., future research activities will comprise projects that make use of the `alps.net.api`—for example a general purpose ALPS workflow/execution engine for the .NET environment.

**Acknowledgments.** Over the last years multiple person have been involved in the creation of this tool and its foundations.

We would like to especially acknowledge the work of Nico Baumann who created the initial incarnation of what now has become the `alps.net.api`.

# References

1. Domingue, J.H. (ed.): Handbook of Semantic Web Technologies: With 96 tables. Springer, Berlin (2011)
2. DotNetRdf Development Team: DotNetRdf project GitHub (2022). https://github.com/dotnetrdf/dotnetrdf
3. DotNetRdf Development Team: DotNetRdf project (2022). https://dotnetrdf.org/
4. Elstermann, M.: Proposal for using semantic technologies as a means to store and exchange subject-oriented process models. In: S-BPM ONE 2017, Darmstadt, Germany, 30–31 March (2017)
5. Elstermann, M., Ovtcharova, J.: Abstract layers in PASS – a concept draft. In: Zehbold, C. (ed.) S-BPM ONE 2014. CCIS, vol. 422, pp. 125–136. Springer, Cham (2014). https://doi.org/10.1007/978-3-319-06191-7_8
6. Elstermann, M., Wolski, A., Fleischmann, A., Stary, C., Borgert, S.: The combined use of the web ontology language (OWL) and abstract state machines (ASM) for the definition of a specification language for business processes. In: Raschke, A., Riccobene, E., Schewe, K.-D. (eds.) Logic, Computation and Rigorous Methods. LNCS, vol. 12750, pp. 283–300. Springer, Cham (2021). https://doi.org/10.1007/978-3-030-76020-5_16
7. Elstermann, M., Krenn, F.: The semantic exchange standard for subject-oriented process models. In: Proceedings of the 10th International Conference on Subject-Oriented Business Process Management. In: S-BPM One 2018. Association for Computing Machinery, New York (2018). https://doi.org/10.1145/3178248.3178257
8. Fleischmann, A.: Distributed Systems - Software Design and Implementation. Springer, Berlin (1994)

9. Fleischmann, A., Borgert, S., Elstermann, M., Krenn, F., Singer, R.: An overview to S-BPM oriented tool suites. In: Mühlhäuser, M., Zehbold, C. (eds.) Proceedings of the 9th International Conference on Subject-Oriented Business Process Management. S-BPM ONE. ACM (2017)

10. Fleischmann, A., Schmidt, W., Stary, C., Obermeier, S., Boerger, E.: Subject-Oriented Business Process Management. Springer, Berlin (2012)

11. I2PM: Towards a standard for subject-oriented modelling and implementation (2021). https://github.com/I2PM/PASS-Standard-Book-Tex-Project/releases. Accessed 16 Feb 2022

12. Institute for Innovative Process Management: Standardisation effort (2022). https://i2pm.net/category/interest-groups/standardisation. Accessed 16 Feb 2022

13. Microsoft: Microsoft documentation:net framework (2022). https://docs.microsoft.com/en-us/dotnet/framework/migration-guide/versions-and-dependencies

14. W3C: Web ontology language (OWL) (2012). https://www.w3.org/OWL/. Accessed 05 Feb 2021

15. Wolski, A., Borgert, S., Heuser, L.: A CoreASM based reference implementation for subject-oriented business process management execution semantics. In: Betz, S., Elstermann, M. (ed.) Proceedings of S-BPM ONE 2019, S-BPM ONE. ACM (2019)

# Understanding and Harnessing the Potential of Conversational AI for S-BPM

Victor Kurtz[✉], Jakob Bönsch, and Jivka Ovtcharova

Institute for Information Management in Engineering (IMI), Karlsruhe Institute of Technology (KIT), Kriegsstraße 77, 76133 Karlsruhe, Germany
utehj@student.kit.edu

**Abstract.** Conversational AI in the form of chatbots is likely to play an important role in modern business processes. In this paper a taxonomy was developed presenting which connections can be drawn between the domain of subject-oriented business process management (S-BPM) and Conversational AI - and whether they are valuable. This taxonomy consists of three major pillars. First, it was considered how chatbots can be expressed using S-BPM. Secondly, an automated specification of chatbots based on subject-oriented process models was examined. Lastly, the support of subject-oriented business process modeling via the guidance of chatbots was considered.

**Keywords:** Parallel Activity Specification Scheme · PASS · Conversational AI · Chatbot · Azure · Microsoft · Bot · Framework

## 1 Introduction

Business process modeling is an integral management tool for most companies. Consistent modeling ensures reliability for corporate processes. A high level of detail in process models makes optimization potentials of the processes visible. Business process modeling thus enables an increase in efficiency of the deployment of personnel, materials, and operating resources, which not only saves costs but also has a significant impact on customer satisfaction. A success factor of process modeling is the flexibility in adapting processes to changing boundary conditions [1].

Business processes are diverse. They can range from manufacturing tasks on the shop floor level, over engineering activities to the preparation of reporting for management. A proper modeling language for this environment needs to be able to represent and manage this heterogeneity and diversity [2].

Subject-orientation is a paradigm that places the active process parts in the center of the description. If this paradigm is operationalized for the description of processes, one speaks of subject-oriented business process modeling (S-BPM) [3]. S-BPM is commonly operationalized by the formal modeling language Parallel Activity Specification Scheme (PASS). This language combines a manageable modeling scope with great expressive power [4].

M. Elstermann et al. (Eds.): S-BPM ONE 2022, CCIS 1632, pp. 41–57, 2022.
https://doi.org/10.1007/978-3-031-19704-8_3

A subtopic of the research field on Artificial Intelligence (AI) is dedicated to the development of software that can understand and generate natural language. AI is used in this context mainly to enable the understanding of a broad range of expressions and to give the machine's responses a human feel. Research on this topic is titled Conversational AI. Humans can interact with Conversational AI by talking to chatbots [5]. The underlying concept explored in this work is what kind of role or relationship chatbots may take in context of or with S-BPM. A rather obvious observation may be the ambivalence of chatbots in subject-oriented process description:

On the one hand, it can be involved in a business process as an active subject. On the other hand, it can be the product or deliverable of a development process. This ambivalence has not yet been described in the literature on subject-orientation and is therefore used as a starting point. In addition, various use cases for chatbots are conceivable to simplify or supplement S-BPM. To get a comprehensive overview of useful links between Conversational AI and S-BPM and to generate ideas for a prototype, three research questions arise:

- How can chatbots be perceived from a S-BPM perspective?
- What kind of framework is needed to automatically specify chatbots based on a subject-oriented process model?
- How can chatbots be used to simplify the usage of S-BPM?

These research questions were answered using scientific findings on S-BPM and Conversational AI, as well as technical experiments and comparing features or concepts of PASS and the Microsoft (MS) Bot Framework. In the following paragraph, the pertinent primary literature and utilized software products will be presented. This is followed by the results of the research. Based on this, a prototype was designed, which will be explained in Sect. 4. Finally, the scientific work will be discussed in Sect. 5.

## 2   Materials and Methods

This chapter covers relevant primary literature and software products needed for understanding the content of this work. That is, S-BPM and the Parallel Activity Specification Scheme supplemented with MS Visio as well as Conversational AI and the MS Bot Framework.

### 2.1   S-BPM and the Parallel Activity Specification Scheme

In subject-orientation, a process is defined by the communication among participating subjects, with each subject possessing an individual workflow. Accordingly, two modeling levels are considered in PASS: The Subject Interaction Diagram (SID) and the Subject Behavior Diagram (SBD) [6]. A process model contains exactly one SID and several SBD's [4]. The SID provides an overview of the subjects involved in a process and how they communicate with each other.

For the creation of PASS models, MS Visio, which is part of the Office suite, is used. Visio is a visualization program, and its flow can be modified by macros. For PASS modeling, special shapes were made, and certain functionalities of the subject-orientation were automated with macros[1].

The shapes available for the SID are shown in Fig. 1.

**Fig. 1.** Basic modeling elements for subject interaction diagrams.

While the behavior of interface subjects remains unknown or irrelevant to the process, a behavior diagram (SBD) is created for each fully specified subject. Such an SBD describes the behavior of the subject at process runtime. Additionally, a subject can be marked as start-subject if it initializes the process. It is assumed that a subject is permanently in a specific state including a final state. By fulfilling the exit condition of a state (receiving or sending messages or receive and send states, or by completing an activity for do states), the state is changed. This is modeled with the shapes shown in Fig. 2:

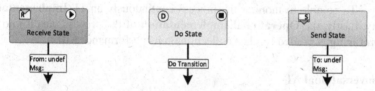

**Fig. 2.** Basic modeling elements for subject behavior diagrams.

A unique selling proposition of the modeling language PASS lies in the formality of both the structural semantics as well as the execution semantics. The former specifies how the language is structured in the Web Ontology Language (OWL). The second defines the execution logic of a PASS model [7]. For this purpose, there is a PASS reference interpreter, which is implemented by means of the technology of the Abstract State Machine (ASM) [8].

## 2.2 Organizational Implementation of S-BPM

It requires a strategic decision to implement S-BPM in any organization, be it corporate, private, or public. This does not only include the usage of a new process modeling

---

[1] Further functionalities, such as a model check, are made possible via an add-in. The shapes, macros and the add-in are developed and maintained at the Institute for Information Management in Engineering (IMI) at KIT. The software is available for download here: https://subjective-me.jimdofree.com/visio-modelling/

language, but even more so a completely new way of thinking about processes is introduced [9]. Ensuring acceptance by employees is therefore critical for the success of the introduction of S-BPM. Fleischmann et al. [6] identified different roles that contribute to the success of the S-BPM strategy:

**Facilitators** support organizational development and are active above all in transition phases between task packages. Facilitators enable targeted communication among stakeholders and support them individually in their professional and personal development (within the framework of the S-BPM strategy). **Governors** assume responsibility for establishing certain framework conditions under which the other stakeholders can act successfully in a subject-oriented manner. **Experts** have domain-specific expertise and are called upon by the other stakeholders as soon as they are dependent on the respective expertise. **Actors** are the subjects modeled in the process. They execute processes and thus play a key role in shaping the subject-orientation of the company. They are supported by experts and facilitators. They can identify weak points in processes and make further suggestions for improvement.

Fleischmann et al. [6] also define different task packages that are iteratively passed through during the modeling process: **Analysis** is usually the first step in which the process is decomposed and aligned with the company's strategy. During **Modeling** a graphical overview of the process is developed. **Validation** means to review the effectiveness of the process. The **Optimization** of the process is achieved by adjusting the maximum consumption of a particular resource. After that, the **Organization-specific Implementation** of the process is necessary to embed it into an existing or new process landscape. To be able to monitor the process continuously an **IT Implementation** is necessary. Lastly, the **Operational Implementation** of the process puts it into action and **Monitoring** is needed for data collection on its performance [6].

### 2.3 Conversational AI

This branch of AI is dedicated to the imitation of natural language by computers for the interaction with humans. This topic gained publicity since Alan Turing designed the Turing Test in 1950. In this Test, humans must decide whether they interact with another human or an artificial intelligence [10]. The chatbot with the name ELIZA, published in 1966, was the first of its kind and brought chatbots to greater attention. ELIZA was a rule-based system, which means it did not utilize machine learning algorithms. Chatbots today, like Siri and Alexa, are powerful Conversational AI systems. The recent high frequency of this topic - since about 2016 - can be explained by the simplification of the creation, deployment and usage of chatbots [5, 11, 12].

A chatbot is basically a web app that can be connected to different channels (Facebook, Slack, etc.) via an endpoint [13, 14]. On an abstract level, a chatbot consists of the components shown in Fig. 3:

The goal of **NLU** is to extract the following components from a user message:

**Intent**: What do the users want to achieve with their query? **Entity**: On which topic, which object do the users want to know something about? **Context**: What entities did the users ask about in previous queries? [11].

**Dialog Management** is a meta-instance of the chatbot in which a strategy for further conversation is established based on the identified goal of the user. From this, the

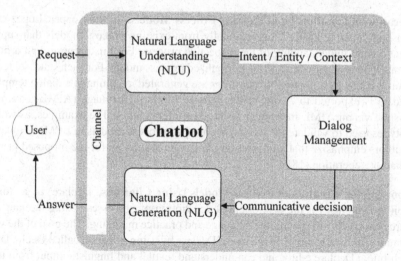

**Fig. 3.** High-level hierarchy of a chatbot.

chatbot's response is derived on a conceptual level and passed to the NLG to provide needed information, or to inquire about it. The NLG processes this data and creates a response consisting of natural language. This is sent to the user [15]. In theory NLU and NLG could include any kind of communication means with humans such as audio or video. The most common form is simple text-based conversation.

**The Microsoft Bot Framework** offers two different approaches on bot development. On the one hand, bots can be created by writing source code, using the **Bot Framework SDK** [16]. The Bot Framework SDK is licensed open-source and is available in C#, JavaScript, TypeScript, and Python and uses.NET Core as its target framework. The SDK v4 was used in C# and offers developers numerous tools and concepts for bot development, as well as templates for chatbots that can be extended as desired.

On the other hand, bots can also be configured via a visual design tool, the **Bot Framework Composer** [17]. This program offers the possibility to design, test and deploy the bot directly to the Azure cloud. No programming knowledge is required for any of these steps. Chatbots created with Composer are based on so-called "Adaptive Dialogs", which are structured according to a hierarchical principle and enable a high degree of flexibility in the way the bot responds. There is exactly one initial dialog that can call child dialogs. During runtime, the child dialogs can call the initial dialog or other child dialogs. Adaptive dialogs are specified in JSON format and interpreted using an associated JSON schema. Both the adaptive dialog and the associated schema can be customized, giving developers extensive options for specifying the behavior of the bot at runtime. Using Composer, the JSON files are automatically generated, and a standard schema is used to interpret them.

### 2.4  Connecting Business Process Management with Conversational AI

While not specifically related to S-BPM, there are two previous approaches on connecting Conversational AI and Business Process Management relevant for this work:

**Generation of Chatbots from Existing Process Models.** In their paper, Lopez et al. propose to generate chatbots automatically from existing process models that support navigation and understanding of the respective process. For this purpose, first a finite-state machine is generated from the normalized process model. For each state, sentences in natural language and possible questions are generated, resulting in a dialog template. This data is exported to Artificial Intelligence Markup Language (AIML) and made accessible via an AIML interpreter in the form of a chatbot. The examples, as well as prototypes used to validate the work, are based on process models in BPMN. However, the authors emphasize that any modeling language is suitable for the proposed process for chatbot generation [18].

**Supporting the Creation of Process Models Using Chatbots.** Declare is a formal modeling language for the task-oriented description of processes. Using the language requires knowledge to specify the language and practice modeling. The goal of the work of Alman et al. was to simplify the use of Declare by using a chatbot called Declo. Declo is built into a Declare editor and can understand textual and linguistic input from users and convert it directly into graphical elements. Declo is also able to recognize negations. Tasks (can, should, must), subjects, business objects, conditions (activation, correlation, and time) can be considered in the model. In the user interface of the editor, the model can also be edited in real time [19].

## 3  Theoretical Findings

The main objective of this work is to establish a taxonomy of how S-BPM and Conversational AI can be tied together. The proposed structure is shown in Fig. 4.

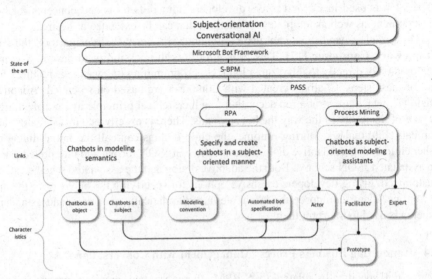

**Fig. 4.** Taxonomy for considering Conversational AI in the context of S-BPM.

The findings spread across three links. Each link is described in a separate section. Since the individual sections are hardly linked in terms of content, they are each concluded with a summary and do not provide an explicit thematic transition.

## 3.1  Chatbots in Modeling Semantics

According to Schmidt et al. the modeling of business processes correlates with the sentence elements of natural language – subject, predicate, and object. Subjects are active participants in a process, predicates are tasks and activities and objects are business objects [20]. Following this idea, a chatbot can take on two roles within a business process, the subject, and the object. A summary of the different roles and their respective implications for S-BPM is given in Table 1. After that, a detailed description of the findings follows.

**Table 1.** Summary of the significance of modeling ambivalence of chatbots

|                    | Subject                                                                                                                                                                                     | Object                                                                                                                           |
| ------------------ | ----------------------------------------------------------------------------------------------------------------------------------------------------------------------------------------- | ------------------------------------------------------------------------------------------------------------------------------- |
| Role of chatbot    | Active process participant                                                                                                                                                                 | In production                                                                                                                    |
| Modeling dogma     | Descriptive                                                                                                                                                                                | Normative                                                                                                                       |
| Modeling features  | • Chatbot as a simple subject<br>• Hides the functional logic of the bot<br>• Only shows the interaction with the user and possibly other software                                        | • Chatbot as SID<br>• Shows the logic of the bot<br>• Dialogs are modeled as subjects, each of which is specified in the SBDs |
| Application        | Business process modeling                                                                                                                                                                  | Software development                                                                                                            |

**As an object:** the components of a chatbot are modeled as a PASS process model. That model itself is considered a data object. This object can be referred to within another business process model. In the following, these components are adaptive dialogs. Figure 5 shows the structure of a chatbot with the purpose of a weather query. The user specifies a location and by querying an application programming interface (API), the current data is automatically retrieved by the chatbot and passed to the user. This is achieved via two dialogs, each implemented as classes.

This model is difficult to understand for observers who do not know how adaptive dialogs work. The same applies to the behavior diagram shown in Fig. 6, which is strongly based on the runtime behavior. Since understandability is one of the most important properties in process modeling, a modeling convention becomes necessary for the representation of chatbots. An approach on a suitable modeling convention is discussed in the next section.

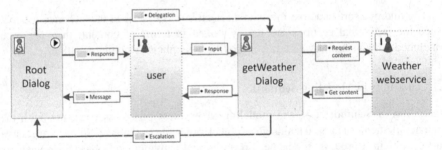

**Fig. 5.** Communicating parts of the chatbot system for a weather query.

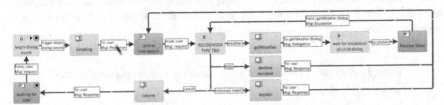

**Fig. 6.** Behavior diagram of Root Dialog shown in Fig. 5.

The model of Fig. 5 is an example for a bot specification that is referred to in the message "Process Model (Bot Specification)" displayed in Fig. 8. The bot therefore is a (business) **object**[2] in the process shown in Fig. 8.

**As a subject**: A chatbot during process runtime can be described as an active participant (subject) in the process. Figure 7 shows the SID of the same bot that was discussed for Fig. 5.

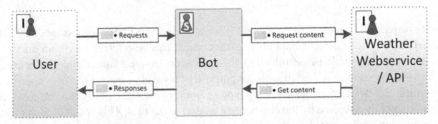

**Fig. 7.** Simple process model of the chatbot-user interaction for a weather query.

The software architecture is not visible, only the desired or realized interaction of a user with the software at runtime is shown. This is advantageous in situations when business processes need to be modeled where a chatbot plays a crucial role in the success of the process (e.g., customer service) and therefore the interaction with it needs to be explicitly modeled to avoid misrepresenting the chatbots importance or leaving it out.

---

[2] To clarify: In Fig. 5 the components of the bot are described as subjects but the bot - or rather the model - is considered to be an object.

Additionally, by modeling the explicit behavior of the chatbot, the different possible outcomes of the process are traceable.

Due to its clarity, the representation in Fig. 7 is better suited for use in larger process models. For the technical specification of a chatbot, however, it contains too little detail. For people who are inexperienced in chatbot development, this type of modeling is easier to understand than the representation in Fig. 5. This applies equally to the creation and interpretation of the model.

## 3.2   Subject-Oriented Specification and Automated Creation of Chatbots

A similar approach like the one which the chatbot DECLO (see Sect. 2.3) is based on, is to take a subject-oriented process model and to automatically generate a chatbot out of it. Figure 8 shows a concept for implementing this idea. Fully specified subjects are parts that either still need to be created or existing programs that need to be adapted. Interface subjects are parts that can be used in their present form. The model validation program operationalizes the modeling convention to ensure correct execution of the PASS parser. The PASS parser converts the process data from the Visio add-in (see Sect. 2.1) into source code for the chatbot using the mapping from the model validation program. This code is reviewed by a developer before the bot is deployed and ready to use[3].

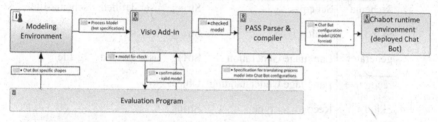

**Fig. 8.** Concept for the development of a program for the automated bot generation.

One of the bigger advantages of PASS is that it is a formal language for describing processes [9]. This opens the possibility to automatically outsource parts of a specified communication by machines. Following this idea, the next section discusses the automated creation of a chatbot starting from PASS models. The method used to explore this idea is structured as follows:

1. Creation of a simple bot using MS Bot Composer (see Sect. 2.3)
2. Creation of a PASS model of the respective bot
3. Creating the software to read the PASS model
4. Injecting the readout information into a pre-built bot skeleton
5. Testing and debugging the bot

---

[3] The content message "Process Model (bot specification)" could be a model like the one shown in Fig. 5

To create a simple and functional bot, a template by Microsoft is used. This bot is used to predict the weather based on the input of an American zip code, like the one in Sect. 3.1.

As summarized in Table 1, a normative process model contains more information about the software architecture of the chatbot. Since a formal specification is needed is obvious to use it for the automated creation of a chatbot. However, the perquisite of understanding the technical functionality of chatbots is contradicting this. The automatic generation of a chatbot specification from PASS is only useful if the modeling of the chatbot's behavior can be performed even by people who do not know its functionality. For this reason, a descriptive[4] model of the chatbot should be used as the subject for the specification.

A modeling convention ensures that a parser can reliably convert the individual modeling elements into source code for the bot project. For this purpose, dialog modules of the MS Bot Framework are assigned to the individual modeling elements. The parts of an adaptive dialog specified in JSON are described in the following table (Table 2):

**Table 2.** Analysis of the degrees of freedom in specifying JSON for adaptive dialogs.

| Name | Dialog module | Type[a] | Possibilities | Reference |
|---|---|---|---|---|
| $schema | Scheme | String | user defined | .schema-file |
| $kind | Dialog type | String | 9 | |
| generator | Language Generation | String | user defined | .lg-file |
| recognizer | Language Understanding | Object | | |
| $kind | Recognizer type | String | 6 | |
| intents[b] | User intention | Array | user defined | |
| intent | Identifier | String | user defined | |
| pattern | adaptive expressions | String | user defined | |
| triggers | Trigger of actions | Array | user-defined | |
| $kind | Trigger type | String | 20 | |
| actions[c] | Trigger response | Array | user-defined | |
| $kind | Action type | String | 31 | |
| activity | Action property | divers | user-defined | user-defined |

[a] The data type of this identifier within the JSON file.
[b] The shaded fill shows the membership of this array as a subset of the object recognizer.
[c] Analogous to the previous footnote.

[4] See Table 1

A total of 12 shapes are available in standard PASS: start subject, interface subject, fully specified subject, message, send state, do state, receive state, start state, end state, send transition, do transition, receive transition. These are used to provide the required data for a correct bot creation shown in Table 3. The fourth column of the table gives possible solutions for modeling in PASS. The dialog modules in rows with entry "user-defined" must get the data from the shapes of the PASS model, the rest can be selected via lists. These dialog blocks that require manual input are generator, intent, pattern and activity. The intent, i.e., the user's intention, can be anticipated by naming the receive state during bot modeling. The corresponding pattern is entered in the receive transition. The messages sent by the bot are defined in the generator dialog module. These messages can be entered in send transitions.

Activities are the basic communication type for the Bot Framework. In view of the complexity of the activity class, the limits of a modeling convention were reached. The addressed modeling convention can clarify which standard classes and methods of the bot framework respectively take over tasks. However, task-specific functions cannot be predefined. Task-specific functions of the sample bot discussed in Sect. 3.1 are:

- Calling API
- Selecting the appropriate display for weather forecasts
- Checking a postal code (also depending on the country)
- NLG of the chatbot

This once again demonstrates the superiority of the MS Bot Framework Composer. The program provides both the modeling convention and intuitive customizability. Compared to a standalone development of a chatbot, numerous details will get lost with the approach of automatically generating a bot from a PASS model.

### 3.3  Chatbots as Subject-Oriented Modeling Helpers

Chatbots are intended to converse with humans and help them on a specific task. Subsequently a specialized bot could be used to automate the elicitation of business processes knowledge from stakeholders and automatically create subject-oriented process models. In Fig. 9 can be seen how the architecture of a system for subject-oriented modeling supported by Conversational AI could look like. As for Fig. 8, fully specified subjects are parts that either still need to be created or existing programs that need to be adapted. Interface subjects are parts that can be used in their present form.

In Sect. 2.2, the tasks and stakeholders that are important for the development and implementation of an S-BPM strategy were presented. Based on these task packages, it was discussed in expert interviews how chatbots can support them. Table 3 gives an overview of the results of that discussion.

Of the six task packages shown in Table 3, these four areas are further discussed for the application of Conversational AI: analysis, modeling, validation, and operation. In Sect. 2.2 the following roles were presented: facilitators, governors, experts, and actors. While chatbots in operation count as actors, facilitators and experts are significantly involved in the phases of analysis, modeling and validation. Due to the complexity of business process management and the responsibilities, chatbots cannot be considered as

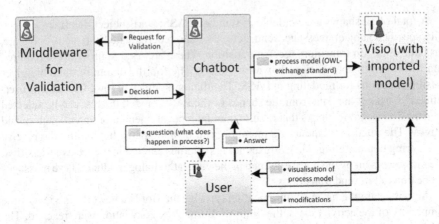

**Fig. 9.** Concept for a system using Conversational AI to assist with subject-oriented modeling.

**Table 3.** Areas of application for chatbots in the context of subject-orientation.

| Task packs | Potential applications | Effort/Benefit |
|---|---|---|
| Analysis | • Documenting the process through conversation<br>• Explicate implicit knowledge | Very good |
| Modeling | • Parallel graphical provision of the process during documentation. Explanation of individual process steps by voice assistance<br>• Help in the application, basic constructs of the modeling method | Good |
| Validation | • Forwarding of the model to experts<br>• Parallel formal validation of analysis and modeling | Medium |
| Optimization | • Increase availability of database entries through API<br>• Create regular reporting<br>• Communicate with monitoring software that detects bottlenecks from process data<br>• In execution: connecting e.g., customers to process execution via chatbots - chatbot as UI to a workflow engine | Poor |
| Org. Implementation | • Inquire and note connections to other processes | Poor |
| IT | • Collaborate with other bots to make processes known in their respective IT systems | |
| Operation/Management | • Use as a process participant | Medium |

autonomous decision makers. Therefore, the role of the governors will be left out for the time being. In the following section, the remaining roles are interwoven with the task packages to work out suitable use cases. The role of chatbots as actors - active process participants - has already been discussed. This application is possible, but must be taken care of a reasonable cost-benefit ratio.

The role of the **expert** is important in many companies because they contribute tacit knowledge. Due to the lack of experience, chatbots cannot do this, but they can provide explicit knowledge as needed if they could access a structured database. In many companies, this is already implemented in practice in the form of frequently-asked-questions bots (FAQ bots). For this use case, however, the reference to subject-orientation is missing in the context of this work.

The role of the **facilitator** can, apart from the emotional component, be automated well or very well in the form of a chatbot (see Table 3, column 3). The following tasks are particularly suitable for further technical convergence of subject-orientation and chatbots. The complexity of the implementation increases from top to bottom.

- Demand-oriented provision of knowledge for subject-oriented process modeling
- Digital and formal documentation of a process through natural language conversation
- Real-time validation of the formal (not contentual) correctness of a model
- Parallel graphical modeling of the process to be analyzed

Hoppenbrouwers and Rouwette [21] emphasize in their work the need for a con-strained behavior of facilitators during modeling, as well as the positive effects of a structured log of the communication through which the model is perceived.

# 4 Albert – A Subject-Oriented Chatbot

Albert[5] was developed as a minimum viable product (MVP) to prove the possibility of realizing the modeling process using only written words. The focus of the development laid on the chatbot itself. Once the planned functional scope has been defined, the first step in the technical implementation of the prototype is to decide how the bot is to be developed. The MS Bot Framework offers a graphical approach with Composer and a code-based approach with the SDK. Since the research field of subject-orientation is to be scientifically extended using chatbots in this work, the following two requirements were placed on Albert's software:

- Low code: Low threshold for further development
- Modularity: High reusability of written code

## 4.1 Development

The chatbot was programmed in C# using the MS Bot Framework SDK as well as the MS Bot Framework Composer. With this approach, the basic conversation flow can be adjusted using the no-code environment of the composer while the subject-oriented

---

[5] The project can be cloned and tested with: https://github.com/itsme-bigv/PassBot1/tree/unstop pableDialog.

functionalities are coded in C# using a custom library with PASS functionalities[6]. By taking this approach, the two requirements set in the previous section are met.

## 4.2  Capabilities

The MVP is capable of creating the very basic SO modeling elements and exporting them into an.OWL-file. In the following, it is shown how a straightforward conversational editor for working with PASS models is operated. First, as shown in Fig. 10 a new model has to be created.

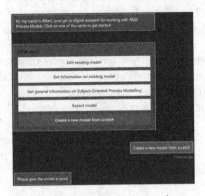

**Fig. 10.** Start of the conversation.

After giving the model a name and telling Albert that you want to edit the model, the basic functionalities are offered as shown in Fig. 11.

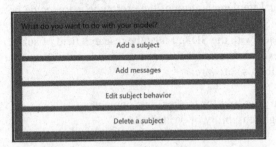

**Fig. 11.** Basic modeling capabilities.

After adding subjects, messages and behaviors, the model can be exported into the respective project folder as.OWL-file.

---

[6] The library is being developed at the Institute of Information Management in Engineering (IMI) and can be integrated using the package manager nuget: https://www.nuget.org/packages/alps. net.api/

# 5   Discussion

In Sect. 3.1, a fundamental consideration of the perception and description of chatbots in S-BPM was made. By describing a chatbot as an object and a subject during a business process, it was discovered that by using PASS, one can detail out the behavior of the chatbot in a respective SBD or just model it as a black box (interface subject). In both cases, the active role of the chatbot in the process is captured as a subject. That way, its importance is never lost, no matter what level of modeling detail you want to deploy.

In contrast to S-BPM, more classical modeling languages, like BPMN, encourage a modeler to either leave the chatbots activity out of the model due to it being "just" a piece of software and therefore a means of communication with other entities. Or the modeler would be forced to always describe every activity of the chatbot due to the procedural paradigm (task-oriented nature) of most classical modeling languages.

In Sect. 3.2, a modeling convention was considered necessary to automatically derive a specification of chatbots from a PASS model. For this purpose, the modeling elements of PASS and the MS Bot Framework were compared. The necessary implementation of the task-specific activities of a chatbot turned out to be a critical point, from which on further research was stopped. The ratio of effort and benefit was found to be too poor. The goal of avoiding the manual programming of a chatbot is the same as that of the MS Bot Framework Composer, which is already very mature in its functionality. This goal goes far beyond that of the paper by Lopez et al. [18]. The method used in this paper seems to be too complex to implement. However, it is independent of the modeling language.

The results in Sect. 3.3 are promising for operationalization. Chatbots are particularly well suited for the provision of domain knowledge, as well as for the automation of recurring tasks. Therefore, in the context of subject-orientation, they are suitable to support the modeling process of business processes. On the one hand, chatbots can be used to explain the specifics of subject-orientation on demand. On the other hand, entire modeling processes can be accompanied by digital and formal documentation. The prototype described in section four is based on these results. Albert - a chatbot - serves as conceptual proof of a meaningful link between subject-orientation and Conversational AI. However, Albert's existing functionality is not sufficient for smooth deployment and requires further development. Alternatively, the development can be done code-based with the Bot Framework SDK in one of the available languages. This approach offers greater freedom in realizing the capabilities of the chatbot, but at the same time requires a much deeper understanding of chatbot technologies, as well as experience in developing web apps. The use of the user-friendly Composer was therefore deliberately chosen to facilitate further development. Nevertheless, the use of Composer meant an overhead due to the necessary configuration of the JSONs and a more complex project management. The functionality is also therefore not comparable to that of the chatbot Declo by Alman et al. [19]. The advantage of Albert, however, is that it can create full-fledged models without a graphical editor, making the chatbot a speech-based editor. This makes it possible for blind people to create process models. In addition, the model quality is not affected by the speech processing, which is the case with Declo.

This work represents the starting point for a stronger integration of subject-orientation with chatbot technologies. As indicated in the previous section, it is important to consider how the results of this work change if a different bot framework is used. For this purpose, an open-source framework is recommended, which is less dependent on the Microsoft ecosystem.

# References

1. Becker, J., Kugeler, M., Rosemann, M.: Prozessmanagement. Springer, Heidelberg (2012)
2. Obermeier, S., Fischer, H., Fleischmann, A., Dirndorfer, M.: Geschäftsprozesse realisieren. Ein praxisorientierter Leitfaden von der Strategie bis zur Implementierung. Springer Vieweg, Wiesbaden (2014)
3. Fleischmann, A., Stary, C.: Whom to talk to? A stakeholder perspective on business process development. Univ. Access Inf. Soc. **11**, 125–150 (2012). https://doi.org/10.1007/s10209-011-0236-x
4. Fleischmann, A., Borgert, S., Elstermann, M., Krenn, F., Singer, R.: An overview to S-BPM oriented tool suites. S-BPM One 30–31 (2017)
5. Gentsch, P.: Conversational AI: how (chat)bots will reshape the digital experience. In: Gentsch, P. (ed.) AI in Marketing, Sales and Service: How Marketers without a Data Science Degree can use AI, Big Data and Bots, pp. 81–125. Springer, Cham (2019). https://doi.org/10.1007/978-3-319-89957-2_4
6. Fleischmann, A., Schmidt, W., Singer, R., Seese, D. (eds.): S-BPM ONE 2010. CCIS, vol. 138. Springer, Heidelberg (2011). https://doi.org/10.1007/978-3-642-23135-3
7. Elstermann, M.: Proposal for using semantic technologies as a means to store and exchange subject-oriented process models. In: Proceedings of the 9th Conference on Subject-Oriented Business Process Management. ACM, New York (2017). https://doi.org/10.1145/3040565.3040573
8. Elstermann, M., Wolski, A., Fleischmann, A., Stary, C., Borgert, S.: The combined use of the web ontology language (OWL) and abstract state machines (ASM) for the definition of a specification language for business processes. In: Raschke, A., Riccobene, E., Schewe, K.-D. (eds.) Logic, Computation and Rigorous Methods. LNCS, vol. 12750, pp. 283–300. Springer, Cham (2021). https://doi.org/10.1007/978-3-030-76020-5_16
9. Elstermann, M.: Executing Strategic Product Planning - A Subject-Oriented Analysis and New Referential Process Model for IT-Tool Support and Agile Execution of Strategic Product Planning. KIT Scientific Publishing, Karlsruhe, Baden (2020)
10. Turing, A.M.: Computing machinery and intelligence. Mind 433–460 (1950). https://doi.org/10.1093/mind/LIX.236.433
11. Adamopoulou, E., Moussiades, L.: An overview of chatbot technology. In: Maglogiannis, I., Iliadis, L., Pimenidis, E. (eds.) AIAI 2020. IAICT, vol. 584, pp. 373–383. Springer, Cham (2020). https://doi.org/10.1007/978-3-030-49186-4_31
12. Ram, A., et al.: Conversational AI: The Science Behind the Alexa Prize. Alexa.Prize.Proceedings (2018). https://developer.amazon.com/alexaprize/proceedings
13. Sürig, C.: Wo gehts denn lang? Entwickler.de (2017)
14. Intuz: A comprehensive guide on web application architecture (2021). https://www.intuz.com/guide-on-web-app-architecture#a
15. Galitsky, B.: Developing Enterprise Chatbots. Springer, Cham (2019)
16. Microsoft: Bot Framework SDK documentation (2021). https://docs.microsoft.com/de-de/azure/bot-service/index-bf-sdk?view=azure-bot-service-4.0

17. Microsoft: Bot Framework Composer Documentation (2021). https://docs.microsoft.com/en-us/composer/
18. López, A., Sànchez-Ferreres, J., Carmona, J., Padró, L.: From process models to chatbots. In: Giorgini, P., Weber, B. (eds.) CAiSE 2019. LNCS, vol. 11483, pp. 383–398. Springer, Cham (2019). https://doi.org/10.1007/978-3-030-21290-2_24
19. Alman, A., Balder, K., Maggi, F., Aa, H.V.: Declo: A Chatbot for User-friendly Specification of Declarative Process Models BPM (2020)
20. Schmidt, W., Fleischmann, A., Gilbert, O.T.: Subjektorientiertes Geschäftsprozessmanagement. HMD **46**, 52–62 (2009). https://doi.org/10.1007/BF03340343
21. Hoppenbrouwers, S., Rouwette, E.: A dialogue game for analysing group model building: framing collaborative modelling and its facilitation. Int. J. Organ. Des. Eng. **2**(1), 19 (2012). https://doi.org/10.1504/IJODE.2012.045905

# Application

# A Comparative Study of Simulation Tools for Business Processes

Matthes Elstermann[1]([✉]) and Christoph Piller[2]

[1] Institute for Information Management in Engineering,
Karlsruhe Institute of Technology, 76131 Karlsruhe, Germany
`matthes.elstermann@kit.edu`
[2] Viessmann Climate Solutions SE, Viessmannstraße 1,
35108 Allendorf (Eder), Germany

**Abstract.** This work is a report on a comparison study done in an industry context with the goal to evaluate three different tools meant to model, simulate, and subsequent evaluate business processes as part of business process management and robot process automation effort. The three compared tools are the SAP Signavio Process Manager, the subject-oriented Simple Simulation Tool, and the Process Simulator from GBU mbH. The tools and their simulation approaches are introduced and the results, where applicable, as well as the general handling compared. Each tool has its intended purpose and pros and cons under different given circumstances. The reader is given the understanding to differentiate between the tools in order to evaluate which tool is meeting which requirements.

**Keywords:** Business process management · Process simulation · Subject-orientation · Signavio · S-BPM · SiSi

## 1 Introduction

### 1.1 Initial Situation

The journey for this study started, as part of an important process automation project at the administration of a big institution for higher education. The goal was to adopt Robotic Process Automation (RPA) solutions. Before being able to make an educated decision, the responsible persons needed a quick and inexpensive analysis of the potential of that process automation, ideally later shown with a pilot project. To do so, first modeling and then a run time simulation of the given business process use-case were considered.

Multiple possible solutions for that endeavor were available or found as part of the study. From there the research question of this worked derived: How does each solution handle the presented use case and what is to gain from it for the overall endevor?

At the starting point of the project, the condition of the project was as following:

M. Elstermann et al. (Eds.): S-BPM ONE 2022, CCIS 1632, pp. 61–78, 2022.
https://doi.org/10.1007/978-3-031-19704-8_4

- Little resources for the topic business process management and process automation. Only few persons are available for analysis, modeling, and simulation of a process. No one is specifically dedicated (typical for a small or medium sized enterprise).
- Therefore, analysis and simulation of processes must be done in the most efficient way. I.e., with as little resources as possible and as significant results as possible.
- Ease of use is also of importance since no dedicated process modeling expert or even a dedicated process team is available (typical for SMEs).
- Aim of a process simulation in such cases is a quick cost-time evaluation of a process.
- Derived from such a cost-time evaluation, possible savings due to improvements and automation a Return of Investments calculation can also be done.
- Due to the general setting (not many resources), a long time investment in a subscription based solution with additional extensive BPM and workflow capabilities are not necessary and a one-time-buy solution is preferable.

A proper and detailed simulation of a business process can be handled as an entire project inside a business process management project (Sect. 2).

Usually, it is recommended to have all information regarding necessary resources (money, manpower, equipment, facilities, materials, information/technology) available and allocated for such a project [7]. If this is the case, a simulation project can be started theoretically. Nevertheless, we had a different starting point, which is explained above.

The three tools evaluated in this study were selected arbitrarily by availability given the involved personal and the institutional situation.

## 1.2   Framework Conditions

Besides the circumstance that there are only little resources available, some conditions must be met, in order to be able to simulate a business process.

First of all, the business process that is to be simulated must be modeled. This model should include all relevant process steps necessary to fulfill the business process.

For each business process step, an at least approximated or known duration or duration interval must be given. Furthermore the personnel and used software costs must be known.

Ideally, knowledge about the impact of automation is also available and modeled. Whereby this condition is not crucial, as it only will give you results about the possible savings. If not available sound assumptions need to be made.

## 1.3   Selection of Tools

As mentioned, the tools to be evaluated were partially selected arbitrarily. Given was an evaluation version of a cloud-based tools suit from *Signavio* [11], based on the BPMN 2.0 modeling language. The expected relatively high costs due to many unused features as well as especially the subscription based business model were the reasons to look for alternatives. Especially with on-time purchasing options.

Both other tools are based on Microsoft Office Visio which was available in general due to a standard office subscription for the whole organization.

The *Simple Simulation* (SiSi) tool [3] was selected, due to previous experience with the subject-oriented modeling paradigm and the modeling language PASS.

Finally, the *Process Simulator* [10] was chosen for its equally simple availability as a Visio plug-in and simple flow-chart based modeling concept.

All chosen tools fulfill the minimum requirements of being able to model a process including assumptions about run-time and probabilities, run the simulation based on that, and output the resulting data in a GUI or via export to a spreadsheet format.

## 2 Simulation of a Process

Before discussing the simulated business process used for the comparison itself, it is important to get a general understanding of the process simulation topic.

One principle goal of creating models for business processes is to ensure a common understanding among the members of an organization. Given a suitable formal notation for the created models, simulation can be used to ensure a quantitative evaluation of the process itself which may be an important aspect of the business process management (BPM) approach [1].

In general, three different sub-areas are distinguished for quantitative evaluation of business processes. The aggregated, the instance-related, and the resource-related evaluation.

The aggregated evaluation provides quantitative insights to general key figures of the entire process (generated and finished process instances etc.).

The instance-related evaluation provides quantitative insights to specific key figures of a single process instance itself (throughput and wait times broken down up to a single activity).

The resource-related evaluation provides quantitative insights to process times of the specific process-executing entity.

In order to start with a simulation and be able to work with the simulation results, following steps should be conducted. First of all, you should make a project plan. After that you can start with analyzing the process and define respectively collect the necessary data. Then you are good to create and conduct the simulation. With the results you can check the correctness of your simulation model, interpret the results, experiment with the variables and finally, present the end results.

In general, following data must be gathered for an effective simulation:

- process time - the time or time distribution an activity or action in a process takes
- Gateway rules - the probabilities of path branching in a process to occur

- Additional data can be: waiting times, transmission times, arising expenses, priorities
- Number of employees, machinery - details about the process execution system
- Frequency - the number of process instances to be run on the execution system

Given the initial situation, not enough resources were available to conduct such a accurate simulation project. Nevertheless, it is important to keep the most important goals and data for such a simulation in mind. Although the simulation of the business process must be done as efficient as possible, the generated results must also be as significant as possible.

## 3   Contract Termination Process

The basis for the comparison of the tools was a relative simple and small process. The business process basically concerned terminating contracts by customers.

When customers want to cancel their contract they have the possibility to notify the respective support and service team or alternatively, the so-called finance team, a support and service team specifically for finance related topics, e.g. postponement of payments, payment reminders, change of payment interval etc. It was created because of the big amount of finance related requests.

If customers are notifying the finance team about their contract termination, the team is not forwarding the information directly to the support and service team. The finance team must make a first check of the received information. Afterwards the information is forwarded and the support and service team will further process the documents no matter where they stem from. If customers have sent all needed documents, the support and service team can make the respective modifications in their online learning system. If information from customers is missing, the support and service team has to demand the missing information from customers.

When all the modifications in the online learning system are done, the support and service team is creating a task for the finance team. Then, the finance team must terminate the contract in the company's ERP system. Finally, customers will receive a confirmation of their contract termination.

Due to the circumstances that all tools are using different modeling languages and partially different modeling paradigms, the previously described process was modeled for each tool individually.

### 3.1   Contract Termination Process Modeled with BPMN 2.0 in Signavio

The process modeled with BPMN 2.0 [9] in Signavio includes the main activities and gateways (see Fig. 1), making use of the swimlane mechanism to differentiate between "Customer", "Support and Service Team" and "Finance Team".

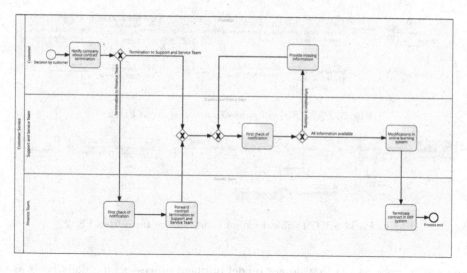

**Fig. 1.** BPMN process in Signavio

## 3.2 Contract Termination Process Modeled with PASS

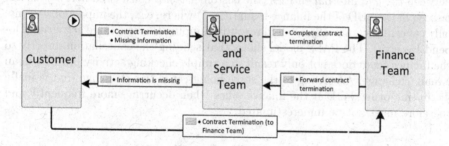

**Fig. 2.** PASS subject interaction diagram

The second evaluated tool uses the paradigm of subject-orientation and the modeling language PASS created by [4,6]. Therefore it is split up into, first, a single subject-interaction diagram (SID - Fig. 2 and then individual subject behavior diagrams (SBD - Figs. 3, 5, and 4).

As analyzed in detail by [2], one big drawback of the SO/PASS approach can be seen from these models directly. SO/PASS requires to explicitly model and name communication and exchange of information (the red receive states (R) and green send states (S) in contrast to the yellow do states (D)). This obviously inflates the model structure that essentially is still the same process. However, the necessary effort can be mitigated by the employed tool [5]. Furthermore, this explicit communication modeling might be actually an important factor in the modeling approach as it results in better, more easily understandable models,

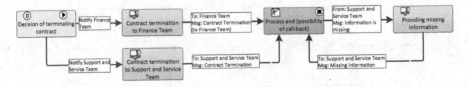

**Fig. 3.** PASS SBD of subject customer from Fig. 2

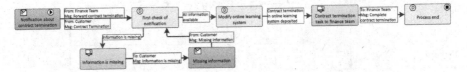

**Fig. 4.** PASS SBD of subject support and service team from Fig. 2

especially from people that do not model business processes on a daily basis as it would be the case for the given scenario [2,8].

Stated by the stakeholder for this project, the PASS model also shows the true complexity of the process and therefore its potential of improvement. This complexity does not stem from the activities, but indeed from the interaction between the two internal entities (the customer is not considered here). This can be seen in the SBD of the finance team (Fig. 5) where, e.g., the impact of students only canceling via the office would result in skipping the first three activities (Do-Send-Receive). The PASS model shows that sending the cancellation directly to the finance team does not only result in a simple checking activity but also in an e-mail exchange. According to the stake holder, it is this exchange that is really disrupting other work at the finance office when occurring more frequently and therefore must not be underestimated.

### 3.3  Contract Termination Process in a Flow Diagram

The third evaluated tool uses a simple flow-chart-type notation. Following the same simple modeling paradigm as the BPMN model. Therefore, this flow chart based model (Fig. 6) is very similar to the BPMN model.

The main differences are on the one side, that no swim lanes have been created for the different roles, but roles had to be assigned to every task specifically. Furthermore, no closings of opened gateways is occurring.

## 4  Simulation of Contract Termination Process

As initially stated, for the improvement of the contract termination process and in order to quantify suggested improvements, an overview about process costs, needed time, and bottlenecks was required. As only limited resources were available for the project, there was no room to start a sophisticated process

**Fig. 5.** PASS SBD of subject finance team from Fig. 2

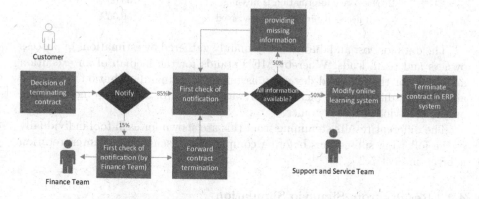

**Fig. 6.** Flow-chart based process in process simulator

simulation sub-project. Thus, all relevant data (time and costs) was gathered while parallel to modeling the processes.

## 4.1 Input Data of the Contract Termination Process

In all three cases, the process was simulated with the following input data (Tables 1 and 2):

**Table 1.** Times and costs inputted into all simulation models

| Role/Subject | Activty | Cost per Execution | Times |
|---|---|---|---|
| Support and Service Team | Pre-check receipt contract termination | 0,20 € | MED 05m DEV 01m |
| | Apply termination in learning system | 0,30 € | MED 10m DEV 05m |
| Finance Team | Pre-check receipt contract termination | 0,20 € | MED 05m DEV 01m |
| | Forward termination to service team | 0,10 € | MED 02m DEV 30s |
| | Apply termination in ERP system | 0,30 € | MED 10m DEV 05m |
| Customer | Contract termination | 0.00 € | 00h 00m |
| | Provide missing information | 0,00 € | 00h 00m |

**Table 2.** Probability of gateways in all simulation models

| | | |
|---|---|---|
| 1 | Contract termination to support and service team | 85,00% |
| | Contract termination to finance team | 15,00% |
| 2 | Necessary information is missing | 50,00% |
| | All necessary information received | 50,00% |

The data for cost and duration was mainly gathered by estimations of process owners and team leads. Whereby MED stands for the median of an execution and DEV for the standard deviation assuming a normal distribution. The costs and activity duration for the customer was set to zero, as we have no influence on the behavior of the customer.

The different results stemming from this are shown for each tool individually in the following subsections before a comparative discussion and interpretation is given in Sect. 5.2.

### 4.2 Results from Signavio Simulation

The usage of Signavio for modeling a process as well as simulating a process was simple. For modeling, all usable shapes are displayed in the left menu bar (Fig. 7). When you hoover over one of the shapes, a short description of the function of the shape is also displayed. Additionally, the syntax of the process model is checked by the software.

When the modeling of the process is finished, the user can go to the simulation area. There, the costs, frequencies, resources and duration of every activity can be set (Fig. 8). If this data was already entered during the modeling, inside the attributes of every shape, the user can use this area for a final check of the entered data.

Finally, a modeler can set up different scenarios, with different data for comparison reasons and choose to simulate one run or a run of several days.

The simulation was run with a scenario for one day, with the given frequency and available employees. The Tables 3 and 4 display the results of costs and duration for every activity.

### 4.3 Results from SiSi Simulation

For SiSi, data input is done while modeling for each shape individually. However, if needed a batch setting dialog can be opened to edit all data in a SBD at once (See Fig. 9).

If all model elements are prepared, the simulation dialogue can simple be called from the task bar. Here (Fig. 10) some additionally simulation parameters can be set, the simulation can be started, and the results can be exported.

In contrast to Signavio and due to the subject-oriented nature, SiSi is listing the results per subject. Tables 5 and 6 show the computed costs per subject as well as the run-time per subject for one process instance. Results per day can be derived by simply multiplying a single instance times by the number of instances expected by day as it is done for Signavio from the start (Table 7).

**Table 3.** Simulation results for Signavio

| Activity | Duration (d) | Finished Instances | Average | Minium | Maximum | Total costs |
|---|---|---|---|---|---|---|
| Notify company about termination | 1 | 17 | 0,00 € | 0,00 € | 0,00 € | 0,00 € |
| First check of notification | 1 | 1 | 4,01 € | 4,01 € | 4,01 € | 4,01 € |
| Forward contract termination | 1 | 1 | 1,34 € | 1,34 € | 1,34 € | 1,34 € |
| First check of notification | 1 | 18 | 4,42 € | 2,66 € | 6,10 € | 80,64 € |
| Provide missing information | 1 | 6 | 0,00 € | 0,00 € | 0,00 € | 0,00 € |
| Modifications in online learning system | 1 | 12 | 7,08 € | 1,02 € | 11,01 € | 84,92 € |
| Terminate contract in ERP system | 1 | 11 | 8,35 € | 2,38 € | 14,36 € | 92,17 € |

**Table 4.** Simulation results for Signavio

| Activity | Finished Instances | Average | Minimum | Maximum | Total execution time |
|---|---|---|---|---|---|
| Notify company about termination | 17 | 0h:00m 00s | 0h:00m 00s | 0h:00m 00s | 0h:00m 00s |
| First check of notification | 1 | 0h:04m 34s | 0h:04m 34s | 0h:04m 34s | 0h:04m 34s |
| Forward contract termination to Support and Service Team | 1 | 0h:01m 29s | 0h:01m 29s | 0h:01m 29s | 0h:01m 29s |
| First check of notification | 18 | 0h:05m 04s | 0h:02m 57s | 0h:07m 05s | 1h:31m 15s |
| Provide missing information | 6 | 0h:00m 00s | 0h:00m 00s | 0h:00m 00s | 0h:00m 00s |
| Modifications in online learning system | 12 | 0h:08m 08s | 0h:00m 52s | 0h:12m 51s | 1h:37m 35s |
| Terminate contract in ERP system | 11 | 0h:09m 40s | 0h:02m 30s | 0h:16m 52s | 8h:25m 23s |

**Table 5.** Simulation output for the SiSi: Costs

| Subjects | Cost Average | Cost Min | Cost Max |
|---|---|---|---|
| Customer | 0,00 € | 0,00 € | 0,00 € |
| Support and Service Team | 15,45 € | 8,30 € | 28,70 € |
| Finance Team | 9,29 € | 4,47 € | 18,00 € |
| **Summed up:** | **24,74 €** | **12,77 €** | **46,70 €** |
| Incl. Fixed Costs: | 24,74 € | 12,77 € | 46,70 € |

**Table 6.** Simulation output for the SiSi: Overall time and subject-times

| Overall Process Runtime: | Mean | Min | Max |
|---|---|---|---|
| | 0h:27m 13s | 0h:09m 00s | 1h:27m 00s |

| Subjects: | Required Work Time: | Overall Active Time: | Inactive/ Waiting Time: | Time until first Activation: | Time From Process Start to End: |
|---|---|---|---|---|---|
| Customer | 0h:00m 00s | 0h:03m 14s | 0h:03m 14s | 0h:00m 00s | 0h:03m 14s |
| Service Team | 0h:17m 30s | 0h:17m 30s | 0h:00m 00s | 0h:00m 07s | 0h:17m 37s |
| Finance Team | 0h:10m 45s | 0h:13m 26s | 0h:02m 41s | 0h:13m 47s | 0h:27m 13s |

**Table 7.** Simulation output for the SiSi: Detail cost per subjects

| Subject: Support and Service Team | Average | Best Case | Worst Case |
|---|---|---|---|
| Labor Cost per Process Execution: | 14,58 € | 7,50 € | 27,50 € |
| Additional Cost per single Execution : | 0,87 € | 0,80 € | 1,20 € |
| **Overall Cost per Execution** | **15,45 €** | **8,30 €** | **28,70 €** |
| Subject: Finance Team | Average | Best Case | Worst Case |
| Labor Cost per Process Execution: | 8,96 € | 4,17 € | 17,50 € |
| Additional Cost per single Execution : | 0,33 € | 0,30 € | 0,50 € |
| **Overall Cost per Execution** | **9,29 €** | **4,47 €** | **18,00 €** |

**Fig. 7.** Modeling palette in Signavio

## 4.4  Results from Process Simulator Simulation

Also MS Visio based, modeling of the process is similar to modeling any process in Microsoft Visio as all usable shapes are available in the left menu bar (Fig. 11). Furthermore, a so-called Syntax-Highlighting and IntelliSense software, included in the Process Simulator application, is supporting during the modeling and checking for possible model errors.

For the simulation of the modeled process, a specific Process Simulator tab appears in the upper menu bar (Fig. 12). From there you can run the simulation and set up different scenarios. The data itself is entered inside the shapes.

Since the Process Simulator software is focusing mainly on production and logistics the results look accordingly and structured around the usage of different resources, as shown in Table 8. In the last column you can see the utilization of the different activities, which number appears in many working sheets.

The results from the Process Simulator simulation are focusing on the utilization and idle time of the different entities, which are assigned to the activities. Thus, the results basically cannot be compared to the results from Signavio and SiSi. The reason for that is that what the process simulator is actually doing is

**Table 8.** Simulation output for the process simulator

| Name | planned time (Min) | capacity | occurrence | av. duration | av. content | max content | current content | capacity util. in % |
|---|---|---|---|---|---|---|---|---|
| Cancel enrollment | 480 | 1 | 79 | 5,99 | 0,99 | 1 | 1 | 98,55 |
| Send cancellation an | 480 | 999999 | 78 | 0 | 0 | 1 | 0 | 0 |
| Pre-check cancellation by StudSek | 480 | 20 | 59 | 5,08 | 0,62 | 1 | 0 | 3,12 |
| Information present | 480 | 999999 | 58 | 0 | 0 | 1 | 0 | 0 |
| Process cancellation | 480 | 20 | 16 | 10,75 | 0,36 | 1 | 1 | 1,79 |
| Terminate contract | 480 | 7 | 15 | 9,81 | 0,31 | 1 | 1 | 4,38 |
| Pre-check cancellation by Finanzteam | 480 | 7 | 15 | 1,94 | 0,06 | 1 | 0 | 0,87 |
| Cancellation to StudSek | 480 | 7 | 15 | 6,33 | 0,2 | 1 | 0 | 2,83 |
| Provide necessary Information | 480 | 1 | 33 | 5,91 | 0,41 | 1 | 1 | 40,66 |
| Cancellation Input Buffer | 480 | 999 | 94 | 28,25 | 5,53 | 20 | 15 | 0,55 |
| Pre-check receive cancellation StudSek Input Buffer | 480 | 999 | 110 | 104,85 | 24,03 | 51 | 51 | 2,41 |
| Process cancellation Input Buffer | 480 | 999 | 25 | 104,64 | 5,45 | 12 | 9 | 0,55 |
| Terminate cancellation Input Buffer | 480 | 999 | 15 | 0,94 | 0,03 | 1 | 0 | 0,003 |
| Pre-check receive cancellation Finanzteam Input Buffer | 480 | 999 | 15 | 1,035 | 0,03 | 1 | 0 | 0,003 |
| cancellation to StudSek Input Buffer | 480 | 999 | 15 | 1,20 | 0,03 | 1 | 0 | 0,003 |
| Provide necessary information Input Buffer | 480 | 999 | 33 | 1,14 | 0,08 | 1 | 0 | 0,008 |

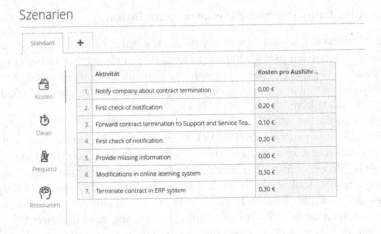

**Fig. 8.** Simulation settings in Signavio for costs

a mix of modeling and simulating an actual process as well as the underlying *process execution system* itself in detail. This is fine for linear production processes, but neither practical for the intended task nor in the scope of Signavio and SiSi. It is also not reflecting the problem, originally sought out to be solve with a simulation tool (see Sect. 1.1).

# 5 Comparison and Interpretation of the Simulation Results

As shown, the contract termination process was simulated with three different tools. In this section, we compare and analyze the simulation results themselves as well as the handling and pricing of the different tools.

As mentioned, the results of the Process Simulator could not be taken into account here, as they were not comparable to the results of Signavio and SiSi simulation, due to its different focus and orientation at production processes rather than business processes. The results were partially too detailed and contained many domain specific metrics. In other regards to achieve comparable result, as mentioned, the whole "production system" would have needed to be modeled to a degree not deemed worth the effort for the required task.

## 5.1 Comparison of the Simulation Results

In this subsection the costs and duration of one process instance are compared (Table 9 and Table 10).

## 5.2 Interpretation of Simulation Results

Obviously the Signavio and the SiSi tools come to somewhat different results. While the average numbers are relatively closely related, especially the maximum or worst case times diverge widely.

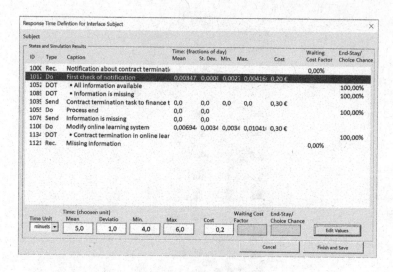

**Fig. 9.** Batch setting simulation parameters in SiSi

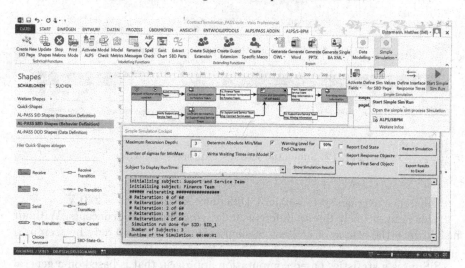

**Fig. 10.** Modeling and simulation GUIs of SiSi within Visio

**Table 9.** Comparison of results: Cost

|  | Support and Service Team | Finance Team | Total |
|---|---|---|---|
| Average Costs (Signavio) | 11.50 € | 13.70 € | 25.50 € |
| Average Costs (SiSi) | 15.45 € | 9.29 € | 24.74 € |
| Minimum Costs (Signavio) | 3.68 € | 7.73 € | 11.41 € |
| Minimum Costs (SiSi) | 8.30 € | 4.47 € | 12.77 € |
| Maximum Costs (Signavio) | 17.11 € | 19.71 € | 36.82 € |
| Maximum Costs (SiSi) | 28.70 € | 18.00 € | 46.70 € |

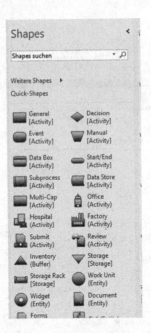

**Fig. 11.** Shape palette in process simulator

**Fig. 12.** Simulator settings in process simulator

Difference average costs = 2.98% Difference average time = 2.31%

This is most likely due to different underlying simulation concepts. Without insight into the source of at least Signavio the following can only be seen as a speculation.

SiSi uses a statistics based computation approach, that is based on a general "maximum recursion depth" setting to determine how many iterations are run if circles appear in the process.

The Signavio solution very likely runs a certain number of instances based on the chances, removes certain extreme outliers (e.g. a 5% quantile) and then averages over the remaining instances. The rest depends on the paths taken of the individual times. E.g. in a one-day run, the notification was sent only one time to the Finance team (out of 17 customers, who wanted to terminate their contract), which means that the two activities "First check of notification" and "Forward contract termination" from the Finance team were only conducted one time. The duration of it is therefore not really significant and could explain the big difference between Finance team duration in both tools. Nevertheless, we

**Table 10.** Comparison of results: Times

|  | Service Team | Finance Team | Total |
|---|---|---|---|
| Average Duration (Signavio) | 13m 12s€ | 15m 43s€ | 28m 55s€ |
| Average Duration (SiSi) | 17m 30s€ | 10m 45s€ | 28m 15s€ |
| Minimum Duration (Signavio) | 03m 49s€ | 08m 33s€ | 12m 22s€ |
| Minimum Duration (SiSi) | 09m 00s€ | 05m 00s€ | 14m 00s€ |
| Maximum Duration (Signavio) | 19m 56s€ | 22m 55s€ | 42m 51s€ |
| Maximum Duration (SiSi) | 33m 00s€ | 21m 00s€ | 54m 00s |

have similar differences with duration of activities from the Support and Service Team.

Another aspects of the simulation results is that Signavio is not differentiating between teams (only one summary of the run-time for every swimlane) but only displaying activities. We assume that for business processes, which are focusing on services between at least two different subjects, the subject-oriented view of a process could be preferable compared to an activity-oriented view.

An advantage of Signavio (as well as Process Simulator) is the creation of different scenarios[1] and the direct comparison of the results of them. This makes it more efficient evaluating the quantitative effect of a possible improvement or automation. In SiSi, different scenarios can only be achieved by having multiple copies of the file containing the process model and modifying them individually to describe different scenarios.

## 5.3   Comparison of Tool Handling

All three tools are intuitive and, given a sufficient basic education in business process modeling, should be usable by most employees.

Signavio and SiSi results are showing what was needed for the use-case. The process simulator claims to be usable for those as well, but is definitively more meant for production process simulation including the modeling of the execution system. This results in more complex modeling activities and less intuitive and direct results.

Signavio is a cloud based tool integrated into the Signavio cloud platform. As part of SAP AG it is not very likely that the platform and the models contained on it will be lost in the near future. However, export and re-usage of the models is limited by the given functionalities. Equally, modification and access of the models is only possible for users registered (and paid for) on the Signavio platform.

SiSi and the Process Simulator, both, are MS Visio based tools and handled like classic MS Office solutions. With Visio not having yet a suitable in-browser

---

[1] A simulation scenario allows to set different versions for times and costs without having to change the process model itself.

variant like its step-siblings MS Word, or Power Point they are limited to classic application usage on machines running the Windows operating system. Export functions of Visio into PDF, or pictures formats etc. are available by standard.

With SiSi, the standard .vsdx (Visio) files contain all data even if the simulation is not available without the SiSi tool itself. Any MS Visio installation or the Visio-Web-Viewer can be used to view or even partially modify the model by other involved persons. Next to the Visio in-build export functionalities, SiSi includes dedicated Word-export function for process reports, Excel-exports for the simulation results, as well as the option to export process models to the open PASS-exchange standard format.

For the process simulator the model is saved as a Visio document (.vsdx) and the simulation scenario is stored in a separated file that can only be opened by the process simulator.

## 5.4   Comparison of Pricing Structure

Naturally, prices are of importance for decisions. The comparison is as following.

Signavio is offering different modules for their Software as a Service (SaaS) solutions, e.g. Process Editor and Simulation, Workflow Manager etc. Every module is offered via a yearly subscription-per-user model. In order to model and simulate processes, a yearly 4-digit euro amount per user is demanded.

The Process Simulator is offering a package for their Visio add-on solution. Therefore, a 4-digit amount per workplace is demanded, whereby the number is almost 50% less than for the needed Signavio modules.

SiSi is free for academic and evaluation use upon request. Commercially, it is available as one-time license purchase and/or as part of a support service agreement with the developer. This in principle would allow permanent usage of the tool without a yearly subscription. Exact pricing is not disclosed and on negotiable terms, depending on usage scenario. However, it is expected to be less than half of the other product's yearly costs.

## 6   Final Thoughts and Outlook

In general, results from Signavio and SiSi are both usable for a quick simulation with the goal to check quantitative impacts of a process improvement and automation beforehand. It was possible to estimate a ROI for the automation project with the given simulation results and the estimated savings due to the process automation. Thus, the stakeholders as well as the process participants could be persuaded to implement the automation. The big difference is the aspect of subject-orientation vs. (more-) activity-orientation in modeling, as well as in the results.

The tool from Process Simulator is ruled out, because of the not-usable simulation results for this use case. Besides that, the handling of the tool (process modeling as well as simulation) and the fact, that it is configured as a Microsoft Visio add-on can be considered as "a plus".

The tool from Signavio delivers almost everything a process enthusiast needs to model and simulate processes. The handling of the tool (process modeling as well as simulation) is very intuitive. The biggest issue is a quite expensive pricing. Furthermore, the simulation results are mainly activity-oriented. Besides the known deficiencies of BPMN 2.0, this activity orientation of the simulation results have room for improvements.

The tool from SiSi persuades with an easy handling (process modeling as well as simulation), with the fact, that is configured as a Microsoft Visio add-on and its low price hurdle. Aspects, which can be improved here, include the user interface of the simulation that looks rather 'old-school'. Additionally, the missing option of creating different scenarios within one file is a disadvantage compared to the other two tools, which is somewhat counterbalanced by the ability to handle all in single files where the other tools either are cloud based and do not give users access to the data files (for better or worse) or, in the case of the Process Simulator they split both aspects in two different files that would need to be kept together when sending or archiving the models and their simulation scenarios.

Overall, this analysis and comparison and evaluation was the result of an existing and partially very specific use-case that explicitly required light-weighted and easy to use tools. All made statements were based on the evaluation of the stakeholders involved in the use-case scenario. Continuing this work, a deeper investigation of the differences between Signavio and SiSi would make sense that considers, e.g., other use-case requirements. Nevertheless, on the business side, the results should be compared with the real change of data after the automation of the contract termination process. Thus, the significance of such a way of process simulation can be checked. Finally, a deeper investigation of the Process Simulator would make sense as the company claims on their website, that business process simulation is possible.

# References

1. Becker, J., Kugeler, M., Rosemann, M.: Prozessmanagement: Ein Leitfaden zur prozessorientierten Organisationsgestaltung. Springer, Heidelberg (2013)
2. Elstermann, M.: Executing Strategic Product Planning - A Subject-Oriented Analysis and New Referential Process Model for IT-Tool Support and Agile Execution of Strategic Product Planning. KIT Scientific Publishing, Karlsruhe (2019)
3. Elstermann, M., Ovtcharova, J.: SiSi in the alps: a simple simulation and verification approach for pass. In: Stary, C. (ed.) Proceedings of the 10th International Conference on Subject-Oriented Business Process Management, S-BPM One 2018. Association for Computing Machinery, New York (2018)
4. Fleischmann, A.: Distributed Systems - Software Design and Implementation. Springer, Berlin (1994). https://doi.org/10.1007/978-3-642-78612-9
5. Fleischmann, A., Borgert, S., Elstermann, M., Krenn, F., Singer, R.: An overview to S-BPM oriented tool suites. In: Mühlhäuser, M., Zehbold, C. (eds.) Proceedings of the 9th International Conference on Subject-oriented Business Process Management, S-BPM ONE. ACM (2017)

6. Fleischmann, A., Schmidt, W., Stary, C., Obermeier, S., Boerger, E.: Subject-Oriented Business Process Management. Springer, Berlin (2012). https://doi.org/10.1007/978-3-642-32392-8
7. Kerzner, H.: Project Management. Wiley, Hoboken (1992)
8. Moattar, H., Bandara, W., Kannengiesser, U., Rosemann, M.: Control flow versus communication: comparing two approaches to process modelling. Bus. Process Manag. J. (2022)
9. OMG: Business process model and notation (BPMN) (2013). https://www.omg.org/spec/BPMN/2.0.1/. Accessed 05 Feb 2021
10. www.process simulator.de: Process simulator company web-site (2022). https://process-simulator.de/
11. www.signavio.com: Signavio company web-site (2022). https://www.signavio.com/de/

# Subject-Oriented Business Process Models of SMEs: Case Study, Best Practices and Evaluation

Jakob Bönsch[✉][iD], Katharina Reh, and Jivka Ovtcharova

Karlsruhe Institute of Technology, Karlsruhe, Germany
boensch@kit.edu
http://www.imi.kit.edu

**Abstract.** This work presents best practices for creating business process models with the existing process modeling notation PASS - the Parallel Activity Specification Scheme. The modeling techniques are shown with regard to the business process model of a small German enterprise which was used as a case study. It's processes have been recorded, analyzed and modeled in three submodels with more than thirty connected diagrams. The usefulness of this business process model of the company has been evaluated with a questionnaire in regards to four main requirements. Requirement 1: Clear and understandable language; Requirement 2: Visibility of optimization potential; Requirement 3: Knowledge separation; Requirement 4: Flexibility and incremental adaptability. According to their different background and modeling knowledge, the questionnaire shows different results for diverse user groups. Nevertheless, it is shown that S-BPM and the proposed modeling techniques yield great benefits in regards to all four main requirements of the model.

**Keywords:** S-BPM · Subject-orientation · Business process model · SME · Case study

## 1 Introduction

Small and medium-sized enterprises (SMEs) are the backbone of European and even more so the German economy. Here, especially the crafts sector, with its many traditional family businesses, has an immense impact on the German corporate landscape. These businesses must face up to the challenges of digitization and Industry 4.0 to make sure to further prosper in the 21st century. Effective, but also cost-efficient concepts and tools must be developed and tested for this purpose.

The real innovation potential of this era is not in the technologies used for Industry 4.0, but more so in the way the new technology is incorporated into

M. Elstermann et al. (Eds.): S-BPM ONE 2022, CCIS 1632, pp. 79–94, 2022.
https://doi.org/10.1007/978-3-031-19704-8_5

business processes and the way it is used to facilitate interaction of humans with each other and with IT systems. Acknowledging this sometimes even necessitates the redesign of business processes and corporate culture. Only by combining all these elements (human capabilities, smart products and services, and business processes) the potential of Industry 4.0 can be fully exploited. In this work we'll focus on the latter: business processes. It is of no news to the S-BPM[1] community that the business processes are essential to the success of a company.[2]. However, only having good processes in place is not enough. Often times, especially in traditional family businesses and their like, the knowledge about the processes is tacit. Everybody "just knows" what to do. This is good and fine as long as there are no changes to the system. However, once new employees, altered products or product variants with a change in complexity or even a change in leadership enter the picture, only tacit knowledge about business processes fails to get the job done. "Knowledge is sticky" [12] and people are reluctant to share their knowledge for many reasons. Nevertheless, only knowledge that is readily available and flows, is good knowledge. There are two steps to making knowledge flow. First, all tacit or implicit knowledge has to be turned into explicit and formalized knowledge. Second, the explicit knowledge has to be accessed and understood properly. Here, process description means like S-BPM are helpful tools as they can be used to explicitly formalize knowledge in a way that is designed to be understood by humans [6].

The first aim of this work is to detail how a mapping and analysis of the socio-technical work systems can be done with the Parallel Activity Specification Scheme (PASS), that is the only fully subject-oriented modelling language. Second aim is to evaluate how such a business process model can be used to facilitate the transfer of knowledge. All of this is discussed in the context of a case study at Wiegand Fensterbau (WF). WF is a typical German SME of the woodcraft sector. The family business with over 100 years of tradition is facing the challenge of meeting the opportunities of the 21st century.

## 2 Methodological Approach

First this section will introduce PASS and the requirements that are to be met by its use. Afterwards the requirements of the case study will be detailed and the methodical approach will be elaborated.

### 2.1 The Parallel Activity Specification Scheme

In the realm of subject-orientation (SO) the PASS has been established as an useful description means. Especially in context of S-BPM, PASS diagrams are prevalent and sometimes even referred to as S-BPM diagrams [2]. If you are familiar with PASS you can skip reading this short introduction of its basic

---

[1] S-BPM – Subject-oriented Business Process Management.
[2] As this has been stated in many ways since the first S-BPM One in 2009, e.g. [8,11], until the most recent S-BPM One in 2020, e.g. [9].

principles. The upcoming descriptions are based on [1,5,6] and the standard PASS ontology.

PASS consists of two main types of diagrams that are used to describe business processes: Subject Behavior Diagrams (SBDs) and Subject Interaction Diagrams (SIDs).

**Subject Behavior Diagrams.** An SBD is used to detail the activities of any one acting entity in a process. As shown in Fig. 1, there are three different blocks in SBDs that are connected with different kinds of transitions. All of these blocks depict states. A subject is always considered to be in exactly one state at any given time. The start state is the state a subject assumes upon starting the process and the end state is a possible final state for completing the process. As can be easily seen by their individual colors, there are three types of states: Do states (yellow), Receive states (red) and Send states (green). Do states are used to describe the purely subject-internal behavior, while receive and send states are used to depict the behavior that is needed for interaction with other subjects.

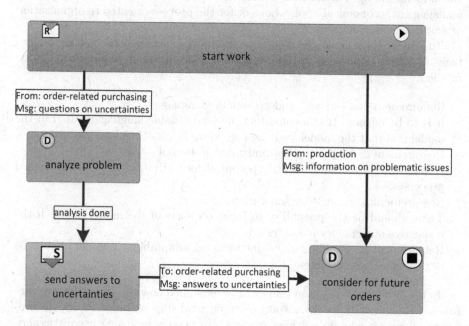

**Fig. 1.** Example of an SBD. Extraction of the business process model of WF. (Color figure online)

**Subject Interaction Diagram.** This interaction between subjects is described in SIDs. An SID consists of subjects and messages. For each fully-specified subject in an SID a corresponding SBD is created. If the subject behavior of a subject is not known, irrelevant or described elsewhere, an Interface subject can be used instead of a fully-specified subject.

## 2.2  Requirements for the Case Study

The goal of this work is to examine whether the following requirements which are derived from the modeling purpose and correspond to proposed advantages of the PASS modeling language can be validated for the application of PASS in SMEs. The main purpose of modeling the business processes of WF was discussed and selected in cooperation with the junior director of WF, Mr. Wiegand. During these meetings, the documentation of the organisation can be stated as one reason for creating a model of the company. The description of the current business processes will increase the transparency and improve the communication about the processes. Additionally, the model can be used for knowledge management, e.g. for tutorials. Therefore, relations between knowledge, the structure of the organisation and their members shall be linked to achieve more transparency and understanding. Further, the model can also be used for continuous process management, economical applications or for the process-oriented re-organisation or employees management.

To achieve these goals, the requirements shall be specified based on the advantages of PASS elaborated in [1]. Eventually, there are four requirements to be fulfilled:

- Requirement 1: Clear and understandable language
  It is to be ensured that a consistent, understandable language is used in the model and that the model is giving a good overview of the business processes.
- Requirement 2: Visibility of optimization potential
  It should be possible to identify potential for optimization of the described processes.
- Requirement 3: Knowledge separation
  There should be the possibility to focus on parts of the model in which the respective stakeholder is interested.
- Requirement 4: Flexibility and incremental adaptability   model should be flexible to adapt incrementally.

In the following subsection there will be explained how these requirements are fulfilled theoretically by the subject-oriented modeling language PASS. According to [3] people who do not have expertise in process modeling usually experience PASS models as intuitive because they are based on the natural structure of English language and it consists of just a few symbols. This shows that PASS can be shown as a "consistent, understandable language". Since the process has to be described very detailed within the messages sent and received by a subject, inconsistencies can be discovered and possibilities for optimizations can be made visible. As described in [10], the large process models are naturally separated into smaller parts and sub-processes by the usage of SBDs, so stakeholders can individually focus on parts in which they are interested. Since the mentioned separation of the model, the flexibility and adaptability is shown. It is possible to model decentralized and parallel and to extend, change or replace individual sub-processes.

## 2.3 Methodological Procedure

This section details the approach we took in recording and modeling as well as the evaluation of the model. Each of these three steps was conducted by a person who was initially unfamiliar with the company WF and its processes. Just familiarizing with the business processes and understanding the ins and outs of the company took about two months as no suitable process documentation was available beforehand. The entire project, including model revisions and evaluation took about six months. This time scale alone shows the need for improved means to transfer knowledge about an SME like WF to new employees or external stakeholders.

**Recording.** For the project, the employees of the enterprise were interviewed about their work tasks as well as observed during their daily work to get the necessary information about the processes of the enterprise. The interviews followed in principle the structure of a professional work assignments analysis [7]. Additionally, the described processes were regularly discussed and verified with the director of WF.

**Modeling.** Following the interview and observation of each employee, the individual working processes were mapped in the modeling program *Visio* with custom stencils for the elements of PASS. After creating a new diagram, the modeler validated each recorded process with the corresponding employee before she began to interview and observe the next one. In this manner, the model was created in iterative fashion. Even more model reviews were used to integrate ideas from discussions with the director of WF and experienced PASS modelers. Some of these changes just concerned the layout and were of similar nature as the modeling guidelines presented in [4]. However, the model reviews and discussions also yielded results in terms of best practices that were identified. In contrast to [4] the best practices that are presented in Sect. 3.2 are not regarding as much the proper layout of the diagrams but rather identify important choices for modeling business processes and suggest suitable solutions for the underlying concerns.

**Evaluation.** After describing all relevant business processes in one PASS model, it was shown and explained to seven stakeholders. Six of these are people who do not have any relation to the enterprise and come from various backgrounds. None of them have any prior knowledge of SO or a meaningful background in process modeling. The seventh person is the junior director of WF. He has some knowledge of SO and PASS from a lecture in university. However, this is very limited and not founded on extensive knowledge on process modeling in general.

**Evaluation sheet for the business process model of the company Wiegand Fensterbau using the subject-oriented PASS language in Visio in the context of the master thesis of Katharina Reh**

*Please evaluate the following statements about the business process model just presented about the company Wiegand Fensterbau. The data will only be used within the scope of the master thesis.*

|   |   | Does not apply at all | Applies rather not true | Applies rather true | Fully applies |
|---|---|---|---|---|---|
| 1 | The language in the model is consistent and easy to understand. | □ | □ | □ | □ |
| 2 | The contents are clearly presented. | □ | □ | □ | □ |
| 3 | The language used within the model is unclear. | □ | □ | □ | □ |
| 4 | Process optimizations are difficult to identify through the model. | □ | □ | □ | □ |
| 5 | The correlations and the real-world reference can be clearly seen. | □ | □ | □ | □ |
| 6 | Optimization measures can be easily identified in the model. | □ | □ | □ | □ |
| 7 | It is possible to take a closer look at individual task areas. | □ | □ | □ | □ |
| 8 | It is difficult to focus on concerns and special circumstances of the respective individual parties. | □ | □ | □ | □ |
| 9 | A focus can be placed on the behavior of individual parties. | □ | □ | □ | □ |
| 10 | The model could be supplemented and extended at will. | □ | □ | □ | □ |
| 11 | The model is fixed and can be extended or changed only with difficulty. | □ | □ | □ | □ |
| 12 | The model can be adapted to the real process over and over again. | □ | □ | □ | □ |

13. How do you rate the model overall? What improvements would you like to see?

_____

_____

_____

_____

**Thank you for your participation!**

**Fig. 2.** Translation of the German evaluation sheet for the business process model of the WF, translated with the DeepL translator. – www.deepl.com.

As the model is very complex and there are many co-processes, the model was explained by the model-constructor in a order related way. That means that she constructed a realistic example order and explained this complete process from order entry to the possible complaints based on the model. Afterwards, the seven different stakeholders and the model-constructor herself got an evaluation sheet where they had to evaluate the fulfilling of the requirements by estimating given statements about the advantages of PASS. The evaluation sheet consists of four sections with three declarations and the following answer options: strongly disagree - rather disagree - rather agree - strongly agree. The evaluation sheet was originally created in German; the translated version can be found in Fig. 2.

# 3    Case Study: Business Process Model of a Small Enterprise

Wiegand Fensterbau (WF) is a typical small German woodcraft family business, specialized in the production of front doors and windows. WF was founded in 1907 and is currently managed in the fourth generation by Dirk Wiegand and his son. The company can be divided into three departments: windows, doors and lift-slide doors. WF attaches great importance to innovative products with a high customer benefit and therefore specializes, among other things, in passive house windows and doors. A large proportion of the products are individual designs for new buildings or restored houses. The company regularly operates throughout Germany and in individual cases also receives orders from Belgium, France, Norway, Austria and Switzerland. The scope of the company with about 35 employees covers the areas of consulting, planning, manufacturing, installation and testing of products.

## 3.1    The Complete Business Process Model

For our research a business process model of the entire company WF was created. The complete model of WF consists of about 30 diagrams: three SIDs, 27 SBDs and one diagram to depict which persons can enact which subjects as a kind of qualification matrix. In the SIDs the interaction of 45 subjects, including 18 interface subjects, with about 200 messages is specified. Figure 3 shows one of the three SIDs, the shop floor. The other two SIDs are on the one hand the general office processes directly associated with order processing and on the other hand all "other office processes" like marketing, etc. In the corresponding SBDs more than 500 achievable states are depicted.

## 3.2    Best Practices

The documentation of this model is way too extensive to be fully displayed here. However, as the business process model has been created with an iterative approach, many changes have been made to the initial drafts. Thereby, some best practices for the modeling of business processes of SMEs were identified and will be presented here:

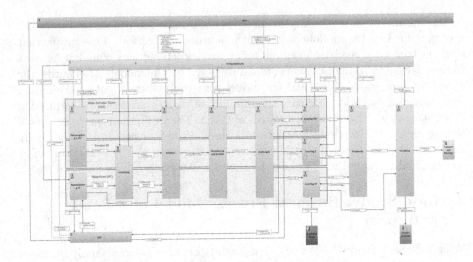

**Fig. 3.** Schematic SID for the shop floor at WF.

**Distinction Between Person and Role.** The first important modeling decision for PASS models lies in the definition of the subjects and their main tasks. This tailoring of subjects is not new to PASS practitioners and was described, giving some decision aids, already in [6]. However, as this might be the most important decision for any PASS model it is highly influential on its quality. A common pitfall in the tailoring of subjects is to map all responsibilities of one person to one subject. Especially in SMEs some employees will take on very different responsibilities. Also some tasks are carried out by whomever has the time to do so. To properly describe this in the process model, it is necessary to have a clear concept and the distinction between a person and a role. While a role can be easily mapped to a subject, a person is to be considered as a subject carrier[3]. The clear distinction between roles yields the benefit of context separation. This allows users of the model to only have an in depth look at the parts of the model that are relevant to them. In addition if responsibilities are shifted from one employee to another, a proper tailoring of subjects can prevent a change to the entire process model. We found it very useful, especially for the authorities in the company, to create a kind of qualification matrix that shows which employees are suitable or desirable subject carriers for which subjects, i.e. which person has which role in the company. However, this kind of diagram is not part of a classic PASS but was added as a informal extension to the model.

**Level of Granularity and Color Coding.** Highly connected to the tailoring of subjects is the decision on a level of granularity for the model. However,

---

[3] A subject carrier is the executing entity for the behavior of a given subject. The same subject carrier can execute the behavior of multiple or even all subjects in one process model. E.g. a PASS model can be used to clearly describe the technical functionality of a computer program but all subjects are executed by the same processor.

this decision is way more implicit. The level of granularity is the measure that is correlating to the complicatedness[4]. In PASS complicatedness increases to some extent by an increase in the number of subjects and messages in the SIDs but mostly through the number of states in the SBDs. However, a disproportional increase in the number of transitions does increase the complexity of the described process and not only the complicatedness. Defining the complexity of a business process is no modeling, but a business decision. Therefore, while managing the business process complexity is still an important aspect to S-BPM, it is not further regarded here. To manage complicatedness of the model it is necessary to define a proper level of granularity in the SBDs. It is to decide how finely the Do-States are to be broken up. We found it to be ineffective to display too much detail in the process model as it is not designed to give a step by step guide as some kind of instruction manual. Nevertheless, no activities are to be excluded on purpose. In some cases it was useful to attach a comment to the state that detailed which steps are included in a given Do-State. As messages directly correlate to the Receive- and Send-States in the SBDs the same approach can be taken for these model elements. As the number of subjects is fixed after subject tailoring and the number of messages is defined in the SBDs, the level of granularity can be hardly adjusted in the SIDs. Here, we found color coding a suitable option to cope with the complicatedness of the model. An example of this can be seen in Fig. 3. The three main product lines of WF are here visibly separated by the colored boxes in the background. Any production area that is necessary for more than one of the product lines is represented by an enlarged symbol for the subject. This representation is similar to the idea of swim lanes. Color coding was also used for the subjects themselves. Subjects that are considered to be part of the office are blue, the shop floor yellow, management orange, etc.

**Linkage of SIDs.** Another way to manage the complexity of a model is to divide the entire model into multiple SIDs that are linked by interface subjects. This is especially useful if there is a subset of subjects that have a lot of interaction between themselves but are only sparsely linked to the remaining subjects. A probable example for this could be dividing the model into one SID for the office processes and another SID for the shop floor. The interaction between these two domains is minimal and almost exclusively realized through message exchange with the management subject. To increase the usability of the model the interface subjects of the different domains were linked to the corresponding SIDs. This linkage enables a possibility to smoothly transition from one diagram to the other. As a guideline: Any process model with a dozen or more subjects should be considered to be divided into multiple linked SIDs.

**Structure of the Process Flow.** Processes can be represented in a model either cyclically or as a start-finish process. Choosing between these two forms

---

[4] Complicatedness is not to be confused with complexity. While throwing a dice thrice and adding the numbers shown is more complicated than throwing it twice and adding the numbers, it is no more complex.

of representations is a typical modeling decision and is closely connected with how the system boundaries are set. Cyclic processes always end in the initial state after a completed run. This means that the start and end state is the same. A so-called re-initiation by the same executing entity, i.e. a renewed activation of the process, is not usual with this type of processes, since the process flow can be continued automatically again at the beginning. Re-initiation would result in multiple entities, e.g. people, executing the process simultaneously and being at different steps in the process at any given time. Start-end processes have a start state and one or more end states. After a process is completed, a re-initiation must be performed to reactivate the process. This type of modeling is often chosen, for example, when the process to be represented is a transformation process: An input of any kind is transformed into a different output. In PASS, both types can also be used within one model, e.g. by representing the behavior of one subject cyclically while another has start-end behavior. However, having the same structure for all subjects makes the model more easily understandable. As using start-end processes means that no loops are applied which lead back to the start state, which simplifies the representation by mapping fewer arrows and the return to the state of origin might lead to confusion, we found this way of modeling to be more suitable for business processes in SMEs.

**Universal Receive-Start-State.** A lot of the subjects are triggered by receiving some kind of message. Therefore, a lot of SBDs start in a Receive-State. However, especially in office and management tasks many quite different paths of action are taken according to the message that is received. Nevertheless, PASS requires a single start state for all of these different possible paths. In Fig. 4 can be seen how different received messages lead to different paths of action. Additionally not only messages can be received but also time transitions for reoccurring activities or user cancel transitions are suitable modeling options. Having this initial unified start state allows to clearly separate paths of action for different scenarios.

### 3.3   Results of the Evaluation Sheet

After demonstrating the created model and best practices, in this chapter, the results received by the evaluation sheet will be presented. Since the purpose of modeling in this enterprise includes different stakeholders with distinct knowledge and backgrounds, the four requirements are analyzed separately for three different user groups. First, the results gained from a small group of users who do not have any relation to the enterprise or the modeling language will be evaluated. The group of questioned people consists of academics and non-academics, people with and without technical training or studies, and a range of age between 20 and 55 years. Afterward, the opinion of the director and then of the modeler will be analyzed separately for each requirement.

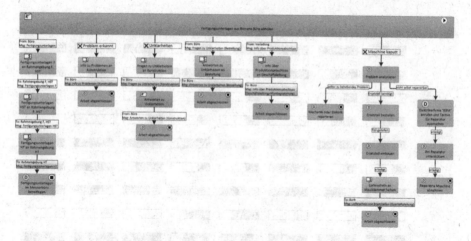

**Fig. 4.** Schematic SBD of the foreman at WF.

The results of the evaluation sheet are graphically summarized in Fig. 5. All of the results are described here in depth and will be discussed in Sect. 4.3.

## Clear and Understandable Language

1. External users
   The group of external users who do not have any relation to the enterprise and the modeling processes do all *rather agree* or *strongly agree* that the language is consistent and understandable and the contents are clearly presented. So the main tendency is the same, only the strength of agreement is different.
2. Director
   The director answered all questions concerning the language and the overview with *rather agree*.
3. Modeler
   The modeler herself fully agrees with the director in stating that she *rather agrees* with the statement that the language is consistent and understandable and the contents are clearly presented.

## Visibility of Optimization Potential

1. External users
   Regarding the possibilities for optimization, the answers of the external group are very wide-ranging and do also differ between the positively and negatively worded question. There is no clear result given. However, almost all of the questioned persons do *strongly agree* that contexts and the reference to the reality can be clearly recognized.
2. Director
   The director, on the other hand, does have a very clear result and does *strongly agree* with any statement about the visibility of optimization possibilities within the model.

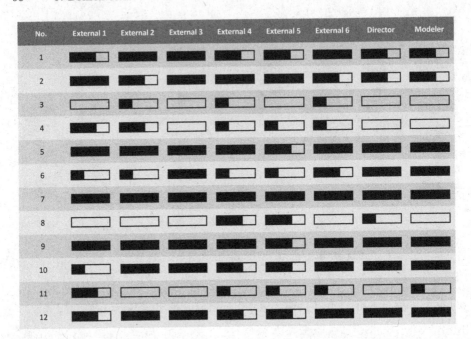

**Fig. 5.** Summary of the results of the evaluation sheet given by six external users, the director and the modeler.

3. Modeler

The opinion of the modeler does also correspond with the director's. She can clearly see optimization possibilities regarding the model of the enterprise.

## Knowledge Separation

1. External users

Regarding the possibility of focusing on certain parts of the model, the answers of the external users were pretty clear. The examined users almost do *totally agree* to the statements no. 7 *It is possible to take a closer look at individual task areas.* and no. 9 *A focus can be placed on the behavior of individual parties.*. The negatively worded statement has been answered with the same tendency but not as clearly as the positive ones.

2. Director

Speaking of the questions of this third requirement, the answers of the director do fit in with the external users' ones. He also does *strongly agree* with the described statements no. 7 and no. 9 and does *rather disagree* with the negatively worded statement.

3. Modeler

Also, the modeler's answers do correspond completely with the external users' and do only differ in a tendency with the director's.

**Flexibility and Incremental Adaptability**

1. External users
   The opinion of the external users differs very much in the section of flexibility
   and given incremental adaptability. Regarding the possibility to supplement
   and extend or change the model, the questioned persons have chosen three
   different answer categories - in the positively worded statement (no. 10) as
   well as in the negative worded (no. 11). The estimation of the statement about
   the possibility to adapt the model to the real process is more unique: Every
   user has answered this statement with *rather agree* or *fully agree*.

2. Director
   The director estimates the three statements about flexibility and adaptability
   with the highest agreement in the positive worded sentences and with the
   lowest agreement in the negative worded sentences.

3. Modeler
   Regarding the estimation of the modeler, there is only the tendency of statement no. 11 (*rather agree*) different from the director's one.

# 4    Discussion of the Results

The benefit of a process model is not correlated with its size. Therefore, it is
important to clarify what use the model has and even more so which limitations.
After that we'll shortly discuss how to apply the best practices in your own
research and/or modeling endeavors. Last but not least the results of the case
study are evaluated and put into perspective.

## 4.1    Benefits of an Extensive Business Process Model

The business process model itself is to be considered complete and suitable for its
application in operational tasks at WF. It's scope even extends past the initial
requirements and includes various speciality processes that are not executed on
regular basis. Therefore, it is clearly helpful for turning tacit knowledge into
explicit knowledge. Especially by combing the view of the employees with the
management view, a more complete and accurate representation of reality is
achieved. Even during the iterative modeling process, the first optimizations of
the business process where implemented by the management. Nevertheless, PASS
and Visio are tools that are not commonly used throughout SMEs. No matter
that the PASS stencils are free to use, as Visio is not this remains a barrier for its
application. In addition to that prior knowledge of process modeling (especially
in PASS) and/or Visio is a prerequisite to handle a model with as many layers
as the process model of WF.

## 4.2    Caveats of the Best Practices

The best practices presented here are to be understood mainly as preliminary
work for further research. They represent a starting point for a repeatable and

more holistic approach of modeling business processes in SMEs. Therefore, we have chosen to not only include the identified practice in this paper but also the reasoning behind them. A practitioner should use this best practices as guideline to not arbitrarily disregard one of the underlying questions. However, it is intended for practitioners to make modeling decisions that contradict the presented best practices, whenever there is a reason to give another answer to one or more of the underlying questions. The goal for future work is to further refine and extend this set of practices to be an even better help for PASS modelers. Especially as the five practices described here are not interconnected in a meaningful way. It would be helpful to design a procedure that could either be applied while modeling or one that could be used to refine initial models.

### 4.3 Evaluation of the Case Study

First of all it is to be said that the evaluation results of the director and the model-constructor are clearly biased as they were involved in the model creation. Nevertheless, we included their evaluation results here because the director and model-creator are the two main stakeholders of the created model. They are the only people with genuine interest in the application of the model and therefore give valuable insights. Summarized, it can be stated that the model generates an added value in comparison to a purely verbal explanation. During the description of the example order process, an easy-to-understand structure was given to the very complex business processes for the users. Some users did not always understand the deeper subject-specific concerns. Hereby, it is to be considered if it is important for everybody to understand every working task in detail or if the main purpose is to give an overall view of the structures and processes of the enterprise.

The two requirements *clear and understandable language* and *knowledge separation* are completely fulfilled, regarding the estimation of the external user group, the director, and the modeler.

The question about the *visibility of optimization potential* has been answered differently by distinct users. This could depend on the heterogeneity of the group: The more prior knowledge about the general processes of a company and experiences in process optimization somebody has, the easier it is to detect optimization possibilities in a model. This assumption is confirmed by the answers of the director and modeler who do have more experience and deeper insights into the enterprise and the modeling language. Both did agree that optimizations can be detected in the model. As the director or modeler are part of the target group who do have to identify optimization possibilities and to make changes in the business processes, their opinion is valued more highly in this concern.

Regarding the requirement of *flexible adaptability*, the result is similar to the previously described one. The different answers of the external user group may come from different understandings of the question. It stands out that the director and modeler do have the same opinion on this concern, too.

Generally, it can be stated that the modeler and director do almost always have the same opinion regarding the utility of the model. This makes sense since they both do have more experience with the modeling language and the business processes and deeper insights into the enterprise. The external user group does not always see all existing possibilities of using the model. This is not to be interpreted as a "negative" result in this way because the possibilities of using the model have not to be fully utilized by everyone but by the distinct stakeholders like for example, Mr. Wiegand.

## 5  Conclusion and Outlook

All in all it was shown that subject-oriented business process modeling is a powerful tool to supplement the knowledge management of SMEs. The presented case study shows that it has its benefits even in a company with less than 50 employees. However, this work does not include any comparison to another modeling notation (like e.g. BPMN) and therefore can be only considered as comparison to textual process descriptions. An iterative approach to optimizing the PASS business process model of WF led to five best practices or modeling decisions that should be considered carefully. First of all, the tailoring of subjects already predefines a large portion of the model complexity. Second, the level of granularity in the SBDs, i.e. the number of states is to be specified. Based on these decisions it can be evaluated whether it's possible to divide the model with multiple SIDs and link them with interface subjects. In regards to modeling the subject behavior it is recommended to use start-end process flow design and universal receive-start-states. The business model created in the case study was then evaluated in regard to four main requirements: Requirement 1: Clear and understandable language; Requirement 2: Visibility of optimization potential; Requirement 3: Knowledge separation; Requirement 4: Flexibility and incremental adaptability. In a qualitative survey it could be shown that all four requirements are met at least to some extent. When only considering the assessment by distinct stakeholders of the model it is satisfying the set of requirements fully.

However, further research is needed to convert this preliminary work on best practices for modeling business processes with PASS into a structured modeling approach. It is also to be examined whether standard PASS or abstract layered PASS (ALPS) is the better solution to model more complex business processes. S-BPM still remains a low-threshold way to improve business processes and implement strategies for knowledge management. In the end, making sticky knowledge flow in SMEs remains an important task to secure economic success.

**Acknowledgements.** The presented research was supported by the German company Wiegand Fensterbau. We want to thank the entire company and especially Roman Wiegand for the opportunity to conduct this case study and the cooperation throughout the entire process. Internet: www.wiegand-info.de.

# References

1. Elstermann, M.: Executing strategic product planning - a subject-oriented analysis and new referential process model for it-tool support and agile execution of strategic product planning. https://doi.org/10.5445/KSP/1000097859
2. Elstermann, M., Bönsch, J., Ovtcharova, J.: Subject-oriented value-stream mapping with SiSi. In: Freitag, M., Kinra, A., Kotzab, H., Kreowski, H.-J., Thoben, K.-D. (eds.) S-BPM ONE 2020. CCIS, vol. 1278, pp. 232–250. Springer, Cham (2020). https://doi.org/10.1007/978-3-030-64351-5_16
3. Elstermann, M., Katter, H., Ovtcharova, J.: S-BPM prozessmodellierung als werkzeug für die entwicklung moderner nutzerzentrierter service-produkte. In: Stuttgarter Symposium für Produktentwicklung (2013)
4. Elstermann, M., Seese, D.: A proposal for modeling standards for subject-oriented modeling with PASS. In: Oppl, S., Fleischmann, A. (eds.) S-BPM ONE 2012. CCIS, vol. 284, pp. 16–32. Springer, Heidelberg (2012). https://doi.org/10.1007/978-3-642-29294-1_2
5. Fleischmann, A.: Distributed Systems: Software Design and Implementation. Springer, Heidelberg (1994). https://ebookcentral.proquest.com/lib/kxp/detail.action?docID=6499166
6. Fleischmann, A.: Subjektorientiertes Prozessmanagement: Mitarbeiter einbinden, Motivation und Prozessakzeptanz steigern. Hanser Verlag, München (2011). https://doi.org/10.3139/9783446429697. http://www.hanserelibrary.com/doi/book/10.3139/9783446429697
7. Haasler, B.: » BAG-Analyse «-Analyseverfahren zur Identifikation von Arbeits-und Lerninhalten für die Gestaltung beruflicher Bildung. Institut Technik und Bildung, Bremen (2003)
8. Heuser, L.: The relevance of management of business processes and orchestration. In: Buchwald, H., Fleischmann, A., Seese, D., Stary, C. (eds.) S-BPM ONE 2009. CCIS, vol. 85, pp. 3–12. Springer, Heidelberg (2010). https://doi.org/10.1007/978-3-642-15915-2_1
9. Lederer, M., Elstermann, M., Betz, S., Schmidt, W.: Technology-, human-, and data-driven developments in business process management: a literature analysis. In: Freitag, M., Kinra, A., Kotzab, H., Kreowski, H.-J., Thoben, K.-D. (eds.) S-BPM ONE 2020. CCIS, vol. 1278, pp. 217–231. Springer, Cham (2020). https://doi.org/10.1007/978-3-030-64351-5_15
10. Moser, C., Elstermann, M., Kannengiesser, U.: Examining the PASS approach to process modelling for digitalised manufacturing: results from three industry case studies. Enterp. Model. Inf. Syst. Architectures (EMISAJ) **17**, 1:1–1:24 (2022). https://doi.org/10.18417/EMISA.17.1
11. Singer, R., Zinser, E.: Business process management—S-BPM a new paradigm for competitive advantage? In: Buchwald, H., Fleischmann, A., Seese, D., Stary, C. (eds.) S-BPM ONE 2009. CCIS, vol. 85, pp. 48–70. Springer, Heidelberg (2010). https://doi.org/10.1007/978-3-642-15915-2_5
12. Szulanski, G.: Sticky Knowledge: Barriers to Knowing in the Firm. Sage Strategy Series, Sage Publications, London and Thousand Oaks (2011). https://search.ebscohost.com/login.aspx?direct=true&scope=site&db=nlebk&db=nlabk&AN=251794

# Business Process Management Bridging Marketing and IT: Transformation Model for Customer Journey Maps and BPMN

Tobias Six[1], Matthias Lederer[1(✉)], Werner Schmidt[2], and Marco Nirschl[1]

[1] Technical University of Applied Sciences Amberg-Weiden, Hetzenrichter Weg 15, 92637 Weiden, Germany
ma.lederer@oth-aw.de
[2] Technische Hochschule Ingolstadt, Esplanade 10, 85049 Ingolstadt, Germany

**Abstract.** Many notations are known for modeling business processes, each has many specific advantages and disadvantages, as well as different distributions. Digital trends such as marketing automation and e-commerce make it increasingly important to align process models from marketing with notations from IT process management. This paper presents a mapping approach to synchronize customer journey maps, which are widely used in marketing, with BPMN diagrams. A transformation between these notations is currently unknown in the literature and has the potential to merge the knowledge of the business department with that of the technical department. In addition to the transformation of individual notation elements, the paper also presents exemplary use cases of an application.

**Keywords:** Business process management · Model transformation · Customer journey map · Mapping · BPMN

## 1 Introduction

In the business process management (BPM) discipline, it is accepted that common visual frameworks facilitate communication and understanding within cross-functional work [1]. Particularly in large organizations, information, [including process notations], has different meanings for different departments, sectors, or people and can therefore develop in many directions [2]. "For nearly three decades, computer professionals have been trying to create methodologies which express business information processes in term that are easily understood by business executives" [3]. In particular, business process modeling notation is playing an increasingly important role in achieving this goal. Especially in this context, the model-based cooperation with IT departments plays an essential role in supporting enterprise executives and BPM consultants in implementing, automating, and improving workflows [2, 4]. However, research conducted by [5] identified that many companies do not have management practices to communicate business goals to IT staff. They also noticed gaps in communication between them on almost all subjects [6]. Early efforts on bridging the communication gap between a business and its IT systems have resulted in several business analysis and modelling techniques.

M. Elstermann et al. (Eds.): S-BPM ONE 2022, CCIS 1632, pp. 95–114, 2022.
https://doi.org/10.1007/978-3-031-19704-8_6

For *IT departments*, most recently, BPMN (Business Process Modeling Notation) is rapidly consolidating its position "as the established standard for modelling business processes" [7]. The aim of the Business Process Management Initiative (BPMI) was to develop a notation in BPMN that can represent processes graphically. The process visualization was intended to be used and understood by both the business and the technical side. According to the official notation standard, "the structural elements of BPMN allow the viewer to be able to easily differentiate between sections of a BPMN Diagram" [8]. Nevertheless, the spread of the notation shows that the technical advantages come to the fore. A central advantage of BPMN is the simulation of processes. Especially for quantitative analyses of process models (e.g. Process Mining, Process Analytics), simulation is an excellent opportunity. Meanwhile, "it is widely acknowledged today that simulation experiments are a reliable and credible source of insights concerning the support of decision making in organizations" [9]. There is the possibility of testing a process scenario before it is applied in the actual market. For managers, these advantages of BPMN can serve as a basis for decision-making. Compared to testing in the real environment, simulating eliminates many costs and associated risks. Furthermore, the effort of a simulation is more manageable [9].

For *marketing departments*, the customer journey – the "journey" of a potential customer through the purchase decision process – nowadays takes place across many different channels, including offline and online. Therefore, an analysis of the customer journey, understood as the process a client has, improves the customer experience. "The Customer Journey is a potential strategic marketing tool that looks at the entire buying or decision-making process up to the point of using a service. It offers the potential to align the entire company with the improvement of the customer relationship and thus an increase in added value" [10]. The focus of notation used (e.g. Customer Journey Maps) is thus not on technical aspects, but rather on questions of human perception as well as a deep understanding of the experiences along the customer-oriented marketing and sales process. There have already been numerous approaches to the customer journey map, but all of them are from a technical point of view and less from an IT-supported process perspective. When it comes to simulating processes, people often compare a model's current state with its future state, which should be an improvement. These holistic models can identify difficult or impossible characteristics to perceive when looking at individual areas or structures because a model allows you to focus on specific aspects and leave unimportant things out [11]. By simulating the processes behind the customer journey or the customer journey itself, it is possible to identify previously unrecognized problem areas. If you wanted to simulate a process that was modeled with BPMN, for example, you had to convert your model into the specific language of the simulation tool because there was only a limited selection of tools and possibilities. This transfer into the new language meant double work and a high error rate for analysts.

*In general*, business process modeling aims to provide a language "that is readily understandable by all business users, from the business analysts that create the initial drafts of the processes, to the technical developers responsible for implementing the technology that will perform those processes, and finally, to the businesspeople who will manage and monitor those processes" [8]. Therefore, it is essential to introduce a set of well-supported standard modeling notations to bring business and IT users on the same level for collaborative topics and projects to avoid confusion in the best possible way. Both business and IT perspectives must be included. In the past, business experts often developed process representations that had to be manually translated into execution models in the further stages of the project. Such migrations are vulnerable to errors and can lead to distortions of important information [12]. For the collaboration between the marketing and IT departments, it is therefore necessary to bring together the ideas and concepts of the business-oriented modeling (Customer Journey Map) with the technical standard (BPMN). In science, this idea of synchronization is often solved by model transformations, i.e. descriptions and rules on how content from one notation can be transferred to the model of the other notation. This paper aims at such a transformation in order to continue to use the specific advantages of both notations and to support internal cooperation against the background of digitization.

To achieve this research goal, this paper first presents (Sect. 2) the state of the art and the focus of the two notations. Then, methods of model transformation (Sect. 3) are used to present the approaches for mapping the notations in Sect. 4. Finally, in Sect. 5, the theoretical rules are illustrated by a case study.

## 2  Related Work

### General: Process Modelling

In general, a model "is an abstract representation of reality that excludes much of the world's infinite detail" [1]. These are generally used to reduce the complexity of an object by eliminating details that contain less relevant information. However, depending on the purpose of the model, the scope of the issue to be modeled may differ [1, 13]. "A process model is an abstract description of an actual or proposed process that represents selected process elements that are considered important to the purpose of the model and can be enacted by a human or machine" [1]. However, the abstraction levels of such models can be completely different. Depending on requirements, detailed processes can be modeled, or abstract phases of a production process can be described [1, 14]. "Process modeling claims a more disciplined, standardized, consistent and overall more mature and scientific approach" [15]. Therefore, the modeling must cope with an increasingly heterogeneous group of interested parties. Process owners need to understand the models and the end user, who can come from the IT direction as well as from the business perspective. Actually, the future trend is going toward these end-users modeling their business processes more and more actively as well as to date-driven optimization of models [16]. The fundamental prerequisite for user-friendly process modeling is configurability and scalability and provides the communication enabler between IT functions and business requirements [15].

**IT Focus: BPMN**

The Business Process Model and Notation (BPMN) is a standard for business process diagrams. Its latest version 2.0.2 was released by the Object Management Group (OMG) in January 2014 [17]. It describes a flowchart-oriented notation and is widely used in practice. On the one hand, the notation enables the graphical design of process diagrams from a business point of view by business analysts (business level) and, on the other hand, it is formal enough for IT developers to transfer these models to software environments for the IT support of the processes (technical level) [18]. [19] refers to this property as the bridge between representation and execution language. Hence, BPMN helps overcoming the gap between a business model and its technical implementation in IT-based workflows. With suitable software in the form of workflow engines, the models can be executed [20], which represents a significant contribution to process automation. This fact makes BPMN a promising candidate for transforming customer journeys into IT-supported business processes as outlined in Sect. 3.

**Marketing Focus: Customer Journeys**

In today's global marketplace, customers interact with companies through various channels and in this way create touchpoints, which can be both online and offline. The touchpoints can be observed in different phases. Nevertheless, they have to work perfectly as a unit because customers do not evaluate their experience with a company according to individual contact points but rather see it as an overall entity. An excellent designed online shop, therefore, does not compensate for the lack of after-sales contact points such as returns management or the hotline [10, 21, 22].

However, with the help of an extensive analysis of the customer journeys, detailed insights into the thoughts and emotions of the target group can be gained and marketing activities can be aligned. Thus, the buying process or the brand experience can be supported and improved [10]. The customer journey can be seen as customers' experiences with a firm across multiple touchpoints throughout the purchase stages [21, 23]. So, the buying process can be divided into different phases (e.g. [24]). An example of a five-phase customer journey (Awareness, Consideration, Acquisition, Service & Loyalty) is shown in Fig. 1. In the first phase, the customer recognizes a certain need and tries to solve it. During the Consideration phase, the customer is screening different alternatives and is still deciding whether to buy the product. During the third phase, the customer has decided on a product and is convinced to purchase it. The customers enter the service phase if they are dissatisfied with the products they have received or need support in general. Classic touchpoints in this phase are hotlines or Frequently Asked Questions (FAQ). The last stage, Loyalty, is concerned with recovering the customer. He recommends the product to friends or even repurchases it from the company.

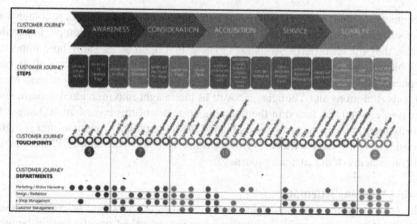

**Fig. 1.** Sample Customer Journey [25]

The touchpoints addressed can be divided into physical and digital. Physical touchpoints can be, for example, trade fairs and word-of-mouth, while Google or social media are examples of digital touchpoints [26]. [23] state in their research that there is still insufficient research about the relationships between individual touchpoints. They also suggest that customer journey mapping should be accomplished with different methodologies than the existing service blueprint. Finally, they "see a need to dive deeper into customer decision journeys, to identify opportunities for intervention or influence" [23].

**Table 1.** Comparison of different modeling approaches [27]

| Modeling approach | This paper | Signavio | gbtec | DSML/HSJML |
|---|---|---|---|---|
| Goal | Mapping the marketing and IT gap | Understanding the complete customer journey | Improving the customer experience | Improving the customer experience |
| Customer Journey | Yes | Yes | Yes | Yes |
| Stages | Yes | Yes | No | Yes |
| Steps | Yes | Yes | Yes | Yes |
| Touchpoints | Yes | Partly | Yes | Yes |
| Departments | Yes | No | Yes | No |
| Service providers | Party | No | No | Yes |
| Micro moments | Yes | No | No | No |
| Emotions | Yes | Partly | No | No |
| Moments of truth | Yes | Yes | No | No |
| Data Structure | Partly | No | No | Yes |

There are three standard concepts of a customer journey by Signavio, gbtec and the domain-specific modeling language approach by [27]. Table 1 provides an overview of the contents covered by the respective mapping approaches. Two of the three contents are rather software solutions. However, the existence of all modeling attempts is justified because they all set different emphases. These first approaches show how important this topic will be in the future. According to the standard, BPMN elements allow for a completely different level of detail. Components of the Customer Journey such as Micro Moments, Emotions and Thoughts, as well as the insight into individual departmental processes, can only be found in the mapping structure of this contribution. Especially the insight into the business processes behind the touchpoints is precious and is highly focused. The result section (Sect. 3) will show that there are many more BPMN symbols than components of the customer journey.

**Existing Mapping Attempts**

In the process-oriented literature dealing with issues of marketing-oriented customer centricity, there are numerous indications that the described transformation between customer journeys and BPMN represents a relevant research gap. For example, the so-called Customer Journey Mapping (CJM) aims at representing the individual steps of the customer and visually mapping his decisions as well as his feelings and thoughts [28]. As a consequence, this can happen in a mapping towards classical process diagrams. However, previous approaches have mostly always focused on the customer journey and neglected a more formal description of business processes as well as the underlying IT support. [28], for example, has taken a simple modeling approach to reach the widest possible audience that does not require a lot of modeling knowledge. In doing so, the contribution focuses on both touchpoints and persona attributes. The approach is process-oriented, but a formal mapping to the widely used BPMN is missing [28]. Another well-known mapping concept according to [29] also remains on a simple level and again focuses mainly on representing the touchpoints a customer encounters during his shopping experience [29]. Looking at the current scientific discourse, it can be summarized that there are simple models of customer journey mapping with the primary perspective on customer experience. In contrast, the mapping described in this paper is based or targeted on an existing modeling language and adds the business process component, a major requirement for process digitalization.

## 3    Methodology

This section describes the methodology for building the transformation and its rules from Customer Journey Maps to BPMN and vice versa. It explains how the diagrams can be derived from each other. The specific methodology is based on the recommendations and guidance of [30–33].

[30] say model transformations consist primarily of transformation rules that describe how one or more elements of the source language or notation are transformed into one or more elements of the target language/notation [33]. Often, these rules are pragmatically visualized illustratively or expressed abstractly in a transformation language (e.g., at the metamodel level). Concrete transformations (e.g., an organization using the rules developed here) are then instances of these metamodels in the second case. [34] note that the terms transformation and mapping (and hence mapping rule, mapping model, transformation program) are not used consistently. If one attempts a differentiation,

transformation is the concrete instance (the application of transformation rules at the model level), while mapping describes the connection between metamodel elements [35]. This paper follows transformation; a meta-model development may follow in further research.

The starting point of such a model-to-model transformation is first the specification of a target state model and definition of the source model. Since the BPMN diagrams show a higher standardization as well as a larger number of symbols and complexity, this notation is the target model. In addition to these formal-technical reasons, the business orientation of process modeling also speaks in favor of this approach. It is recognized that IT should technically implement (e.g., by automation, web-services, etc.) the business requirements (e.g., specifications in the journey). For a transformation, a finite number of transitions must then be described, to define which elements of the source model (customer journey map) correspond to which (possibly also alternative) BPMN elements. Even if arbitrary and hierarchically nested references and dependencies of transitions are possible, only simple transformation rules are to be described. According to [30], such transformation rules must in principle cover two subtasks: (i) describing mappings between elements of the source metamodel and elements and (ii) describing the execution of the mappings [35].

In the first subtask, mappings are composed of a so-called Left-hand Side (LHS), which references elements of the source metamodel, and a so-called Right-hand Side (RHS), which references elements of the target metamodel. Both the LHS and the RHS of the figure were solved using qualitative text analysis. The idea behind this approach was to obtain semantic correspondences between LHS and RHS through a content-based discussion in the text analysis. Such correspondences then provided the clues for the individual transformation rules, and thus for a mapping of individual notational elements [35]. Following the approach of [30], starting from the source model, all elements were transformed into search terms and strings, which were then searched in the OMG standard description for BPMN as the target model, and compared in terms of content. In a multi-stage and iterative procedure, the element in the target model that comes closest to the semantics of the element of the source system was identified via a content analysis [35]. For the description and execution of the transformation rules, two further subtasks were then performed. They are intended to satisfy the requirements of [31] enriched with interpretation from [35]: (a) In *matching*, the left-hand side is used to search the source model, determine application points (i.e., model cutouts) for the mapping, and extract any parameters. This connection was not yet solved in the context of a meta-model. Rather, the transformations were documented in a two-column table as a result of the content analysis. Since the qualitative analysis of the element meaning sometimes makes it necessary that an element of the target system covers two different elements of the source system, in this case defaults for naming were used. These follow recommendations from Unified Modeling Language (UML) notations (e.g. upper and lower case, syntax and structure of the name like "result [condition/effect]" etc.) [35]. (b) In the subsequent *expanding*, the Right-hand Side described by the mapping is used to create, parameterize, as well as link the corresponding elements of the target model. This contribution fulfills this task with illustrative examples and case explanations. The elements are included as representations in the tables in Sect. 4, while Sect. 5 explains and visualizes the transformation rules and their application in a use case.

# 4  Results

In this section we describe the individual rules and elements for the model transformation in detail. Structuring subsections are ordered by categories of basic BPMN modeling elements.

### Roles: Involved Parties and Their Arrangement

BPMN provides two symbols that point out process participants and their activities: Pools on the one hand and lanes. Pools in the way they are used for the modeling of customer journeys, are leading the focus on collaboration, i.e., the interaction of processes of several partners. Thereby, the different participant roles are represented in other pools [8, 17, 36]. When modeling customer journeys, it is vital for companies to understand both the company and customer perspectives of the buying process and to identify the most impactful aspects at each stage [23]. Typically, three overarching roles are involved in the customer journey. On the one hand, these include the user, the company, and its business partners. The user, who can also be referred to as the decision-making unit (DMU), plays a fundamental role because the entire process is tailored to him. Consequently, the user and his activities, which will be explained in more detail later, are to be modeled within his pool or a lane within his pool. The business partners and the company itself are represented in own pools to emphasize the relationship and interaction of these components. The company pool should also be displayed with different departments, which are represented as lanes, in order to be able to capture the exact processes of the individual departments and their effects on the customer journey in detail [23].

**Table 2.** Mapping rules for roles

| Customer Journey Element | BPMN Symbol | Notation (if needed) | Description |
|---|---|---|---|
| 1. Roles | | | |
| User | Pool/Lane (OMG 2013 p. 27) | Pool Name = User | Isolated area for modeling the Customer Journey Steps, Path, Micro Moments, etc. |
| Business partner, company | Pool/Lane (OMG 2013 p. 27) | Pool Name = Name of the business or name of the business partner | The company as well as their partners get their own pool for activities. |
| Departments | Lane (OMG 2013 p. 27) | Pool name = Name of the business = Lane name = Marketing / Distribution / E-Shop Management etc. | The departments involved within the company - which in turn acts as a pool (see above) - are represented by lanes. |
| System | Pool/Lane (OMG 2013 p. 27) | Pool Name = System, Lane Name = Touchpoint | The system is modeled as an extra pool between the user and the company to highlight touchpoints within the system. |

In addition to the three main roles, a further pool is introduced, representing the 'system'. It stands for a layer outlining all customer interactions, like digital touchpoints, with a Customer Relationship Management System. The system pool serves to document the touch points provided by the layer. When arranging the pools, it is essential to interpose the system pool between the one for the user on top and the one for the company with its departments. This allows for clearly visualizing the relationship or the points of contact between the company and the user with the help of message flows. In principle, the names of the pools and the lanes should begin with a capital letter so that they can be distinguished from the following labels. Apart from that, nothing else needs to be considered in the labeling. In general, however, labeling will be of great importance so that a clear document language can be demonstrated, and symbols can quickly be grouped mentally. Table 2 gives an overview of the previously explained rules. Alongside the mapped elements, the table contains a short description and shows what the notation looks like.

## Activities: Core of the Process Model

Activities form the core of a process. Their symbol is used in the customer journey modeling as well as the element for collapsed sub-processes [8, 17]. During the customer journey, a potential customer takes numerous small steps and activities, such as clicking on a paid advertisement or, later on, passing through the checkout process in the particular online shop. There are many different ways for the customer to reach their destination. Therefore, the modeling is done via the activity symbols, since these are the customer journey steps before the customer achieves his or her desired goal of a purchase, subscription or similar. Furthermore, all possible variants can be depicted through the labeling of the activity symbols. The activity description is formatted in lower case letters and with a short and concise description of the task performed (e.g.: clicks an ad to landing page). The symbol for collapsed sub-processes is used for modelling customer journeys in order to describe the "in-session" activities, i.e. the interactions of a potential customer with their own website. The activity elements also serve to model touchpoints (Table 3).

**Table 3.** Mapping rules in the field of activities

| Customer Journey Element | BPMN Symbol | Notation (if needed) | Description |
|---|---|---|---|
| 2. Activities | | | |
| Customer journey Step | Activity (OMG 2013 p. 26) | e.g. clicks an ad to landing page, passes checkout etc. | Map the individual steps of the user within his journey as an activity. For example: clicks an ad to landing page // browses through the online store // passes checkout |
| Touchpoints provided by the system | Acitivty (OMG 2013 p. 26) | e.g. provides Webshop/App, provides hotline | Touchpoints shall be modeled as activities of the system and are only mentioned in its pool |
| E-Shop Activities/ In Session Journey | Collapsed- Sub- Process (OMG 2013 p. 30) Sub-Process Name ⊞ | | For customer journey steps such as "browse e-shop" or "go through checkout", sub-processes can be used to model the user's "in session" activities in a more detailed way without going beyond the scope of the overall BPMN model. |

Although this may sound a little inappropriate at first, this way of representing such contact points between the user and the company has many advantages. Customer touchpoints (CTP) may be places, products, people, or marketing activities that create contact with a brand or a company. Every customer's interaction with the brand leaves traces, which makes touchpoints one of the most important elements in the analysis of customer journeys [22].

The system that is used as a pool (see section before) between the user and the company plays a decisive role. Now, this becomes clearer when modeling the touchpoints. In order to represent these crucial elements of the customer journey properly and, most importantly, in a helpful way, they are represented as activities of the system. For example, the system provides the shopping platform, the hotline, or the advertisement. In this way, a clear view of the contact points between the customer and the company is created relatively quickly. The pool with the touchpoints is connected via message flows with the respective departments of the company or the customer journey step of the user's pool. The start and end events within this system pool, which stand at the beginning and end of the "touchpoint activities", remain unnamed. However, it is possible to give the lane within the pool the name "Touchpoints" to create even more clarity.

**Supporting Artefacts: Enriching the Main Process**
When looking at the artifacts embedded in the process model, two underlying BPMN symbols are relevant: Groups and text annotations [8, 17]. The customer journey can be divided into individual phases. During its long and gradual development, the model that has proven most successful is the AIDA principle. Its four phases, Awareness, Interest, Desire and Action, have become a trendy division in both academic and marketing practice [37]. In the end, it is up to the company itself to decide in how many phases and which ones to divide its customer journey. Each of these phases is modeled by using a group symbol. In this way, the phases do not actively intervene in the process but summarize further related model elements and define their affiliation. Group names are written in capital letters (e.g. AWARENESS) to distinguish them from the rest of the notation style. Although phases could be modeled across several roles, the group elements depicting the customer journey phases remain exclusively in the top pool of the user to keep the model simple. Nevertheless, it is relatively easy to read off the assignment of touchpoints and applications in the individual phases via the message flows that lead to the separate groupings. The moments of truth are another part of the customer journey that can be modeled with the text annotation. The customer journey includes the critical moments in which customer expectations have to be fulfilled. For example, the following four points in time can be distinguished in the purchase decision process: Zero Moment of Truth (ZMOT), First Moments of Truth (FMOT), Second Moment of Truth (SMOT), Third Moment of Truth (TMOT) [38]. While FMOT is the stage at which a potential buyer perceives a product or service for the first time, SMOT involves actual physical contact with the product. At this point, it often emerges whether the customer's expectations correspond to the actual performance. In addition, the ZMOT is positioned before the others and developed during the era of digitalization. It involves gathering information before the start of the purchase process, for example, via blogs, rating sites, price comparison sites, or similar. As soon as the customer has reached the end of the customer journey, he can complete the process with the TMOT by

sharing his experience and providing it to other people for the start of a new journey [30, 39]. Text annotations are suitable for additional supporting information, as explained above. Therefore, these moments of truth are attached to the respective position using the BPMN symbol. Associations are the way to proceed. The notation begins with the name of the respective moment in abbreviated form (e.g., FMOT). In square brackets, the description of what exactly happens at this moment follows. An example of the complete text annotation for moments of truth would be: FMOT [First interaction with the product]. Emotions can influence decision-making processes in many situations, especially in digital customer journeys [39, 40]. This includes identifying points at which the customer reaches emotional highs and lows in order to take steps to counter negative experiences and use positive actions to acquire the customer [40]. Emotions are abbreviated with the acronym "EM" and thoughts with "TH". The structure of the notation for a user emotion appears as follows: EM [negative/neutral/positive]/reason. The structure is similar for thoughts. The only difference is that the thought is described as free text in the square bracket, and no fixed specifications exist, as there are countless variations (Table 4).

**Table 4.** Mapping rules in the field of artefacts

| Customer Journey Element | BPMN Symbol | Notation (if needed) | Description |
|---|---|---|---|
| 3. Artefacts | | | |
| Customer journey Stages | Groups (OMG 2013 p. 28) | e.g. AWARENESS, CONSIDERATION, ACQUISITION, SERVICE, LOYALTY | Identify the customer journey stages Awareness, Consideration, Acquisition, Service, Loyalty using the grouping element and write them in capital letters. |
| Emotions, Thoughts, | Text Annotation (OMG 2013 p. 28) Descriptive Text Here | EM [negativ// neutral // positiv] / Reason TH[...] | Annotate emotions and thoughts of the user in the following style. The respective action is shortened either with EM (emotion) or TH (thought). The expression follows in square brackets and the reason after a slash: EM [negative// neutral // positive] / Reason TH [...] |
| Moments of truth | Text Annotation (OMG 2013 p. 28) Descriptive Text Here | Moment of truth [reason] For Example: FMOT [Sale event is perceived] Zero Moment of Truth (ZMOT), First Moment of truth (FMOT), Second Moment of Truth (SMOT), Ultimate Moment of truth (UMOT) | Key customer moments in the customer journey can be highlighted at the appropriate points using text annotation. The following format is recommended for doing so : [ZMOT: Sale is perceived]. |

## Connectors: Essential Description of the Dynamic

Another essential component of process models is the connectors, including associations and the sequence flow [8, 17]. "The sequence flow describes the time-logic sequence of the flow elements: tasks, events, and the gateways" [42].

For the transformation of customer journey maps into IT-supported business processes, sequence flows are utilized on the one hand in the user pool as a path that users follow during their shopping experience. It connects the individual customer journey steps across all phases. On the other hand, when it comes to modeling departmental processes in the company pool, the sequence flow can be interpreted simply as a connecting element of the departmental activities. Associations are firstly applied for the modeling of text annotations. Secondly, they offer the possibility to connect the user's activities via the touchpoints provided by the system with the individual departments or the whole company. They represent the relationships between the pools. Table 5 summarizes the explained mapping for connectors.

**Table 5.** Mapping rules in the area of connectors

| Customer Journey Element | BPMN Symbol | Notation (if needed) | Description |
|---|---|---|---|
| **4. Connectors** | | | |
| Path | Sequence Flow (OMG 2013 p .27) | | The user's path across all customer journey stages and steps. In the context of departments and systems, it represents the link between their activities. |
| Connection | Association (OMG 2013 p. 27) | | Provides the opportunity to connect the activities of user their touchpoints and the associated department/business. |

## Events: Critical Steps of the Customer Journey

After looking at the sequence flows, the following section will focus on the start, end and intermediate events in BPMN, which control the flow. As a process chain trigger, the start event is used to model customer journeys in the user pool to represent the so-called trigger or stimulus that has inspired the potential customer to engage in the journey. Many purchases result from spontaneous stimuli and decisions and are not pre-planned. The stimulus-organism-response paradigm (S-O-R) describes a model in which the effect of experience-oriented measures (input) on the psyche of the customer and the success-oriented output factors are represented [42]. Regarding the customer journey, the response of the S-O-R model, i.e., the output that follows the process after the stimulus, corresponds for example, as a purchase, a subscription, or simply a newsletter registration. However, it can also arrive after the loyalty phase, and the target can be defined as remarketing or retargeting. In any case, the process or the user journey ends with this output and, if necessary, restarts from the beginning. That description coincides with the description of the BPMN End Event [41]. Therefore, the customer journey in the user pool ends with the end event and is described with the previously defined outcome. Like the Start Event, the End Event is not described in the lanes of the departments and is simply used for syntax purposes [42]. One of the benefits of modeling customer journeys is the identification "specific trigger points that lead customers to continue or discontinue in their purchase journey" [23]. Such critical contact points during the customer journey are called micro-moments. They can be expressed by intermediate events, which mark key elements or intermediate goals within a process. They are located somewhere between the start and the end in a process chain. "The micro-moments concept was introduced by Google in 2015 but has already attracted a lot of attention from marketing practitioners" [43]. Google identified four scenarios as critical points in the user journey. The first micro-moment, "I want to know", includes situations in which users research and obtain information about certain products or services but do not have a direct intention to buy anything. If the potential customer is not acquired in this small time frame, he will be lost due to the ubiquity of micro-moments. In the "I want to go" scenario, a potential customer is looking for a local business or is considering buying a product at a nearby store" [43]. After informing themselves, the customer has decided to go to a certain location, such as a retail shop, or to visit a certain website in order to be convinced by the product. In the third scenario, "I want to do", the customer deals with applying the product via guidance from the internet or by talking to a salesperson. Companies can use tutorials to show customers how their product works and thus keep them in their customer journey (Table 6).

**Table 6.** Mapping rules in the area of events

| Customer Journey Element | BPMN Symbol | Notation (if needed) | Description |
|---|---|---|---|
| | **5. Events** | | |
| Stimulus/Trigger | Start (OMG 2013 p. 29) | Description of the trigger. | Trigger/stimulus that creates a need or incentive to buy. |
| Outcome | End (OMG 2013 p. 29) | Description of the outcome. | By using the end event, the result can be described, which ends the journey for the user. (Remarketing, Retargeting, etc.) Outside the user pool, this event ends the activity chain. |
| Communication between Participants | Message (OMG 2013 p. 33) | | Direct communication between the roles involved. |
| Micro Moments | Intermediate (OMG 2013 p. 29) | MM [Information/ Decision/Action/Purchase] | The following intermediate events should mark milestones for the respective company within the customer journey.  I want to know = **INFORMATION** // I want to go = **DECISION** // I want to do = **ACTION** // I want to buy = **PURCHASE** |

The last micro-moment involves the actual buying process and is called "I want to buy". Here, the customer's decision to buy the product has already been made, and only the supplier or brand may still be undecided. With the conversion of the customer into a buyer, this micro-moment is completed [43, 44]. Due to the dropout rates at these points, it is important for companies to be aware of them and to be able to prevent dropouts. As mentioned before intermediate events can be used to consider the micro-moments. Four characteristics are combined into generic terms in order to simplify their notation and make it more meaningful: I want to know = Information, I want to go = Decision, I want to do = Action, I want to buy = Purchase. Consequently, the labeling of the intermediate events is as follows starts with MM for micro-moment, followed by the right scenario: MM[Information/Decision/Action/Purchase].

**Further Symbols: Optional Details**
Ultimately, this chapter will discuss other possible mapping rules, which are not necessary for the core and the main statement. However, they bring added value for some stakeholders and increase the level of detail. They include the BPMN symbols for gateways, data objects, and data stores. When transforming the customer journey into IT-supported business processes, the data object symbol in BPMN can be appropriate to label the user's activities that lead to data collection on the company side. The data type can be also be specified via labeling, for instance indicating, whether it is web tracking data during in-session activities or backend data after billing. In addition, discussing data origin in the model context can help improving data quality [41].

Table 7. Mapping rules of further Symbols

| Customer Journey Element | BPMN Symbol | Notation (if needed) | Description |
|---|---|---|---|
| 6. Further Symbols | | | |
| Path Gateway | Gateway Controls (OMG 2013 p. 31) | | Gateways offer the possibility to map alternative customer journeys, which may end earlier (e.g. ordered shoes fit vs ordered shoes have to be returned). |
| Customer Journey Data | Data Object (OMG 2013 p. 27) | Tracking Data, Backend Data etc. | Label those activities of the user with data objects, where data is collected from the customer. The data objects are tagged with the specific type of data. |
| Databases | Data store (OMG 2013 p. 207) | Backend-, Frontend Systems, CRM Systems, etc. | If data is used in activities, the corresponding databases can be modeled by tagging them on the data store. |

Adding the Data Store element can create value when modeling the individual departments within the company pool. "A Data Store provides a mechanism for Activities to retrieve or update stored information that will persist beyond the scope of the Process. The same Data Store can be visualized, through a Data Store Reference, in one or more places in the Process" [8]. If a department uses data in a specific activity, the icon can be used to model the data source. An online marketing department, for example, could do that to access web tracking data from a database in order to evaluate certain actions. The naming of the data source only requires tagging the symbol. Table 7 recaps the described mapping rules.

## 5   Exemplary Use Case

In the following, the idea of the transformation into IT-supported business models will be explained in more detail based on the customer journey illustration by [25].

### Level of Detail 1: Involved Roles and Phases of the Customer Journey

First, it is important to take a look at the basic structure or framework of this process model. As process participants, the Customer Journey Map shows the user on the one hand and the company with its individual departments on the other. Another special role has been created that bridges the gap between the two just mentioned and thus also holds the pool in the second place. This pool includes the system and the touchpoints as a lane. The touchpoints are an essential part of the customer journey, if not the most important. Five group elements are visible in the user pool, which represents the various customer journey stages (Awareness, Consideration, Acquisition, Service, and Loyalty).

### Level of Detail 2: The Fundamental Process Structure

The next level of detail in modeling the customer journey in IT-supported business processes starts with the process itself. In the selected example, the customer wants to buy a new pair of shoes, so the start event in the user pool is the customer's request. In order to reach his goal, the first step in the customer journey is a click on an advertisement campaign of a well-known fashion brand, which he finds very attractive. With this click, he enters a stored page in the online shop.

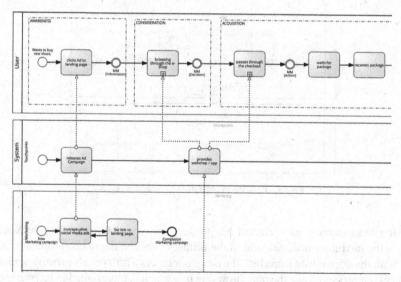

**Fig. 2.** Initial step of specific process modeling

The system makes this campaign available and thus signals to the viewer that this is the customer's first touchpoint with the company. In the company pool, the underlying process of the department is displayed, which makes it possible to establish this contact. In this case, the marketing department was about to launch a new campaign, which they designed and therefore also linked to a Uniform Resource Locator (URL). After the campaign is completed, the system makes the advertising measures available, and the customer can, in this case, come into contact with the company. This is how the basic principle of this modeling works. Individual departments can arrange their daily business in the big picture, i.e., the customer's journey, and learn to understand colleagues' work from other departments. Consequently, it is relatively easy to see how various departments approach the customer and which concrete processes are behind them. To return to the concrete process, we continue to look at the next steps of the potential customer, who has reached a micro-moment after his first interaction with the company. He has probably enquired about new shoes on the internet and then jumped in via the advertisement, which is the reason why he has reached the intermediate event MM[Information]. The customer browses through various product detail pages and product lists in the online shop to find the right product. Beforehand, the system provides the internet appearance in the form of a webshop or an app. The underlying process within the company, which consists of the provision of content from the e-shop management on the one hand and the technical infrastructure from the IT department on the other, is modelled in the company's pool and linked to the system and the user via associations (see Fig. 2). The in-session journey, i.e., the user behavior on the online shop, was included as a sub-process and modeled according to the same mapping rules, as seen in Fig. 3. This sub-process has been presented in a minimalist way, as the focus is on the classic branding customer journey and not on the user experience in the online shop.

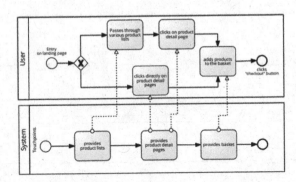

**Fig. 3.** In session activities as a sub-process

After the customer has selected his product and wants to enter the checkout, he reaches the next intermediate event in the primary process: the micro-moment of decision. With the decision on a product, the customer enters a further sub-process, including the checkout process. Like the pure browsing process, it is represented in its own model, similar to the sub-process just shown. In the meantime, the customer has entered the acquisition phase, which can be clearly seen in the group element. While the customer waits for his parcel and finally receives it, the shipping department again runs through a process chain until the package is finally sent and the order is closed. Thus, the shipping department has indirectly established the touchpoint of the first physical product contact. The customer journey splits up in the process chain from this point on. Either the customer decides to purchase the product and thus first reaches the intermediate event of the purchase micro-moment. After the invoice has been paid, this process chain ends with the purchase process's outcome. However, [25] has included the service and loyalty stages in his customer journey map. Therefore, the gateway initiates the complaint process. Meanwhile, the customer has problems making a complaint and turns towards the FAQs and the hotline provided. The system again provides these two touchpoints. The handling process behind the hotline call, i.e., solving the tipped-in ticket with the problem description, can be found in the company pool in the corresponding lane. The service stage ends with the completed returns process, and the potential customer receives a newsletter to enter the loyalty phase. The activities of the last phase are presented analogously to the steps mentioned before.

### Level of Detail 3 - Additional Information Regarding the Process Flow
In a final level of detail of the process model, additional information is added via various BPMN elements, which in principle do not actively influence the process but are nevertheless extremely valuable for interpretation and understanding.

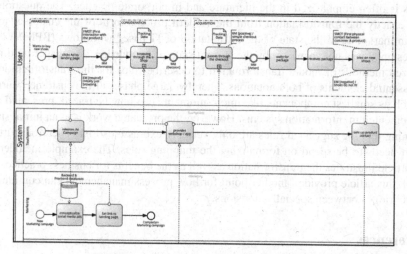

**Fig. 4.** Section of the completed process model

Figure 4 shows a section of the finished process model. In addition to the previous section, the user's emotions during the shopping experience have been added. This information is valuable if you want to take a closer look at certain pain or gain points within the customer journeys and make targeted improvements as a company. In the BPMN model, these emotions and thoughts of the customer are pinned to the respective activity using the text annotation. The emotional expressions are limited to three types. Negative, neutral, and positive emotional states were defined, which the customer can adapt on his journey. On the other hand, in the case of thoughts, several states are possible, as no restrictions were made here. This results from the large number of possibilities. Another element added in the last step of this process modeling is the moments of truth within the customer journey. This was solved by using text annotation and a defined notation analogous to the mentioned emotions. In the example shown, the first product interaction when clicking on the advertising banner, which leads to a landing page in the online shop, is the first moment of truth (FMOT). Accordingly, it is noted and recorded when the customer performs the appropriate action. These critical moments or milestones during the customer's shopping experience are essential information for every company to win over the customer. The second moment of truth can also be found on the process map and includes the customer's first physical product interaction when they open their package and try on the shoes they received. Finally, in the Third Moment of Truth or Ultimate Moment of Truth, the customer either passes on the product via word of mouth or buys products from the company again.

## 6  Summary, Limitations and Future Work

Business process management in general and process modeling in particular have the potential to build bridges between stakeholders. The ability to build a link between strategic ideas for the business and the operational-technical implementation in workflows is often emphasized in the literature and in corporate practice. The question of how exactly the transformation from the modern process form of the customer journey in marketing to the state of the art notation of IT-based workflows (BPMN) is to be designed was not answered by the current state of knowledge. This paper used recognized methods of model transformation to describe rules for the transformation of all essential elements of both notations. Thereby, large phases of the customer journey as well as smallest components like micro-moments can now be traced, presented and implemented in information systems. However, the presented work is in an initial state, meaning that the suggested rules are only verbally expressed so far. Therefore further effort needs to be spend on formalizing the mapping rules. The example included in the article illustrates the transformation as well as the benefits for business practice. All in all, this article provides another point for how process management can continue to build bridges between specialist divisions.

## References

1. Curtis, B., Kellner, M.I., Over, J.: Process modeling. Commun. ACM **35**(9), 75–90 (1992)
2. Davenport, T.H.: Process Innovation: Reengineering Work Through Information Technology. Harvard Business Press, Boston (1992)
3. Carlson, W.M.: Business information analysis and integration technique (BIAIT): the new horizon. Data Base **10**, 3–9 (1979)
4. Lederer, M., Schott, P.: Business process management. In: Khosrow-Pour, M. (eds.) Encyclopedia of Organizational Knowledge, Administration, and Technologies. IGIG, Pennsylvania (2020)
5. Nash, E.M.: IT and business alignment: the effect on productivity and profitability. IT Prof. **11**(6), 31–36 (2009)
6. Martin, V.A., Lycett, M., Macredie, R.: Exploring the gap between business and IT: an information culture approach. In: Proceeding in Action in Language, Organisations and Information Systems (2003)

7. Zhao, L., Letsholo, K., Chioasca, E.V., Sampaio, S., Sampaio, P.: Can business process modeling bridge the gap between business and information systems? In: Proceedings of the 27th Annual ACM Symposium on Applied Computing (2012)
8. OMG: Business Process Model and Notation (2013)
9. Pereira, J.L., Freitas, A.P.: Simulation of BPMN process models. Adv. Intell. Syst. Comput. **444**, 557–566 (2016)
10. Ott, C.S., Keller, B.: Touchpoint management. https://ebookcentral-proquest-com.pxz.iubh.de:8443/lib/badhonnef/detail.action?docID=4840472. Accessed 27 Oct 2021
11. Krogstie, J.: Quality in Business Process Modeling. Springer, Trondheim (2016)
12. White, S.A.: Introduction to BPMN. www.bptrends.com. Accessed 22 Oct 2021
13. Mohapatra, S.: Business Process Reengineering - Automation Decision Points in Process Reengineering. Springer, Boston (2013)
14. Becker, J., Rosemann, M., von Uthmann, C.: Guidelines of business process modeling. In: van der Aalst, W., Desel, J., Oberweis, A. (eds.) Business Process Management. LNCS, vol. 1806, pp. 30–49. Springer, Heidelberg (2000). https://doi.org/10.1007/3-540-45594-9_3
15. Rosemann, M.: Potential pitfalls of process modeling: Part A. Bus. Process. Manag. J. **12**(2), 249–254 (2006)
16. Lederer, M., Schott, P., Knapp, J.: The digital future has many names - how business process management drives the digital transformation. In: Proceedings of the 6th International Conference on Industrial Technology and Management (2017)
17. OMG: BPMN Standard. https://www.omg.org/spec/BPMN/. Accessed 22 Oct 2021
18. Weske, M.: Business Process Management - Concepts, Languages, Architectures. Springer, Berlin (2019)
19. Aagesen, G., Krogstie, J.: Analysis and design of business processes using BPMN. In: vom Brocke, J., Rosemann, M. (eds.) Handbook on Business Process Management. Springer, Berlin
20. Ruecker, B.: Practical Process Automation: Orchestration and Integration in Microservices and Cloud Native Architectures. Farnham, O'Reilly (2021)
21. Nam, H., Kannan, P.K.: Digital environment in global markets: cross-cultural implications for evolving customer journeys. J. Int. Mark. **28**(1), 28–47 (2020)
22. Esch, F.-R., Knörle, C.: Omni-channel-strategien durch customer - touchpoint-management erfolgreich realisieren. In: Binckebanck, L., Elste, R. (eds.) Digitalisierung im Vertrieb, pp. 123–137. Springer, Wiesbaden (2016). https://doi.org/10.1007/978-3-658-05054-2_7
23. Lemon, K.N., Verhoef, P.C.: Understanding customer experience throughout the customer journey. J. Mark. **80**(6), 69–96 (2016)
24. Puccinellia, N.M., Goodstein, R.C., Grewal, D., Priced, R., Raghubire, P., Stewart, S.: Customer experience management in retailing: understanding the buying process. J. Retail. **85**(1), 15–30 (2009)
25. Buchberger, O.: Customer Journey. http://www.omkantine.de/customer-journey-warum-sie-so-kompliziert-ist-und-sich-trotzdem-lohnt/. Accessed 2 Feb 2022
26. Kantola, J.I., Nazir, S. (eds.): Advances in Human Factors, Business Management and Leadership. Advances in Intelligent Systems and Computing. Springer, Cham (2020)
27. Berendes, C.I., Bartelheimer, C., Betzing, J.H., Beverungen, D.: A DSML for customer journeys in high streets data-driven customer journey mapping in local high streets: a domain-specific modeling language. In: Proceedings of the Thirty Ninth International Conference on Information Systems (2018)
28. Heuchert, M.: Conceptual modeling meets customer journey mapping: structuring a tool for service innovation. In: Proceedings of the Conference on Business Informatics (2019)
29. Halvorsrud, R., Haugstveit, I.M., Pultier, A.: Evaluation of a modelling language for customer journeys. In: Proceedings of the IEEE Symposium on Visual Languages and Human-Centric Computing (2016)

30. Gruhn, V., Pieper, D., Röttgers, C.: MDA - Effektives Software-Engineering mit UML2 und Eclipse. Springer, Berlin (2006)
31. Czarnecki, K., Helsen, S.: Classification of model transformation approaches. In: Proceedings of the 2nd OOPSLA Workshop on Generative Techniques in the Context of the Model Driven Architecture (2003)
32. Mayring, P.: Qualitative Inhaltsanalyse. Beltz, Weinheim (2010)
33. Kleppe, A., Warmer, J., Bast, W.: MDA Explained: The Model Driven Architecture: Practice and Promise. Addison-Wesley, Boston (2003)
34. Sottet, J.S., Calvary, G., Favre, J.M.: Mapping model: a first step to ensure usability for sustaining user interface plasticity. In: Proceedings of the MoDELS 2006 Workshop on Model Driven Development of Advanced User Interfaces (2006)
35. Freund, M.: Entwicklung von Modell-zu-Modell-Transformationen für Benutzungsschnittstellen in der Domäne der Industriellen Automatisierungstechnik. Technische Universität, Dresden (2017)
36. Allweyer, T.: BPMN 2.0 - Business Process Model and Notation. Books on Demand, Norderstedt (2020)
37. Strong, E.: The Psychology of Selling. McGraw-Hill, New York (1925)
38. Rusnjak, A., Schallmo, D.R.A. (eds.): Customer Experience im Zeitalter des Kunden. Springer, Wiesbaden (2018). https://doi.org/10.1007/978-3-658-18961-7
39. Märtin, C., Bissinger, B.C., Asta, P.: Optimizing the digital customer journey. J. Consum. Behav. (2021)
40. Gloppen, J., Lindquister, B., Daae, H.P.: The customer journey as a tool for business innovation and transformation. In: De Fillippi, R., Rieple, A., Wikström, P. (eds.) International Perspectives on Business Innovation and Disruption in Design. Edward Elgar, Cheltenham (2017)
41. Freund, J., Rücker, B.: Real-Life BPMN, 4th edn. Camunda, Lakewood (2019)
42. Engelhardt, J.F., Magerhans, A.: eCommerce klipp & klar. Springer, Wiesbaden (2019)
43. Snegirjova, M., Tuomisto, F.: Micro-moments: New Context in Information System Success Theory. Norwegian School of Economics, Bergen (2017)
44. Google: Micro-moments - Your Guide to Winning the Shift to Mobile. https://www.thinkwith google.com/_qs/documents/34/micromoments-guide-to-winning-shift-to-mobile-download.pdf. Accessed 22 Oct 2021

# A Co-evolution Model of Collaborative Process Design

Udo Kannengiesser[✉] and Christian Stary

Institute of Business Informatics – Communications Engineering, and Business School,
Johannes Kepler University Linz, Linz, Austria
{udo.kannengiesser,christian.stary}@jku.at

**Abstract.** Modelling socio-technical systems such as cyber-physical systems (CPS) is becoming increasingly complex, due to their heterogeneous and highly dynamic nature. Collaboration between multiple stakeholders is needed to deal with this complexity. While collaboration has been studied extensively in process modelling, there is a lack of research in collaborative process design. In this paper, we propose a model of collaboration in process design, based on the co-evolution of design ideas across different process designers. We show how this model can be used for testing hypotheses related to task openness, modes of collaboration, and modelling tools. Research models based on co-evolution are proposed for testing each hypothesis. The co-evolution model can advance our understanding of process design by providing a basis for empirically studying the contextual factors likely to contribute to collaborative ideation.

**Keywords:** Process design · Collaboration · Social creativity · Co-evolution · S-BPM

## 1 Introduction

The design and development of modern, digitalised systems such as cyber-physical systems (CPS) is highly complex due to their heterogenous and dynamic nature. They comprise a variety of networked, digital and physical components and processes (cf. [1]), resulting in the need to involve a range of domain expertise (e.g. mechatronics, communications engineering, product management etc.) and different modelling notations and runtime support for execution and simulation [1–4]. Process modelling is increasingly used as an aid for designing socio-technical systems including CPS by means of describing system behaviour [5]. In cyber-physical settings processes control the various components and their interplay, requiring a variety of design decisions, such as orchestrating subsystems according to their topology (cf. [6]).

Yet, modelling a process is not the same as designing a process. As Reijers [7, p. 3] put it: "There is a fine line between *process modelling* and *process design*. [...] Process models are often useful to capture the design of processes, but they serve other purposes as well, e.g. to analyse or enact a process. Process design, in its turn, entails more than merely the modelling of a process. How to organize a process, which technologies to

M. Elstermann et al. (Eds.): S-BPM ONE 2022, CCIS 1632, pp. 115–130, 2022.
https://doi.org/10.1007/978-3-031-19704-8_7

involve, and to whom to assign responsibilities within a process, are all examples of *design* decisions. Such decisions are driven by the objectives of an enterprise as well as the constraints that are in force. Once such decisions are taken, a design may be specified with a model. The *modelling* decisions, then, concern the representation of the business process." Some (S-)BPM practitioners may argue that the examples of design decisions provided in this quote do not address process modelling *per se*, as they concern downstream stages in the BPM lifecycle, such as details of organisational and technological implementation – aspects that are intentionally omitted in S-BPM modelling. However, the argument remains that modelling is only a subset of what is required for the design of a process or organisation.

Most research in BPM is concerned with process modelling rather than process design. The "process of process modelling" is a common term in this area to refer to the temporal sequence in which process modellers carry out modelling activities. Some empirical studies focus on the quality and efficiency with which textual process descriptions can be transformed into graphical models using different modelling notations (e.g. [8, 9]). Others are concerned with process elicitation that transforms knowledge about as-is processes into process models (e.g. [10, 11]). All of these studies are based on the assumption that the requisite process information needed for creating a complete process model is available. This is not the case in design, where tasks are typically ill-structured [12] and their outcomes are highly dependent on the designers' experience and creativity [13, 14]. While effective and efficient modelling is certainly an important aspect of good process design, it does not account for the cognitive activities needed for generating the ideas to be articulated as process models.

Insights in design research and practice have been used for deriving requirements for process modelling methods and notations [15]. Subject-oriented business process management (S-BPM) [16] provides a modelling approach that has been shown to support process design based on its simplicity, intuitive semantics, separation of concerns and executability. However, process modelling (including S-BPM) has not been empirically analysed from the perspective of process design. In this paper, we lay the foundations for this area of research by proposing a model of collaborative process design. It based on a recent formalisation and generalisation of the widely-known co-evolution model in design [17]. Our model describes design collaboration in terms of joint idea generation of different domain experts. We show how this model can be used for empirically testing various hypotheses related to subject-oriented process design.

Section 2 provides related work on collaboration in process modelling and design. Section 3 develops a co-evolution model of collaborative idea generation. Section 4 describes research models for testing hypotheses related to the impact of task openness, modes of collaboration, and modelling tools on collaborative idea generation. Section 5 concludes the paper by summarising its contributions and suggesting future work.

## 2    Collaboration in Process Modelling and Design

### 2.1    Subject-Oriented Process Modelling

In a number of projects, subject-oriented process modelling (S-BPM) has been shown to support the collaboration between stakeholders in business and production domains

[18–21]. Therefore, in this paper we will focus on S-BPM based process design. The fundamental concepts of S-BPM are outlined in this subsection.

Subject-oriented Business Process Management (S-BPM) is a methodology for modelling and executing enterprise behaviour based on interactions between functional roles called "subjects". Every subject in a process encapsulates its individual behaviour and exchanges messages for coordinating its behaviour with other subjects [16]. Two diagrams are used in S-BPM: a Subject Interaction Diagram (SID) showing the subjects in a process and the messages exchanged between them, and Subject Behaviour Diagrams (SBDs) showing the behaviour of individual subjects. An example of an SID is provided in Fig. 1 for an "order management" process. Note that the "internal" behaviour of the subjects (i.e. the detailed way in which a subject fulfils its role in the process) is not specified in this diagram; it is encapsulated in the SBDs of the respective subjects.

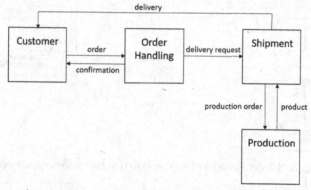

**Fig. 1.** Subject Interaction Diagram (SID) of an order management process. Rectangles represent subjects, and labelled arrows represent messages exchanged between the subjects.

The details of the internal behaviour of every subject is specified using a Subject Behaviour Diagram (SBD). An example is an SBD is shown in Fig. 2, describing the internal behaviour of the "Shipment" subject (cf. Fig. 1). It is a directed graph that connects three types of nodes: Function states (representing actions), Receive states (representing the receipt of a message from another subject) and Send states (representing the dispatch of a message to another subject). The arrows represent state transitions that become active once the preceding state has been executed. Conditions may be added to transitions to enable XOR branching. Parallel branches are not allowed within a single SBD; for representing concurrent behaviours a separate subject must be used for every individual behaviour, and messages between these subjects for coordinating their behaviours.

S-BPM models afford a way of modelling in which different subjects are assigned to different modellers [8]. Every modeller can create the SBD of a subject individually but needs to align it with other modellers whenever the interfaces with the respective subjects are affected. Interfaces are established by the messages in the SID. When modellers collaborate and agree on the definition of a message between their subjects, they need to take that message into account in their internal behaviour models (SBDs).

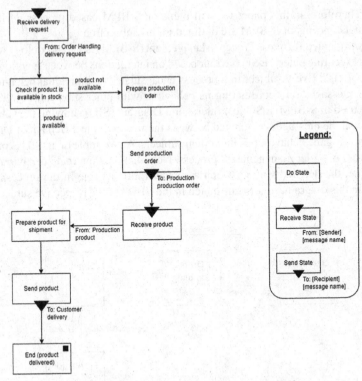

**Fig. 2.** Subject Behaviour Diagram (SBD) of the "Shipment" subject

## 2.2  Collaboration in Model-Driven Design

Traditional understanding of collaborative modelling can be described as follows: "Multiple stakeholders with different roles and different kinds of expertise should be enabled to contribute to the collaborative instantiation and creation of the model" [22, p. 72]. However, in a recent typology of modelling in the context of transformative change, collaborative modelling has been understood as means to "empower stakeholders to take ownership over their reality" [23, p. 7], regardless from which discipline they come from or what interest they have in change processes.

Modelling in general has been recognised as a key activity in the conceptual design of systems in that it creates a shared understanding among various stakeholders about a system representation (cf. [24]). The kind of interest in stakeholder participation can be nominal, instrumental, representative, and transformative [23], each of which supporting a specific flow of control and information in the course of modelling. "Nominal participation increases a project's legitimacy by including stakeholders in spreading the results of the study. Instrumental participation uses participants to increase efficiency and reduce costs. Representative interest ensures participants agree to the solution by ensuring their wishes and concerns are heard. Finally, a transformative interest in participation does not see participation as a means to an end, but as both the means to obtain benefits as well as an end in itself." [*ibid*, p. 9] Although the authors refer in their typology to the generic interest in participatory modelling (bottom-up, top-down) they do not differentiate in terms of design ideas and creative interactions among participating stakeholders. It seems the drivers of collaborative modelling are efficiency and effectiveness of collaboration tasks (as in previous studies, e.g., [24]) rather than understanding the various inputs for design that occur along externalization of knowledge and representational acts on a model.

Stephan [25] provided a survey on collaborative modelling in software engineering, observing a number of collaborative modelling research concepts being or becoming prominent in the last five years. He identified versioning, recognizing model differences, conflict resolution, and inconsistency management due to collaboration of modelers in advanced system development. These issues are adjacent to establishing 'quality' in collaborative modelling, including issues like security and access control rather than ideas and creative design inputs, even though increasingly (potential) users and customers become modelers in agile software development environments.

In their meta-modelling approach Ssebuggwawo et al. [26] analysed collaborative modelling sessions based on a triad of rules, interactions and models. It enables a more detailed analysis than more recent frameworks in model-driven development, such as the one introduced by Franzago et al. [27] who used a triad of management, collaboration, and communication. The fine-grained framework by Ssebuggwawo et al. was utilized to investigate modelling activities and the resulting quality of the modelling process. Quality is captured in terms of excellence, correctness or validity, and the modelling process is described by evaluation, related discussions and negotiations.

Recent findings from analysing model-driven engineering and respective tool support for collaboration indicate various research needs, e.g. to improve collaborative graphical modelling with a focus on users and change history [28]. Thereby user-level edit operations should be preserved rather than identifying differences of model versions after their creation. Persisting the process rather than the result of multiple edit operations leads to chronological details. Enriching them with event sourcing enables understanding the genesis of evolving design representations, variants in behaviour, and new possibilities in collaboration [ibid].

Experiences gained from training students to use model-based design and development methodologies suggest that collaborating modellers should not only be able to differentiate problem from solution spaces, but also to actively shape their collaboration [29]. The development of a shared solution can be facilitated by a variety of settings and interventions:

- *Focus on Roles*: As already studied in the context of S-BPM [16], role-based business process modelling allows to focus on technical know-how to accomplish tasks of work and to focus on negotiating with other business process participants in the course of collaborative modelling to come up with a consistent and integrated process model. As shown by Ertugrul et al. [30], the type of communication, being either ex-ante, ex-post, or ongoing, has an impact on the process of collaboration and the resulting design of models. These findings indicate that pull-based information awareness and on-demand conflict resolution minimize latency and do not disturb the flow of model generation.

- *Focus on Intelligibility*: Not only understanding collaboration within organizations plays a crucial role when recognising roles of stakeholders, but also ensuring the understanding of representations for non-technical persons (cf. [31]). Apart from reducing complexity in models, the modeler's interaction and conflict resolution need to be considered as an integral part of the modelling process.
- *Focus on Evolvement*: Since collaborative modelling supports volatile organisational structures, stakeholders can create dynamic and flexible process models to adapt to changing conditions, e.g., to stay competitive in a networked market. Continuously evolving process designs can be facilitated through explicit management activities, including rule-based transformation, change coordination, operational process continuity, and collaboration traceability (cf. [32]).

These facilitating items are mutually dependent for designing a comprehensive collaboration effort. When targeting evolvement of collaborative modelling in a human-centred way, the intelligibility of representations and interaction among role carriers play a crucial role. So far, methodological and tool support has been focused on a variety of topics when multiple users generate a model. According to Masson et al. [33], the most prominent topics are access control, versioning of model representations in case several users collaborate when generating or editing a common model, and notification management including asynchronous and synchronized collaboration of modelers. Taking into account quality attributes of modelling inputs, they relate to the modelled content in terms of excellence, effectiveness, or efficiency (see above). Other qualities with respect to co-evolving design, e.g., capturing fundamental or complimentary information of core processes, differentiating routine from emergency behaviour, proposing design ideas influencing further development, have not been investigated in detail so far.

## 3   Modelling Collaborative Idea Generation as Co-evolution

Designing is a process that brings about changes in the world. During this process, designers continuously create ideas for the particular design task. The set of ideas created is commonly termed the design space, within which candidate designs are searched [34]. Creating the design space is a distinguishing feature of designing, as not all the knowledge needed to generate a design solution is provided at the outset of the design task. Design spaces are often subdivided into a problem space and a solution space.

Creating ideas during a design process can be thought of as a basic form of creativity. Creativity is concerned with generating ideas that are both novel and useful [35]. Novelty is a relative concept that can refer to the history of humankind (historical or h-creativity) or to the previous knowledge of an individual (psychological or p-creativity) [36]. P-creativity is a precursor of h-creativity. Another type of creativity was introduced by Suwa et al. [37] to refer to ideas that are created for the first time in the current design process (situated or s-creativity). While s-creativity does not necessarily lead to p- or h-creativity, it is always their precursor and the only type of creativity that can be measured in empirical studies such as think-aloud design sessions. In the remainder of this paper we use the term creativity to mean s-creativity.

In collaborative design, novel ideas are generated not only by individuals working in isolation, but as a synergistic result of interaction with other team members [38].

In this context, Fischer et al. [39] speak of individual and social creativity. They view social creativity as a collective outcome that is greater than the sum of individual efforts, contrasting it with traditional "division of labour" accounts that are based only on the individual creativity of team members.

We can describe social and individual creativity using a recent model of co-evolution [17] that provides a formalisation and visualisation for the changes of state within and across different analytic categories during a design process. The model distinguishes two types of change: (1) *endogenous change*, if the change of state of a category is caused by the transformation of a state of that category, and (2) *exogenous change*, if the change of state of a category is caused by the transformation of a state of a different category. Endogenous change corresponds to the notion of evolution. Exogenous change, if it is reciprocal (i.e. occurring in both directions between two categories), corresponds to co-evolution.

The notion of co-evolution was originally introduced in design research to describe the mutual interaction between problem and solution spaces [40, 41], based on the biological metaphor of co-evolution between different species. An example of co-evolving problem and solution spaces is provided by [17]: A race car designer is considering how to solve the problem how to increase the rate of acceleration of the car. The problem prompts the consideration of a possible solution (exogenous change): using a more powerful engine. While elaborating this solution, the designer eventually introduces more effective brakes as another design feature in the solution space (endogenous change), which is subsequently recognised to solve a new problem (exogenous change): allowing the car to decelerate later in the corners of the racetrack.

The term of co-evolution has also been used to characterise mutual influence in various other categorical schemes in design (not just problems and solutions), including the interaction of design ideas between members of a design team [42]. Using this instantiation of co-evolution, we can map social creativity onto the co-evolution of ideas across different designers' design spaces, and individual creativity onto the evolution of ideas within a designer's design space. Here it is not relevant whether the novel ideas relate to the problem or solution space; it only matters which designer generated them.

The co-evolution model of social and individual creativity can be represented using the graphical visualisation proposed by [17]. An illustration is shown in Fig. 3, where all possible endogenous and exogenous changes of the design spaces of three designers ($D^1$, $D^2$ and $D^3$) between two points in time are described conceptually. The transition from $D^1$ at time i to $D^2$ at time i + 1, for example, is an exogenous change of $D^2$. It corresponds to the notion of social creativity, as the change of $D^2$ is induced by $D^1$. The transition from $D^1$ at time i to $D^1$ at time i + 1 is an endogenous change of $D^1$, consistent with the notion of individual creativity.

This visualisation makes explicit a key difference between designing and (only) modelling: Designing generates novel ideas that have not existed before in the current design process, leading to incremental expansions of design spaces. Modelling takes ideas that exist and puts them into a particular form according to notational rules and conventions. It produces no upward increments in the representation of co-evolution. Of course, designing can involve modelling or episodes in which no novel ideas are produced, neither individually nor socially. In such episodes, designers may take turns

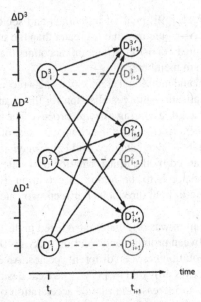

**Fig. 3.** Conceptual representation of endogenous and exogenous changes of the design spaces of three designers $D^1$, $D^2$ and $D^3$ (adapted from [17]), corresponding to individual and social creativity, respectively. A change in a design space is represented by an upward increment and the addition of the prime symbol. When no change has occurred, there is no upward increment.

in modelling or reasoning about existing ideas or concepts, but this would not lead to increments in the graphs as no new ideas are created.

Possible analyses based on the co-evolution model have been illustrated by [17] using empirical data from a think-aloud design session. The session involved three engineering designers (here denoted as D1, D2 and D3) collaborating on a design task. The task was to design a future personal entertainment system. The verbalisations of the designers were segmented and coded using an ontological coding schema [14] and a binary variable representing the novelty of an idea in terms of its first occurrence in the design process. The arbitrated results were analysed and visualised in the same way as the conceptual model shown in Fig. 3, leading to the diagram presented in Fig. 4. The graphs D1, D2 and D3 represent the cumulative occurrence of novel ideas by the three designers and thus the expansion of their design spaces while designing. The distance between the graphs does not mean convergence or divergence of ideas; it simply shows the relative difference in the expansion of design spaces. The various endogenous and exogenous changes of the design spaces indicate episodes of individual and social creativity in the design process. It can be seen that there are a few episodes, particularly towards the end of the design session, in which no novel ideas are produced by any of the three designers. This is because at that time they were either sketching or talking about ideas that have already been articulated earlier. Another piece of information that can be inferred from the graphs, as pointed out by [17], is the relative influence of each designer on the idea generation of the others. This can be interpreted as the extent to which a designer contributes to social creativity. For example, it can be seen there is more social creativity between D2 and D3 than between D1 and D3. On the other hand, the individual creativity of D2 is relatively low compared to the others.

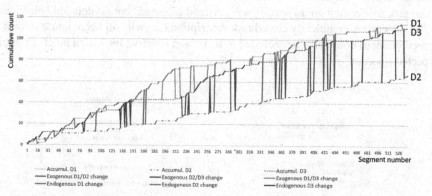

**Fig. 4.** Representation of empirical data as a sequence of endogenous and exogenous changes of the design spaces of three designers D1, D2 and D3 (adapted from [17]).

The co-evolution model of social creativity can be used for analysing data gained from collaborative process design sessions. Here, design tasks need to be underspecified with a focus on designing to-be processes. In such a setting, individual and social creativity can be expected to play a major role in the design process. This is different to previous studies focussing solely on process modelling aspects [8]. In Sect. 4, we present four hypotheses regarding S-BPM based process design that can be tested using the co-evolution model.

# 4 Research Models for Empirical Studies of Collaborative Process Design

In this section, four hypotheses for S-BPM based process design are proposed. For each of them it is shown how the co-evolution model can support their empirical testing.

## 4.1 Task Openness and Social Creativity

The degree to which a process design task is underspecified – here called task openness – can be expected to require an increased amount of creativity (of both individual and social kinds) needed to solve that task. This can be formulated in terms of the following hypothesis:

*H1: Open process design tasks lead to more individual and social creativity than closed process design tasks.*

A research model for testing this hypothesis is shown in Fig. 5. The independent variable is task openness, which generally relates to the knowledge available about the problem or solution space. It can be operationalised in S-BPM by the amount of information provided in the design brief about subjects and messages involved in the design. For example, such a task may simply state "design a process for order management", without specifying subjects such as "customer", "order handling" or "shipment" or messages such as "delivery request" or "confirmation" (cf. Fig. 1). A more constrained (i.e., less open) task description could specify subjects and messages but no detailed behaviours of the subjects. A completely closed task description (i.e. with all behavioural information predefined) could also be included to serve as a baseline for which no creativity is expected to occur.

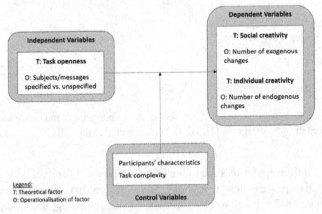

**Fig. 5.** Research model for testing hypothesis H1: *Open process design tasks lead to more individual and social creativity than closed process design tasks.*

The dependent variables include the social and individual creativity occurring in the design session, operationalised by the number of exogenous and endogenous changes of the design spaces of different process designers. The total number of (exogenous and endogenous) changes indicates the overall creativity of the design team. The number of exogenous changes divided by the total number of changes indicates the relative contribution of collaboration to the team's creativity.

Control variables include the participants' characteristics, such as their domain knowledge, their level of experience in process design and modelling, and general personal traits (e.g. cognitive, social and motivational capacities). They also include the complexity of the process design task, such as the number of subjects and messages needed in the process.

This research model primarily serves as a testbed for the basic assumption underpinning our co-evolution model, i.e. that process design fundamentally differs from process modelling. However, it may also be used for investigating the amount of "design" in an otherwise routine modelling task. There is anecdotal evidence in the S-BPM literature that during the elicitation of processes already in operation (which normally should be a routine task not involving any ideation), it often occurs that stakeholders spontaneously articulate ideas for process improvement, thus blurring the distinction between as-is and to-be processes [20].

## 4.2  Modes of Collaboration and Social Creativity

Collaboration in design encompasses different degrees of coupling between the activities of individual domain experts, ranging from closely-coupled to loosely-coupled [43]. In closely-coupled collaboration, "participants work intensely with one another, observing and understanding each other's moves, the reasoning behind them and the intentions" (*ibid*, p. 411). In loosely-coupled collaboration, different experts work individually on different parts of the design but coordinate their efforts in frequent intervals. Based on the fact that closely-coupled collaboration allows more time to be spent on working together in a group than loosely-coupled collaboration, it can be expected that the former leads to increased social creativity. This can be formulated in terms of the following hypothesis:

*H2: Closely-coupled collaboration in process design leads to more social creativity than loosely-coupled collaboration.*

A research model for testing this hypothesis is shown in Fig. 6. The independent variable is the mode of collaboration during the process design task, operationalised by the distinction of a closely-coupled and a loosely-coupled mode. In (subject-oriented) process design, the closely-coupled mode can be realised by applying the so-called "workshop" approach that brings all the different domain experts together to work on the same model of the process [44]. This is the traditional approach for process elicitation and can be done in any notation including S-BPM, although this would violate the (subject-oriented) principle of separation of concerns: namely, that experts work on their own subjects without having to deal with the internal behaviour of other subjects. The loosely-coupled mode corresponds to the approach described by [45] that is well aligned with the separation of concerns in S-BPM, where different subjects are modelled by different experts that work individually on defining their own subjects' behaviour and coordinate with others only when the interfaces of their subjects (i.e. messages) need to be aligned.

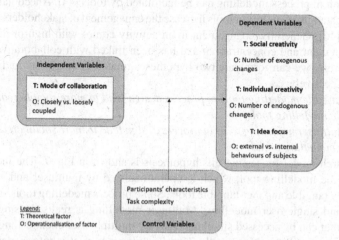

**Fig. 6.** Research model for testing hypothesis H2: *Closely-coupled collaboration in process design leads to more social creativity than loosely-coupled collaboration.*

The dependent variables include social and individual creativity in terms of the number of exogenous and endogenous changes. Although individual creativity is not involved in hypothesis H2, it is still included in the research model. This is to get a more detailed overall picture of the distribution of social and individual creativity, taking into account absolute and relative numbers. The dependent variables also include idea focus, in terms of the subjects' external behaviours (i.e. messages) or internal behaviours. This is to find out more about the potential increase in social creativity in closely-coupled collaboration: Are the ideas being generated related mostly to the internal behaviour of subjects or to their interfaces?

The control variables in the research model are the same as in the previous one.

Hypothesis H2 has been set up in response to outcomes of a recent empirical study [8] of two process modelling approaches – control flow (BPMN) and communication (S-BPM) – that afford closely-coupled and loosely-coupled collaboration, respectively. In the study it was shown statistically that the loosely-coupled approach outperformed the closely-coupled one in terms of higher model quality and reduced modelling time. Yet, the focus of that study was on process modelling, not process design. Therefore, proponents of the control flow approach may argue that the inferior modelling performance of close-coupled collaboration can be compensated by more creative and effective process designs. If hypothesis H2 is confirmed, then an analysis of the dependent variable of idea focus could reveal its cause: If the idea focus is mainly on the subjects' internal behaviours, then the separation of concerns in subject-oriented modelling could in fact be identified as detrimental to social creativity in process design. If the idea focus is mainly on external behaviours, then the increased social creativity would not be linked to a violation of the separation of concerns principle.

### 4.3   Modelling Tools and Social Creativity

Collaboration in process modelling can be facilitated by tools [44]. Anecdotal evidence suggests that tangible, multiuser tools increase the engagement of stakeholders in process modelling [46]. Generally, engagement in an activity comes with high intrinsic motivation, enjoyment and concentration, and has been linked with collaborative ideation [47]. Therefore, we can formulate two hypotheses related to tangibility and multiuser support, respectively: .

*H3a: Tangible modelling tools in process design lead to more social creativity than non-tangible modelling tools.*

*H3b: Multiuser modelling tools in process design lead to more social creativity than single-user modelling tools.*

A research model for testing this hypothesis is shown in Fig. 7. The independent variable is the modelling tool, which is operationalised by multiuser and single-user tools, and by tangible and non-tangible tools. Some process modelling tools[1] allow both multiuser and single-user modelling. Multiuser modelling is realised using a shared repository that can be accessed simultaneously by multiple user clients. Tangible modelling tools are usually multiuser tools. They include cards, post-it notes and multitouch

---

[1] https://compunity.eu/#!/toolsuite,  https://www.metasonic.de/en/products/metasonic-process-suite/.

interfaces [46]. Non-tangible tools include desktop-based editors with more traditional
input devices such as a mouse or stylus.

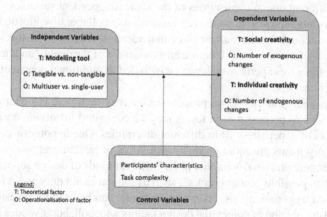

**Fig. 7.** Research model for testing hypothesis H3a: *Tangible modelling tools in process design
lead to more social creativity than non-tangible modelling tools*, and hypothesis H3b: *Multiuser
modelling tools in process design lead to more social creativity than single-user modelling tools*.

The dependent and control variables are the same as in the research model shown in
Fig. 5.

The research model allows testing claims that tangible, multiuser modelling environments support design thinking related to processes [19]. Related studies in tangible
process modelling have been limited to elicitation rather than design [11].

## 5   Conclusion

Collaboration is a ubiquitous feature in most design activities. This is also the case
in process design for business and production, where processes often involve different
organisational departments and lifecycle phases such that multiple domain experts are
needed [48]. While collaboration between stakeholders has been studied in areas such
as BPM, its role in idea generation – which can be seen as the primary characteristic of
designing – has not been paid much attention to. This paper has proposed an explicit
account of collaborative ideation based on an abstraction of the co-evolution model of
design. It can be applied to empirical data to gain insights in the way process designs are
created. It goes beyond existing studies that are limited to activities of (collaborative)
modelling. The paper shows how the co-evolution model can support testing of various
hypotheses related to process design, for which only anecdotal evidence exists to date.

The next logical step in this research would be to run experiments according to the
research models presented in this paper, using protocols of think-aloud process design
sessions. Unlike most studies in process modelling, the data to be captured would include
not only modelling actions (i.e. actions related to creating or modifying process models)
but also the designers' utterances describing design ideas and the reasoning behind these

ideas. Coding schemes and visualisations such as those used by [17] could be applied to analyse the data. While the research models in this paper are focused on S-BPM based process design, it is possible to also use other process modelling approaches by developing different operationalisations of the same independent variables.

The co-evolution model shows the (co-)evolution of collaborative ideation over time, but does not account for the outcomes of that ideation (i.e. whether the ideas being generated are useful). This would require an assessment of the quality and/or originality of process designs by experts, which can be included as additional dependent variables in the research models.

Finally, more hypotheses about process design may be tested. For example, different compositions of process design teams may be compared, involving designers with different levels of expertise or from different disciplines. One hypothesis could be that interdisciplinary teams are more productive in terms of novel ideas produced, as suggested by literature on social creativity [39]. Different kinds of design support may also be compared as possible "collaborators", such as human facilitators and AI-based systems. Based on its genericity, the co-evolution model can be used for investigating any hypothesised connection of contextual design factors with collaborative idea generation.

# References

1. Barišić, A., et al.: Multi-paradigm modeling for cyber-physical systems: a systematic mapping review. J. Syst. Softw. **183**, 111081 (2022)
2. Deng, L., Jiang, Y., Zhang, L.: Spatiotemporal modeling method of cyber-physical system based on object-oriented. In: 2021 IEEE 12th International Conference on Software Engineering and Service Science (ICSESS), pp. 182–185 (2021)
3. Graja, I., Kallel, S., Guermouche, N., Cheikhrouhou, S., Hadj Kacem, A.: A comprehensive survey on modeling of cyber-physical systems. Concurr. Comput. Practice Exp. **32**(15), e4850 (2020)
4. Mittal, S., Tolk, A.: Complexity Challenges in Cyber Physical Systems: Using Modeling and Simulation (M&S) to Support Intelligence, Adaptation and Autonomy. Wiley, New York (2019)
5. Kannengiesser, U., Krenn, F., Stary, C.: A behaviour-driven development approach for cyber-physical production systems. In: 2020 IEEE Conference on Industrial Cyber-Physical Systems (ICPS), pp. 179–184 (2020)
6. Liu, B., Zhang, Y., Zhang, G., Zheng, P.: Edge-cloud orchestration driven industrial smart product-service systems solution design based on CPS and IIoT. Adv. Eng. Inform. **42**, 100984 (2019)
7. Reijers, H.A.: Business process management: the evolution of a discipline. Comput. Ind. **126**, 103404 (2021)
8. Moattar, H., Bandara, W., Kannengiesser, U., Rosemann, M.: Control flow versus communication: comparing two approaches to process modelling. Bus. Process. Manag. J. **28**(2), 372–397 (2022)
9. Weber, B., et al.: Fixation patterns during process model creation: initial steps toward neuro-adaptive process modeling environments. In: 2016 49th Hawaii International Conference on System Sciences (HICSS), pp. 600–609 (2016)
10. Harman, J., Brown, R., Johnson, D., Rinderle-Ma, S., Kannengiesser, U.: Augmenting process elicitation with visual priming: an empirical exploration of user behaviour and modelling outcomes. Inf. Syst. **62**, 242–255 (2016)

11. Luebbe, A., Weske, M.: Determining the effect of tangible business process modeling. In: Plattner, H., Meinel, C., Leifer, L. (eds.) Design Thinking Research. Understanding Innovation. Springer, Heidelberg (2012). https://doi.org/10.1007/978-3-642-21643-5_14
12. Rittel, H.W.J., Webber, M.M.: Dilemmas in a general theory of planning. Policy Sci. **4**, 155–169 (1973)
13. Cross, N.: Expertise in design: an overview. Des. Stud. **25**(5), 427–441 (2004)
14. Gero, J.S., Kannengiesser, U.: The function-behaviour-structure ontology of design. In: Chakrabarti, A., Blessing, L.T.M. (eds.) An Anthology of Theories and Models of Design, pp. 236–283. Springer, London (2014)
15. Kannengiesser, U.: The future: obstacles and opportunities. In: Neubauer, M., Stary, C. (eds.) S-BPM in the Production Industry: A Stakeholder Approach, pp. 209–230. Springer, Cham (2017)
16. Fleischmann, A., Schmidt, W., Stary, C., Obermeier, S., Börger, E.: Subject-Oriented Business Process Management. Springer Nature, Cham (2012). https://doi.org/10.1007/978-3-642-45103-4_25
17. Gero, J.S., Kannengiesser, U., Crilly, N.: Abstracting and formalizing the design co-evolution model. Design Science **8**, e14 (2022)
18. Fleischmann, A., Schmidt, W., Stary, C.: S-BPM in the Wild: Practical Value Creation. Springer Nature, Cham (2015). https://doi.org/10.1007/978-3-642-45103-4_25
19. Fleischmann, A., Oppl, S., Schmidt, W., Stary, C.: Contextual Process Digitalization: Changing Perspectives – Design Thinking – Value-Led Design. Springer Nature, Cham (2020). https://doi.org/10.1007/978-3-030-38300-8
20. Moser, C., Kannengiesser, U., Elstermann, M.: Examining the PASS approach to process modelling for digitalised manufacturing: Results from three industry case studies. Enterp. Model. Inf. Syst. Arch. (EMISAJ) In, J. Conceptual Model. **17**(1), (2022)
21. Neubauer, M., Stary, C.: S-BPM in the Production Industry: A Stakeholder Approach. Springer, Cham (2017). https://doi.org/10.1007/978-3-319-48466-2
22. Faber, A.T.L.: Collaborative Modeling and Visualizing of Business Ecosystems. Doctoral dissertation, Technische Universität München, Germany (2019)
23. van Bruggen, A., Nikolic, I., Kwakkel, J.: Modeling with stakeholders for transformative change. Sustainability **11**(3), 825 (2019)
24. Renger, M., Kolfschoten, G.L., Vreede, G.J.D.: Challenges in collaborative modeling: a literature review. Adv. Enterp. Eng. **I**, 61–77 (2008)
25. Stephan, M.: Emerging concepts and trends in collaborative modeling: a survey. In: Proceedings 7th International Conference on Model-Driven Engineering and Software Development (MODELSWARD 2019), pp. 240–247 (2019)
26. Ssebuggwawo, D., Hoppenbrouwers, S.J.B.A., Proper, H.A.: Collaborative modeling: towards a meta-model for analysis and evaluation, Sprouts Working Papers Inf. Syst. 10(36) (2010)
27. Franzago, M., Di Ruscio, D., Malavolta, I., Muccini, H.: Collaborative model-driven software engineering: a classification framework and a research map. IEEE Trans. Software Eng. **44**(12), 1146–1175 (2017)
28. Pietron, J.: Enhancing collaborative modeling. Proceedings 23rd ACM/IEEE International Conference on Model Driven Engineering Languages and Systems: Companion Proceedings, pp. 1–6 (2020)
29. Dittmar, A., Buchholz, G., Kühn, M.: Effects of facilitation on collaborative modeling sessions with a multi-touch UML editor. In: Proceedings IEEE/ACM 39th International Conference on Software Engineering: Software Engineering Education and Training Track (ICSE-SEET), pp. 97–106 (2017)
30. Ertugrul, A.M., Demirors, O.: An exploratory study on role-based collaborative business process modeling approaches. In: Proceedings of the 7th International Conference on Subject-Oriented Business Process Management, pp. 1–5 (2015)

31. Aleem, S., Lazarova-Molnar, S., Mohamed, N.: Collaborative business process modeling approaches: a review. In: Proceedings IEEE 21st International Workshop on Enabling Technologies: Infrastructure for Collaborative Enterprises, pp. 274–279 (2012)

32. Liu, C., Li, Q., Zhao, X.: Challenges and opportunities in collaborative business process management: overview of recent advances and introduction to the special issue. Inf. Syst. Front. **11**(3), 201–209 (2009)

33. Masson, C., Corley, J., Syriani, E.: Feature model for collaborative modeling environments. In: Proceedings MODELS, pp. 164–173 (2017)

34. Woodbury, R., Burrow, A.: Whither design space? Artif. Intell. Eng. Des. Anal. Manuf. **20**(2), 63–82 (2006)

35. Sternberg, R.J., Lubart, T.I.: The concept of creativity: prospects and paradigms. In: Sternberg, R.J., Lubart, T.I. (eds.) Handbook of Creativity, pp. 3–15. Cambridge University Press, Cambridge (1999)

36. Boden, A.: The Creative Mind: Myths and Mechanisms. Weidenfeld & Nicolson, London (1990)

37. Suwa, M., Gero, J.S., Purcell, T.: Unexpected discoveries and s-invention of design requirements: important vehicles for a design process. Des. Stud. **21**(6), 539–567 (2000)

38. Paulus, P.B., Baruah, J., Kenworthy, J.B.: Enhancing collaborative ideation in organizations. Frontiers in Psychology **9** (2018)

39. Fischer, G., Giaccardi, E., Eden, H., Sugimoto, M., Ye, Y.: Beyond binary choices: integrating individual and social creativity. Int. J. Hum Comput Stud. **63**(4–5), 482–512 (2005)

40. Maher, M.-L., Poon, J.: Modelling design exploration as co-evolution. Microcomput. Civil Eng. **11**(3), 195–209 (1996)

41. Dorst, K., Cross, N.: Creativity in the design process: co-evolution of problem–solution. Des. Stud. **22**(5), 425–437 (2001)

42. Crilly, N.: The evolution of "co-evolution" (Part II): The biological analogy, different kinds of co-evolution, and proposals for conceptual expansion. She Ji J. Des. Econ. Innov. **7**(3), 333–355 (2021)

43. Kvan, T.: Collaborative design: what is it? Autom. Constr. **9**(4), 409–415 (2000)

44. Nolte, A., Brown, R., Anslow, C., Wiechers, M., Polyvyanyy, A., Herrmann, T.: Collaborative business process modeling in multi-surface environments. In: Anslow, C., Campos, P., Jorge, J. (eds.) Collaboration Meets Interactive Spaces, pp. 259–286. Springer, Cham (2016)

45. Oppl, S.: Articulation of work process models for organizational alignment and informed information system design. Inf. Manage. **53**(5), 591–608 (2016)

46. Kannengiesser, U., Oppl, S.: Business processes to touch: engaging domain experts in process modelling. In: Proceedings of BPM Demo Session, vol. 1418, pp. 40–44 (2015)

47. Dorta, T., Lesage, A., Pérez, E., Bastien, J.C.: Signs of collaborative ideation and the hybrid ideation space. In: Taura, T., Nagai, Y. (eds.) Design Creativity 2010, pp. 199–206. Springer, London (2011)

48. Dumas, M., La Rosa, M., Mendling, J., Reijers, H.A.: Fundamentals of Business Process Management, 2nd edn. Springer, Berlin (2018). https://doi.org/10.1007/978-3-662-56509-4

# Short Papers

# A Single Point of Contact for Privacy Management in Cyber-Physical Systems

Thomas Ernst Jost[✉][iD] and Christian Stary[iD]

Institute of Business Informatics - Communications Engineering,
Johannes Kepler University Linz, Linz, Austria
{thomas.jost,christian.stary}@jku.at

**Abstract.** Cyber-Physical Systems (CPS) are a pervasive generation of socio-technical systems that become manifest in complex domains, such as healthcare. This progression challenges system architecting due to the heterogeneity, connectivity, and dynamic adaptation of CPS. In particular, cross-cutting issues, such as privacy management, require dedicated development effort, as they affect both individual components and the behavior of the overall system. The presented research introduces a Single Point of Contact architecture for handling privacy issues at design and run time.

**Keywords:** Cyber-Physical Systems · Cross-cutting concerns · Privacy management · Single Point of Contact · Semantic behavior modeling

## 1  Introduction

There are certain concerns, such as privacy [10] and security [11], that need to be addressed on the system level of distributed systems. In particular, Cyber-Physical Systems (CPS) have introduced challenges due to their heterogeneity, connectivity, and dynamic [13]. Consequently, a CPS architecture has to support system adaptation at design and run time while taking into account decentralized control, modularity, and autonomy of components, including self-capabilities [6]. Most important, concerns addressing multiple dependencies need to be tackled beyond the boundaries of individual components and need to recognize emergent phenomena occurring through the interaction of components (cf. [8], where the need for a multi-disciplinary CPS development process that also focuses on integration and interaction of separate physical and computational components was highlighted). In the following we refer to such challenges as "cross-cutting concerns".

When implementing approaches on the system level, a generic abstraction could help in addressing such issues. In order to demonstrate the potential and feasibility of such an approach, we consider the cross-cutting concern of privacy

M. Elstermann et al. (Eds.): S-BPM ONE 2022, CCIS 1632, pp. 133–143, 2022.
https://doi.org/10.1007/978-3-031-19704-8_8

management[1]. CPS applications, such as smart cities, have the potential to pervade many aspects of a person's live and bring privacy challenges (see [4]). Similarly, interconnected CPS of different organizations in industry also raise issues for involved stakeholders. In such complex and heterogeneous cyber-physical environments, trying to manage privacy for every single individual device, application, service, or sub-system would require a high amount of effort for users and developers. It would also likely lead to redundant actions for each CPS sub-system or component (especially if the same privacy setting would apply to a variety of the involved components). Due to the interactions between different components of the cyber-physical environment, knowledge of a singular aspect is furthermore not sufficient to provide insight into effects on privacy for a specific setting. It also influences privacy-related decision making significantly (see [15]).

To help address such issues, we advocate for the creation of a so-called "Single Point of Contact" (SPoC) architecture for privacy management. The goal is to provide a single interface for affected stakeholders to manage their privacy. This means that they should be able to view information that supports their decision making and configure privacy requirements for the system, which should subsequently be enforced. The SPoC should reduce the complexity of the underlying system and make relevant information accessible and transparent. "Transparency" in the context of this work means for a stakeholder to be able to understand how the system behaves with regard to privacy and how stakeholders can manage privacy requirements and their implementation. Transparency is applied to guide the continuous development of CPS in a way that privacy concerns on the system and component level can be put into operation, in line with Privacy-By-Design principles (see [7]).

In the following section, we will examine existing privacy management approaches from the fields of CPS and IoT (capturing the physical part of CPS) to assess to what extent their architectures already address these initially stated requirements and identify potential shortcomings to inform further requirements. Following that, Sect. 3 exemplifies a generic SPoC architecture for privacy management in cyber-physical environments. It utilizes subject-oriented models for behavior-driven development. Finally, Sect. 4 summarizes the work, draws conclusions, and highlights limitations and opportunities for future research.

## 2   CPS Architecture Design for Cross-Cutting Concerns

The literature regarding solutions to privacy issues in CPS is vast. In addition to primarily technologically focused mechanisms to preserve privacy (see, e.g., [10]), user-centric privacy management approaches were also proposed. They usually aim to create awareness on the user side regarding privacy implications and to allow users to exercise control in some form or another. Table 1 gives an overview over a selection of existing research, including core architectural elements and data for privacy management. Most approaches utilize a system architecture with

---

[1] In the context of this work "privacy management" is the ability to govern which CPS users or components can share and access information about oneself and others.

a clear distinction between components collecting data and those that consume this data. Privacy management is primarily supported with regard to the sharing of data. An exception is the smart building approach in [14], where the collection of data through building sensors can be controlled in addition to the sharing of data with building services. Some approaches [1,3,9,16] also store data at an element of the architecture before it is shared with data consumers.

With regard to the heterogeneity of CPS, these approaches can account for different data collecting elements and different data consumers. The complexity of the system itself is reduced through the architecture, by establishing central elements where data has to pass through to reach a consumer. There can still be a variable number of data consumers and providers, but the possible connectivity and communication of CPS components are limited through that architecture. In terms of autonomy and self-capabilities of components, the responsibility for privacy management is mostly centralized as well, with the viewing of information, configuration of privacy settings, and enforcement being realized by dedicated privacy management components. There are some exceptions to this, as in [16], any device can be used for viewing and configuring settings, and in [17], certain enforcement tasks are handled on the side of IoT devices.

Overall, most approaches can offer a hub or control component for privacy management with regard to the underlying system, confirming the respective requirement identified in the introduction. The functionality itself also meets the requirements for privacy management as outlined in Sect. 1. However, the operational CPS limitations created by incorporating privacy management into the architecture means (i) the privacy management architecture is intentionally confining the functional characteristics of the system, or (ii) the privacy management architecture was tailored to fit the specific architecture of its underlying system. These architectures also entail assumptions about the systems in question, e.g., with respect to the scope of privacy concerns and when triggering privacy management activities. Finally, most of the approaches treat data collecting elements as trusted, thus, leaving open how the initial data collection is controlled.

A generic architecture should be abstract enough to be implemented for a variety of different scenarios and to better account for the inherent characteristics of CPS. Considering the limitations of existing approaches and the aspects already discussed in the introduction, the following requirements need to be met by an abstract privacy management architecture for CPS: (i) it should support general privacy management functionality, including (a) the presentation of information to stakeholders in a way that it facilitates decision making on privacy concerns, (b) the stakeholder-centered configuration of privacy requirements for a specific system and its behavior, and (c) the adaption features for a system to meet those requirements; (ii) it should furthermore address privacy management both on the component and system level to account for certain CPS characteristics as outlined in the introduction, but (iii) without constraining the system's operation unnecessarily, as in architecturally limiting its heterogeneity, connectivity, and autonomy.

Considering these requirements, and given the discussed capabilities of existing approaches, the approach proposed in the following section is a first step towards a generic architecture for handling cross-cutting concerns of CPS.

**Table 1.** Examination of privacy management approaches from the fields of CPS and IoT.

| Ref | Architectural Elements | Data |
|---|---|---|
| [1] | IoT devices (data collection/generation), Policy Enforcement Fog Module (data storage, data sharing, policy enforcement with regard to sharing, policy configuration), local or remote IoT applications (data consumption) | Privacy policies (rules regarding data access) |
| [3] | IoT objects (data collection/generation), various reference architecture components (data storage/data sharing, risk analysis, viewing/configuration of information/sharing decisions, enforcement of sharing decisions/data transformation), data consumers (data consumption) | Request-specific information (e.g., data items, privacy risks, benefits, contextual information, recommended actions), user sharing decisions (which data items and their accuracy) |
| [9] | IoT devices (data collection/generation), interface (viewing/configuration of privacy policies/flexible access control rules), gateways (enforcement through access control and encryption, data sharing), cloud platforms (data storage), cloud services (data consumption) | Configurable privacy policies (service functionality and needed data), flexible access rules, configuration suggestions |
| [14] | Smart building (data collection/generation), IoT assistant (building policy presentation, capturing of privacy preferences through a learned model of preferences, configuration of privacy settings), building management system (enforcement of privacy settings/building policies with regard to data collection and data sharing, data sharing), building and third-party services (data consumption) | Building policies , privacy preferences/settings |
| [16] | IoT devices (data collection/generation, viewing/setting of permissions), central server (data storage/data sharing, enforcement of permissions with regard to data sharing), third party services (data consumption) | Privacy permissions (available and selected) |
| [17] | IoT devices (data collection/generation, enforcement of constraints through privacy mechanism plugins), gateways (communication intermediaries), IoT platform (viewing/setting of permissions, enforcement with regard to data sharing through access control), IoT applications (data consumption) | Privacy permissions (collection of privacy rules pertaining to information type, access purpose, optional constraints, and activation contexts), recommendations (regarding privacy permissions) |

## 3  A Single-Point-of-Contact Architecture

In this section, we outline a generic CPS architecture encompassing a Single Point of Contact for privacy management. The proposed SPoC aims to serve as the primary and singular interface for any stakeholder with regard to privacy concerns. Architectural elements beside the SPoC are CPS components. The term "component" is an abstract term used to designate all the devices, applications, sub-systems, etc., that make up the overall cyber-physical environment in question. Considering the architectural elements of the identified approaches, components in the proposed architecture can hold multiple roles. With regard to privacy-relevant data, they can act as elements that collect/generate, store, share, receive, and process data at the same time. This abstract view can accommodate realization for different CPS architectures and scenarios.

Certain key tasks need to be supported by a privacy management architecture. Specifically, the provision of information, the setting of certain privacy requirements, and the subsequent enforcement of such requirements were part of every single examined approach. In the described architecture, these tasks are divided between components and the SPoC. Components are responsible for enforcing privacy requirements, while the SPoC handles all interactions with stakeholders. This will still result in a reduction of autonomy of individual components, since they need to interact with the SPoC for certain privacy management functionality. However, having a single point for privacy management will prove advantageous for addressing other CPS characteristics. For instance, components can keep their interaction patterns, as long as privacy requirements are met - see also below.

## 3.1 Privacy Information Provision

The SPoC stores information about the components, such as their individual privacy policies, and makes it accessible to stakeholders through a user-interface (e.g., a web application). This information can be viewed to facilitate informed decision-making with regard to the required data. Providing a single access point for privacy-relevant information helps dealing with the potential complexity of the underlying system, e.g., as caused by the heterogeneity of CPS, or cross-cutting concerns, through integrating relevant items. Another benefit is the capability of a SPoC to adapt the (visual) presentation of the network of components according to the dynamic development of a CPS , and keep its topology transparent for privacy management (cf. [7]).

To further help make the system's behavior and the involved components transparent to affected stakeholders, we propose the use of models that can capture structural and behavioral aspects. These models are part of the information provided by the SPoC. Subject-oriented models [5] have already been utilized successfully for the purpose of CPS design (see [18,19]). Subject-oriented modeling considers two types of diagrams for capturing behavior of components and systems: Subject-Interaction Diagrams (SIDs) depict the interaction between subjects through message exchanges, and Subject-Behavior Diagrams (SBDs) depict the internal behavior of each subject through states (function, send, and receive). With regard to privacy management, a SID can show which subjects (CPS components and other actors) exchange which information as part of interactions along a process, including potentially privacy-relevant data being transmitted between them. This way, stakeholders can see when data passes from one party to another. In addition, SBDs can show how privacy-relevant information is used by the different components or parties.

In order to demonstrate the effectiveness of this approach for user-centric design, we consider a use case from the domain of healthcare. A patient lives in a smart home environment, which contains a variety of different devices and sensors. One of these components of the CPS is a smart pill bottle, outfitted with sensors to detect the removal of pills from the bottle, including the number of taken pills. Such CPS have been proposed to offer medication intake support [2]. The sensor data gathered by the bottle is sent to the patient's smartphone application for processing and storage of the medication intake event. The stored data can be used for a variety of purposes, such as comparing it with a patient's prescription schedule and reminding the patient to take the medication via the smartphone. The medication intake history of a patient can also be shared with a connected hospital information system, allowing for the assessment of medication adherence. The interactions between components following a sensor event occurrence, e.g., when a pill is taken from the bottle, were modeled in Fig. 1[2], including the different domains components belong to.

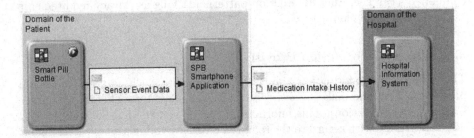

**Fig. 1.** Subject interaction diagram of the sensor event occurrence process, including the sharing of the updated medication intake history with another party. The different domains the subjects belong to are highlighted.

Taking the viewpoint of the patient living in such a smart home environment, reluctance can be expected for sharing pill intake information automatically with other components or parties. Modeling all the processes of the smart home components and providing a SPoC allow stakeholders an integrated view of the system and its behavior. Associating privacy policies with subjects that belong to a certain domain and certain data processing purposes with tasks of the model as part of the SPoC helps in further structuring this information and tying it to representations of the system's behavior. The exchanged messages detail which information with relation to which party is exchanged (through the modeling of structured data as mentioned in [19]). To help address potentially different

---

[2] all models were created using the metasonic suite: https://www.metasonic.de/en/.

information demands of stakeholders, models can be created at different levels of concreteness/abstraction.

Concerning the mentioned CPS characteristics, modeling components as subjects helps to deal with the heterogeneity of CPS, since different types of components (hardware, software) can be abstracted through subjects in a unifying way [18]. Complexity aspects can be tackled through modeling message flows between subjects to depict the interactions between many different components. Complexity can also be reduced through hierarchical process networks [19]. However, the dynamics of CPS can entail a situation that during run time behavior is adapted in ways not fully specified during design time. It could be that components, which were not necessarily intended to exchange data, need to exchange data. For instance, a case of emergency in home healthcare could require to contact additional health experts previously not involved in the patient's case. Dealing with the dynamics of CPS during run time would require models to automatically stay up-to-date with the behavior of the system they depict. To the knowledge of the authors, while there are approaches to create executable code from models (see [12]), mechanisms for model synchronization are currently still lacking. Therefore, CPS dynamics can not be fully captured and communicated by models to stakeholders during run time of the system yet. Synchronizing executable models with current system behavior would open up potential for dynamic privacy management. A stakeholder could track the current behavior of subjects in real-time and view which data is currently used by which component.

## 3.2   Privacy Requirement Definition and Enforcement

Stakeholders can use the interface of the SPoC to define privacy requirements for the underlying components. The examined literature has shown different approaches. In [9], options offered in a privacy policies are configured for each service. Similarly, settings available for each component (depending on their individual capabilities) could be configured through the user interface of the SPoC and communicated to each component, where they are stored and enforced. However, such a strategy could lead to redundant actions on the user side, even though recommendations (as in [3,9]) could reduce effort. Alternatively (or in addition), the definition of certain rules (e.g.: "do not share health data, unless it is anonymized"), could allow to articulate requirements affecting more than one component. This would require an appropriate format for privacy rules and a way to translate them into the settings offered by the heterogeneous components for enforcement.

Different ways of handling implications of privacy requirements on system functionality were shown by the examined approaches. In [17], for each application functionality, certain permissions are required and need to be provided for it to be usable. A similar approach is taken in [9], with service functionality requiring data. In [3], users have the option to reduce the accuracy of the shared data. Although it would allow to maintain the access to certain functionality, the trade-off between privacy and utility needs to be considered.

### 3.3   Privacy Event Notifications

Events in the behavior of a component (such as missing privacy settings when wanting to collect or share data) can trigger the need to notify a stakeholder so that action may be taken (akin to informing users about data request in [3]). A component gives a privacy notification to the SPoC, which is then displayed to the user, informing them about the event and asking them to review privacy information and configure requirements. This means that components can act autonomously, until they lack the necessary information to make a decision. In this case, they need to communicate with the SPoC. Considering the smart pill bottle example, the smartphone application can check its privacy settings before sharing information. This would either lead to the enforcement of these settings, or to calling the SPoC. The corresponding interactions between subjects and the behavior of the smartphone application were modeled in Fig. 2. Not only a lack of configured settings for sharing can trigger such a SPoC call. It could also be included in a component's behavior before any action is taken that is potentially privacy-relevant for a stakeholder, such as data collection or data storage.

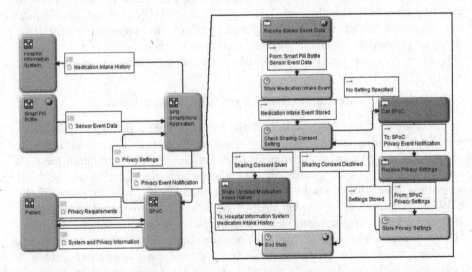

**Fig. 2.** Subject interaction diagram of the sensor event occurrence process, including the integration of the SPoC (on the left). Subject behavior diagram of the smartphone application (on the right).

## 4   Summary and Conclusion

In this paper, we outlined a generic architecture for privacy management in CPS. We described conceptually how it provides privacy management functionality to satisfy respective core requirements. The presentation of information to stakeholders and the configuration of privacy requirements are facilitated on the system level through the SPoC. For the purpose of enforcement, centrally defined privacy requirements are translated by the SPoC into privacy settings of individual components. Thus, enforcement becomes a task of the components. Utilizing these mechanisms, privacy can be addressed both on the component and system level. The used abstraction of a CPS as a network of interacting components, and component's multiple roles concerning privacy-relevant data, make the architecture flexible without unnecessarily constraining CPS characteristics. Components only interact with the SPoC to receive privacy settings or to call upon it if they lack the necessary settings. We justify this reduction in privacy management self-capabilities through the gains of the "outsourcing" and integrating of certain privacy management functionality at the SPoC. To support the presentation in a way it also facilitates the configuration, we proposed models depicting the structure and behavior of a CPS and its components. Subject-oriented modeling was identified as a promising candidate to accomplish this task in a stakeholder-centric form.

With regard to CPS characteristics, subject-oriented models can help abstract heterogeneity and complexity. However, dealing with the dynamic of CPS during run time presents a major challenge. Achieving the synchronization between executable models and the behavior of their associated components is a major step required in this direction. Such a mechanism would open up potentially interesting avenues for cross-cutting concerns in general. Models could incorporate data of the CPS produced during run time to help facilitate monitoring of not only currently processed private data but also other metrics of interest.

Upcoming research needs to focus on creating a running prototype of the architecture. It will be evaluated together with stakeholders, to assess its effectiveness and efficiency with regard to privacy management (including the expressive capabilities of subject-oriented models) and determine necessary adaptions. Future possibilities for research include exploration of subject-oriented models to communicate privacy-related information more effectively. To this end, the notation could be extended to more explicitly depict privacy-relevant information. Finally, other open challenges include dealing with potentially conflicting privacy requirements, since CPS can have multiple users simultaneously. The SPoC also needs to be secured properly to prevent it from becoming a single point of failure. Architectural fallback mechanisms could be explored, such as returning privacy management functionality to individual components in case the SPoC is not available.

# References

1. Al-Hasnawi, A., Lilien, L.: Pushing data privacy control to the edge in IoT using policy enforcement fog module. In: Companion Proceedings of the 10th International Conference on Utility and Cloud Computing, pp. 145–150. ACM, Austin Texas USA (2017)

2. Amin, S., Salahuddin, T., Bouras, A.: Cyber physical systems and smart homes in healthcare: current state and challenges. In: 2020 IEEE International Conference on Informatics, IoT, and Enabling Technologies (ICIoT), pp. 302–309. IEEE, Doha, Qatar (2020)

3. Barhamgi, M., Perera, C., Ghedira, C., Benslimane, D.: User-centric privacy engineering for the internet of things. IEEE Cloud Comput. 5(5), 47–57 (2018)

4. Eckhoff, D., Wagner, I.: Privacy in the smart city-Applications, technologies, challenges, and solutions. IEEE Commun. Surv. Tutorials 20(1), 489–516 (2018)

5. Fleischmann, A.: What is S-BPM? In: Buchwald, H., Fleischmann, A., Seese, D., Stary, C. (eds.) S-BPM ONE - Setting the Stage for Subject-Oriented Business Process Management, pp. 85–106. Springer, Berlin Heidelberg, Berlin, Heidelberg (2010). https://doi.org/10.1007/978-3-642-15915-2

6. Grimm, M., Anderl, R., Wang, Y.: Conceptual approach for multi-disciplinary cyber-physical systems design and engineering. In: Proceedings of TMCE 2014. Budapest, pp. 61–72. Budapest (2014)

7. Hansen, M., Thiel, C.: Cyber-physical systems und Privatsphärenschutz. Datenschutz und Datensicherheit - DuD 36(1), 26–30 (2012)

8. Hehenberger, P., Vogel-Heuser, B., Bradley, D., Eynard, B., Tomiyama, T., Achiche, S.: Design, modelling, simulation and integration of cyber physical systems: methods and applications. Comput. Ind. 82, 273–289 (2016)

9. Henze, M., Hermerschmidt, L., Kerpen, D., Häußling, R., Rumpe, B., Wehrle, K.: A comprehensive approach to privacy in the cloud-based internet of things. Futur. Gener. Comput. Syst. 56, 701–718 (2016)

10. Keshk, M., Moustafa, N., Sitnikova, E., Turnbull, B., Vatsalan, D.: Privacy-preserving techniques for protecting large-scale data of cyber-physical systems. In: 2020 16th International Conference on Mobility, Sensing and Networking (MSN), pp. 711–717. IEEE, Tokyo, Japan (2020)

11. Konstantinou, C., Maniatakos, M., Saqib, F., Hu, S., Plusquellic, J., Jin, Y.: Cyber-physical systems: a security perspective. In: 2015 20th IEEE European Test Symposium (ETS), pp. 1–8. IEEE, Cluj-Napoca, Romania (2015)

12. Müller, H.: Using S-BPM for PLC code generation and extension of subject-oriented methodology to all layers of modern control systems. In: Stary, C. (ed.) S-BPM ONE - Scientific Research, pp. 182–204. Springer, Berlin Heidelberg (2012). https://doi.org/10.1007/978-3-642-29133-3

13. Napoleone, A., Macchi, M., Pozzetti, A.: A review on the characteristics of cyber-physical systems for the future smart factories. J. Manuf. Syst. 54, 305–335 (2020)

14. Pappachan, P., et al.: Towards privacy-aware smart buildings: capturing, communicating, and enforcing privacy policies and preferences. In: 2017 IEEE 37th International Conference on Distributed Computing Systems Workshops (ICDCSW), pp. 193–198. IEEE, Atlanta, GA, USA (2017)

15. Schaub, F., Balebako, R., Cranor, L.F.: Designing effective privacy notices and controls. IEEE Internet Comput. 21(3), 70–77 (2017)

16. de Souza, R.T., dos Santos, G.F., Zorzo, S.D.: User's privacy management in IoT environment using dojot platform. In: Latifi, S. (ed.) 17th International Conference on Information Technology-New Generations (ITNG 2020), pp. 485–491. Springer, Cham (2020). https://doi.org/10.1007/978-3-030-43020-7

17. Stach, C., Gritti, C., Mitschang, B.: Bringing privacy control back to citizens: DISPEL – a distributed privacy management platform for the internet of things. In: Proceedings of the 35th Annual ACM Symposium on Applied Computing, pp. 1272–1279. ACM, Brno Czech Republic (2020)

18. Stary, C., Elstermann, M., Fleischmann, A., Schmidt, W.: Behavior-centered digital-twin design for dynamic cyber-physical system development. Complex Syst. Inf. Model. Quart. **30**, 31–52 (2022)
19. Weichhart, G., Reiser, M., Stary, C.: Task-based design of cyber-physical systems – meeting representational requirements with S-BPM. In: Freitag, M., Kinra, A., Kotzab, H., Kreowski, H.-J., Thoben, K.-D. (eds.) S-BPM ONE 2020. CCIS, vol. 1278, pp. 63–73. Springer, Cham (2020). https://doi.org/10.1007/978-3-030-64351-5_5

# Subject-Oriented Modelling of VDI-4520: A First Draft

Christoph Schubert[✉] and Frank Häuser

Kiel University of Applied Sciences, Kiel, Germany
cschubert.mi@gmail.com, frankhaeuser@gmx.net

**Abstract.** Origin of this article was the question whether the process description of product management, as it occurs in the guideline of VDI-4520, can be replaced by a model created with the concept of Subject-Orientation. Advantages and disadvantages of both description approaches are compared. The most important evaluation criterion is the achievable transparency for all persons and departments involved. Therefore, the goal was to construct a subject-oriented model draft of the Product Management Process based to the VDI guideline. The resulting diagram was created by a novice modeler in this field, without prior knowledge and experience with that uncommon modeling paradigm that is Subject-Orientation and without access to experience. Consequently, using this created the model for the Product Management Process as an example, weaknesses of PASS may have surfaced but at the same time have to be considered under the given circumstances. The weaknesses include semantical issues in processes with few defined subjects and explicit communication in the source material, possibly suggesting that PASS might not be as versatile as literature implies, and in result making the modelling of explicitly non-subject-oriented processes a challenge. This article provides a basis for discussion and further research regarding the applicability of PASS, and the claimed benefit of featuring a higher practical usefulness when executing in practice compared to traditional notations.

**Keywords:** S-BPM · Product Management · Business Process Management · PASS · Subject-Orientation

## 1 Introduction

The relevance of business processes and the capability of designing them in a flexible and dynamic way as a key driver for organizational success has been proven numerous times (Fleischmann et al. 2011: 2). The subject-oriented paradigm supposedly possesses major advantages compared to traditional ways of modelling, in regards to every process imaginable (Elstermann 2019: 126 -137). One of the processes that have not yet been modelled subject-orientedly is the Product Management Process according to VDI-4520. The aim of this research was therefore to create a finished diagram that describes this process in a subject-oriented way using the Parallel Activity Specification Scheme (PASS). The created model was then subsequently used in order to discuss whether claimed benefits and disadvantages of using PASS apply as well. A factor to consider in

M. Elstermann et al. (Eds.): S-BPM ONE 2022, CCIS 1632, pp. 144–151, 2022.
https://doi.org/10.1007/978-3-031-19704-8_9

this endeavor is that the model was created by a modeler without any prior knowledge of neither subject-orientation nor PASS and without receiving assistance from experienced modelers during the creation. On one hand, this potentially impacted the model quality and overall approach, on the other hand it was an ideal situation to evaluation the simplicity of the modeling approach, one of the claimed benefits.

In this paper, first, a draft of a subject-oriented model of the Product Management Process will be created, which will then be compared to a model with the classical process description approach, the "input-output-model" (Elstermann 2019: 96–108). After this, the claimed benefits and disadvantages of PASS are discussed. Thereby it will be attempted to verify whether they can also be applied to the Product Management Process. Finally, results will be summed up in order to highlight potential future research regarding the benefits of using PASS on a complex, explored and defined process.

## 2  VDI-4520 in Subject-Oriented Notation

### 2.1  Modelling the Product Management Process VDI-4520 in a Subject-Oriented Way Using PASS

Using PASS, it should be possible to take all involved subprocesses and sub-subprocesses of VDI-4520 into consideration while modelling. However, before doing so, it should be noted that the Product Management Process is special due to two different factors.

On the one hand, claimed benefits of using PASS as a modelling language base on the fact that the focus is put on subjects and their interaction(Elstermann 2019: 79). However, according to the VDI-4520 guideline the Product Management Process completely refers to a single subject, the product manager, who executes many different tasks and subtasks on his own (VDI-4520 2019). In order to show different tasks in a Process Network Diagram, singular tasks are represented through a respective interface subject (Fleischmann et al. 2011: 95). While the guideline does mention subjects other than the product manager, e.g. the R&D department, these subjects are only relevant for the explicit processes in which they are named, and do not interact with subjects of other (sub-)processes. The only subject that is present in every (sub-)process of the Product Management Process is the product manager. In consequence, since the product manager is merely a single subject it would only receive a single Subject Behavior Diagram (SBD).This would lead to an enormous diagram, resembling a classical process model without being able to utilize any of the claimed benefits of PASS. In order to combat this, additional subjects not explicitly defined in the VDI guideline were interpreted and added, serving the sole purpose of representing their respective tasks as interface subjects (Schubert 2022: 60–62).

In the VDI-4520 guideline, most processes are only mentioned implicitly, without going into the specifics what activities have to be executed in which order (VDI 4520 2019). While communication with process-internal subjects of some sub-processes is explicitly defined, it is continuously limited to "Input from [other subject]" (ibid.). As a result, if only these imprecise information is used without altering it or making assumptions/interpretations about procedural flows or communication, every SBD other than the product manager would only consist of a single do state, framed by a Send State asking for Input/sending the results, and a Receive state. It was assumed that such SBDs would not enhance the value of the model, and consequently they were not created, even though according to (Fleischmann et al. 2011: 218) they are a necessary component of PASS. Additionally and due to the same lack of explicit information arrows that should contain messages between subjects are reduced to the arrows themselves, not specifying the contents of the send information with the exception of those where messages are explicitly defined in the VDI guideline. These alterations have been made in order to keep the model as simple as possible, and also due to the fact that it was assumed that the messages would be limited to "Request: Input" and "Input", since no further contents of communication are explicitly defined in the guideline. This interaction between the interface subjects was modeled in a diagram that was understood to be a Process Network Diagram (PND) with subjects being framed by boxes that are considered "processes", containing the subjects – one each – and being labeled as activities.

By using and connecting those external interface subjects, it is possible to include every subprocess in the subject-oriented modelling of the Product Management Process. This can be further done in another process model by connecting larger subprocesses such as the internal and external analysis to the product manager – again with the assumption that no messages can be defined. Finally, to show the communicational relationships between the various process models/SIDs, a Process Hierarchy Diagram (PHD) was created, visualizing the fact that only bilateral communication is described, and subjects are only communicating with subjects of their respective process.

Figure 1 shows an extract of the model drafted for the Product Management Process according to VDI-4520 in subject-oriented notation. The full model can be found in Schubert 2022 (Schubert 2022: 71).

## 2.2 Descriptive Comparison of the Classical Approach vs. The Subject-Oriented Diagram – a Beginners Point of View

When comparing the created model to the classical model in VDI-4520 the following observations and conclusion were made:

To begin with, the traditional approach features a single diagram, whereas a proper interpretation requires both the Process Network Diagram and also the Process Hierarchy Diagram, and thus two different diagrams (VDI-4520 2019). The VDI diagram separates the product management process in several phases, whereas PASS does not allow a display of causal or temporal[1] divisions in any type of Subject Interaction Diagram (SID) like the PND or PHD. The original diagram only implicitly shows communications, while Fig. 1 emphasizes this aspect through the use of message connectors and at one point with an explicit messages. Arrows as symbols do exist in the VDI-diagram; however, they define a clear temporal and logical procedural flow, which is not intended in the PASS version as SBDs have not been deemed necessary.

In the traditional way of modelling, the Product Management Process possesses the option to display additional information such as perspectives or organizational units; this has not been done in Fig. 1. While PASS does not explicitly forbid the display of any information outside of messages, it is not explicitly encouraged to do so either (Fleischmann et al. 201: 124–126). Furthermore, business objects such as the business or

---

[1] Note by editor: it can be arranged displayed visually, but it has no formal impact.

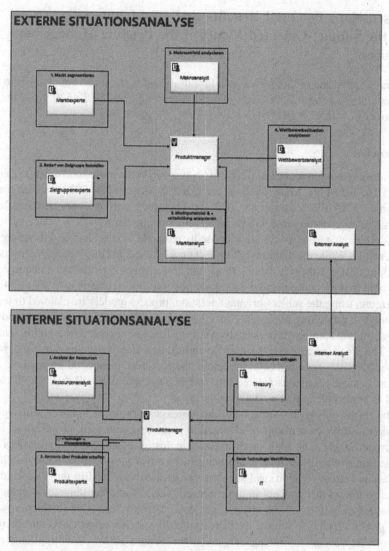

**Fig. 1.** Extract of several SIDs in one PND of the Product Management Process

product-marketing plan can be arranged freely in the VDI diagram, whereas the inclusion of business objects in PASS is possible as information objects sent as messages, but has not been done. Finally, there are several quality gates shown in the reference model, while Fig. 1 does not include quality gates. A translation of quality gates to PASS is not explicitly ruled out, however it requires the use of SBDs where some subject actively needs to evaluate the predefined criteria of a quality gate as done in (Elstermann 2019: 237). This has not been considered in this research.

# 3 Discussion: Potential Benefits and Disadvantages of the Subject-Oriented Model of the Product Management Process

As initially stated the model serves as a first draft and is therefore not claimed to be a perfected, finished and valid subject-oriented interpretation of VDI-4520. Nevertheless, the following evaluation was done.

## 3.1 Benefits

PASS is claimed to possess a lot of benefits compared to the traditional notation (Elstermann 2019: 126–137). Many of these are listed in Moser et al. 2022 and Elstermann 2019 (ibid.: 126–137, Moser et al. 2022: 3). Therefore, only the ones applying to the Product Management Process will be taken into consideration.

Models created using PASS are supposedly readable by machines and therefore easily executable. While the diagram in Fig. 1 cannot be executed due it being very abstract and lacking SBDs. However, adding those and converting the model into adequate software would make a computerized execution possible (Fleischmann et al. 2011 34–35). Furthermore, using the subject-oriented notation, process models are claimed to feature a high level of modelling precision. Since it was possible to include all mentioned sub-processes in this complex process network, Fig. 1 can be regarded as a highly detailed model. The precision could be enhanced even further if all layers defined in PASS would be included; SBDs have not been modelled due to before mentioned limitations. SIDs have furthermore been consolidated into one PND. Therefore, still this benefit can be viewed as applicable in this model.

Subjects not only representing individual roles or workplaces, but instead also giving the option to serve as a means of abstraction is another supposed advantage of PASS (Elstermann 2019). The high precision and inclusion of all sub-processes was only possible due to the usage of this mechanism, however it should be noted that it was necessary to introduce additional subjects not explicitly defined in the VDI guideline in order to utilize this concept in a meaningful way. Would the diagram instead have been modelled only using the original subjects, the only means of abstraction would be the product manager subject itself, resulting in a single subject SID and therefore no proper abstraction. Following this, a claimed benefit of this modelling language is the simple ability to assign activities to subjects (ibid.). This also applies to the Product Management Process; however this is, again, only possible due to the added subjects. However, it was simple to reassign them to other subjects, supporting this supposed benefit. If the model in Fig. 1 would be executed in practice, the created subjects could be assigned to actual subject carrier (such as employees) without much additional effort.

Since PASS is based on the structure of natural language, literature suggests that complete and correct models also should be easily interpretable. Taking a look at Fig. 1, missing elements of actual executional or temporal flow, also due to the missing SBDs, it can be assumed that the audience of this model requires basic knowledge of PASS, in order to properly interpret it (Elstermann 2019: 118).

Additionally, subject-oriented modelling enables a natural separation of context, mainly going back to the fact that a subject's communication relationships are separated from the actual activities through the use of at least two different diagrams (ibid.). Since this draft of the Product Management Process does not feature any SBDs, behavior context is not included. Therefore, this benefit cannot be evaluated with this process description. Finally, notations in PASS are said to be both compact yet powerful at the same time (ibid). When taking into consideration that the Product Management Process is a highly extensive and complex process, Fig. 1 can be regarded as compact, while still including all relevant information for this abstraction layer. This leads to this advantage being fully applicable.

### 3.2 Drawbacks

Some of the disadvantages of using PASS have been mentioned in 3.1. Already. For one, subject-oriented models require the user to possess knowledge over the modelling language and especially the paradigm! Proven in Fig. 1, which is not easily interpretable without knowing the functional semantics of this notation (Elstermann 2019: 118).

PASS is claimed to increase size of models of processes, which would otherwise feature a small and compact model (ibid.) due to always having SIDs and SBDs together. This cannot be verified completely since the Product Management Process is regarded as a complex, rather than a small and compact process anyway, and no SBDs were modelled. However, the required existence of more than one diagram implies that complexity is increased to some extent.

Furthermore, the effort in modelling itself supposedly is increased due to the always-required explicit modeling of communication, which is a disadvantage also evident during the modelling of this research. While not only a person modelling a process has to acquire knowledge of PASS, it was felt that the semantics even had to be adjusted in order to fit this process. Adjustments took place by introducing additional interpreted subjects, not modeling individual SBDs and especially not modeling explicit messages in the interaction diagram (Fig. 1). However on the contrary, it can be argued that these adjustments have also been necessary due to the imprecise definitions in VDI-4520.

## 4 Conclusion

In this research it was attempted to construct a subject-oriented diagram of the Product Management Process, resulting in a first draft. It should be made clear that this model has been constructed by an inexperienced modeler and should not be regarded as a perfect model. By expanding this model, e.g. by including product management aspects that are not explicitly defined in the VDI-guideline and then including actual explicit communication and subjects, some of the before mentioned drawbacks might even be eliminated in the future.

Regarding the application of PASS as a subject-oriented modelling language, some benefits, but also some disadvantages have been verified in this draft. Based on the amount of factors, it seems that benefits predominate. However, it should be taken into consideration that this does not allow a clear statement whether PASS as a representing language for subject-oriented modelling is more beneficial than traditional notations, using the Product Management Process as an example. Due to the fact that this process only focusses on a single subject, rendering many of the claimed benefits inapplicable, a hypothesis follows that Subject-Orientation (SO) is beneficial especially for those processes, where the interaction of subjects is process-determining and not a mere side note like in VDI-4520. Furthermore, it has to be questioned whether this process is one actually executed in practice according to the guideline, since its purpose is mainly to offer theoretical definitions. It is also assumable that the product manager of an organization does not execute all processes and sub-processes on his own, but rather receive support from other organizational units. This thought opens discussion, since it could be argued that the challenging nature of applying PASS to the Product Management Process also bases on the insufficient level of detail defined in VDI-4520. Therefore, no clear answer can be given to what extent the constructed model draft features a practical use for organizations, and in result, the potential benefits. For this a validation and a practical execution has to be done, which is not part of this research. The hypothesis mentioned in the beginning, that both SO and PASS feature advantages for organizations, therefore remains unanswered at this stage. However, it would be valuable to do future research at this point.

**Acknowledgement.** This contribution was accepted as a short paper since it is a valuable show-case for the fact that adopting subject-orientation and subject-oriented thinking is not necessarily as simple and straightforward as it may be perceived by the research community. The work is a demonstration of the challenge to diverge from classical input-task-output process-thinking and truly adopt subject-orientation, especially when source material and pre-training are deeply rooted in and limited by the classical description paradigm.

E.g., in Fig. 1: The "sub-process" (grey rectangles around the subject) are labeled in a way that make it evident that "process" is mainly understood as activity by the authors (e.g. "Markt segmentieren" – Eng.: "to segmented the marked"). Consequently, the subjects are assigned to the activities and the whole model is essentially task/activity oriented. The stated claim that no messages could be defined demonstrates this problem complex further, especially when the "Mark-texperte" (market expert) could have easily send a "Report on the analysis of Market Segments" to the Product Manager. Sternly speaking, it could be said that PASS elements are mostly used as a visualization tool, but SO is at best weakly or not "daringly" enough applied. Hypothetically it can be seen that this is a logical consequence from the attempt of "literally translating" the source material and stay too close to it. Furthermore, the work shows how important "the notion of process" for understanding subject-orientation. In other words what is "a process" or "a sub-process"? Subject-Orientation requires understanding that "a process" is the interaction of multiple active entities and that activities are assigned to active entities, not the other way around like was done above. An interface subject can indeed represent a more complex sub-system of active entities, which is the "sub-process", but that is a different understanding than the "sub-process" idea in VDI-4520.

# References

1. Elstermann, M.: Executing Strategic Product Planning. A Subject-Oriented Analysis and New Referential Process Model for IT-Tool Support and Agile Execution of Strategic Product Planning. Reihe Informationsmanagement im Engineering Karlsruhe, Band 3. Karlsruher Institut für Technologie, zugl. Diss. 2019. Karlsruhe: KIT Scientific Publishing (2019)

2. Fleischmann, A., Schmidt, W., Starcy, C., Obermeier, S., Börger, E.: Subjektorientiertes Prozessmanagement. Mitarbeiter einbinden, Motivation und Prozessakzeptanz steigern. 2011. München: Carl Hanser (2011)
3. Moser, C., Kannengiesser, U., Elstermann, M.: Examining the PASS approach to process modelling for digitalised manufacturing. In: Enterprise Modelling and Information Systems Architectures 2022, vol. 17, pp. 1–24. Springer, Cham (2022)
4. Schubert, C.: Subjektorientierte Modellierung des Produktmanagementprozesses. Fachhochschule Kiel, zugl. Masterarbeit (2022)
5. VDI-Richtlinie 4520: Produktmanagement: Einführungen und Grundlagen. Internes Arbeitspapier 2017. Accessed 16 Mar 2022
6. VDI-Richtlinie 4520: Produktmanagement: Methoden und Werkzeuge in den Phasen des Produktmanagementprozesses. Internes Arbeitspapier (2019)

# Organizing a Self-organized Team: Towards a Maturity Model for Agile Business Process Management

Matthias Lederer[✉] and Julia Thummerer

Technical University of Applied Sciences Amberg-Weiden, Hetzenrichter Weg 15, 92637 Weiden, Germany
ma.lederer@oth-aw.de

**Abstract.** Due to the increasingly volatile environment of companies, agile business process management (BPM) is becoming more relevant. The requirement for self-organized teams, as an essential part of the agile approach, causes major challenges for many companies. The main reasons for this are that (a) it is often not known how self-organized the process teams are so far and (b) which initiatives can further extend the agile principles. This paper presents the findings of a research-in-progress project that aims to develop a maturity model for self-organized teams. Based on a comprehensive literature review, 80 practical indicators were identified for 31 enabling factors (including self assignment, knowledge sharing, shared vision) supporting the pathway to more self-organization in BPM. Process consultants and process departments can use this list to successively prepare teams for the requirements of self-organization in the context of agile BPM. In further research, the presented content will be further developed (e.g. with maturity levels).

**Keywords:** Agile business process management · Self-organization · Maturity model

## 1 Introduction

The demand for flexible project and process execution puts enterprises under increasing pressure [1]. It is accepted that agility enables organizations to react flexibly to changing market conditions and to implement individual customer requirements as quickly as possible [2]. In terms of business process management (BPM), it is recognized that agile techniques can be successfully applied when the process team must plan processes whose conditions are volatile or uncertain [3, 4]. Likewise, agile values help when the context of a process to be described or improved is highly complex or even ambiguous. It can be said that agile methods are increasingly being used when the process landscape is rather unstable. Due to disruptions, new technological possibilities, and many facets that are often summarized under VUCA (volatility, uncertainty, complexity und ambiguity), it can be assumed that the importance of agile process management will increase in the future [3–5].

© The Author(s), under exclusive license to Springer Nature Switzerland AG 2022
M. Elstermann et al. (Eds.): S-BPM ONE 2022, CCIS 1632, pp. 152–164, 2022.
https://doi.org/10.1007/978-3-031-19704-8_10

However, a hasty application and conversion to agile values and practices leads to failure and frustration. Team organization in terms of work coordination is considered as one of the most important responses to the organizational requirements of agile methods [6]. The effectiveness of teamwork coordination is also related to team performance [7]. In the agile approach, teamwork is predominantly meant to be self-organizing (Fowler and Highsmith 2001). In agile process management, not all phases of the classic process life cycle are planned in advance; instead, agile methods are used to adapt processes in a feedback-driven and, above all, iterative manner [3, 8]. For this necessary exchange with customers and especially in the team, the self-organization of the process teams can help a lot - as a general conviction as well as operationally in the organization of sprints.

Many companies struggle with the introduction of self-organizing teams for BPM as it requires a profound cultural change [8, 9]. By evaluating the as-is state of a team's self-organization, appropriate solutions for a successful adoption of agile could be proposed [10]. This paper intends therefore to show and discuss the initial results of a research-in-progress project that can be used to assess the level of teams to self-organize. This planned maturity model helps managers, teams, and the organization to have a realistic view on the self-organization levels of groups to become agile. Self-organization is thus very much in line with well-known and accepted BPM approaches such as BPM 2.0 or case management.

## 2 Related Work

Although the agile approach was initially designed for small team projects in software development, the advantages have also attracted attention outside of this context [11]. Whereas these methods are used extensively nowadays, the agile transition to them is challenging and takes a long time. Not every organization is psychologically and technically capable of effectively implementing agile teams [10]. Literature says that one of the biggest challenges when introducing change-driven development is the transition to a self-organizing team [6]. In a synthesis, [12] describe this concept as "[..] teams of employees who typically perform highly related or interdependent jobs, who are identified and identifiable as a social unit in an organization, and who are given significant authority and responsibility for many aspects of their work, such as planning, scheduling, assigning tasks to members, and making decisions with economic consequences (usually up to a specific limited value)." Self-organized team settings in BPM thus stands as a counter-design or addition to purely data-driven process optimization [13], which can be found primarily in stable processes. In this case, self-organized teams are not used; instead, statistical methods are required to bring workflows under control and to achieve full transparency (e.g., process mining).

Several structured adoption frameworks and indices have been proposed to measure an organization's and a team's agility level respectively. [10] developed the Agile Adoption and Improvement Model (AAIM) for the adoption, assessment and improvement of an agile software development process. The AAIM is organized in three agile blocks, six agile stages and an agility measurement model. Furthermore, [14] propose a 4-step roadmap to lead teams to agility in five essential values, which consider both the project/process and organizational level. The researchers evaluate the degree of agility of an organization using the Agile Measurement Index including extensive questionnaires, a project/process-level assessment and conclude recommendations for agile practices. Similar steps can be found in [10]. [15] argue in a summary that, while researchers have developed various assessment tools and frameworks, most agile adoption frameworks have several characteristics in common. However, there does not exist a consensus on the proposed adoption stages [16].

Self-organization in BPM can be seen on different levels and also in different contexts. In general, agile methods are often stressed in process management because they encourage frequent reviews, adjustments, and teamwork that can lead to innovation and optimization in processes [17]. Systematic literature reviews in the BPM field also show that agile techniques such as self-organization are increasingly being incorporated into BPM methodology to improve business processes [18, 19]. In this context, the desired self-organization can be within the team of process experts (e.g., teams of consultants conducting a re-engineering project) or within the teams of a processes (e.g., participants in the process like front-line workers). In the first case, there is evidence that it seems advisable to minimize central responsibilities and supervision as much as possible to achieve a high degree of self-organization [20]. This may promote the important digital transformation in companies. The second case is in line with trends around social BPM (e.g., BPM 2.0, case management, etc.). Here, for example, social software is used to foster interaction in a bottom-up approach and through the collective intelligence of individuals. Self-organization approaches are intended to support this cooperation of knowledge workers in order to achieve process improvements. The basic conviction behind this is that people are empowered, and they do not necessarily have to be organized in a hierarchy [21]. Furthermore, mixed cases are also conceivable, in which self-organized project groups work together with agile specialist groups. Here, self-organization is understood from the bottom up and combined with guidance from the top down: With the help of facilitators, quality managers and method experts, for example, the aim is to ensure that ideas from process participants are considered in formal process improvement (e.g., process modeling) using agile methods [19]. [22] contrasts the trend toward social BPM – and at the same time toward self-organization – as a decision of an organization towards knowledge society with traditional BPM as organizations in the information society. Decentralized, self-organized planning and execution by knowledge workers are considered as an essential part of the trend. Likewise, stakeholders in the process are integrated into BPM activities through social interaction and collaboration in communities. As a conclusion, the authors describe that BPM work is performed by stakeholders themselves, further increasing the degree of self-organization. This ultimately expresses their appreciation as self-responsible organizational members [22] and is thus fully in line with the transfer of modern work approaches to the BPM discipline (e.g. such as New Work or democratization of work).

Summing up, transitioning to agile BPM, and especially to self-organizing teams as one core principle, is a difficult and long process. The assessment of self-organization needs to be determined through a variety of factors. The approach in this paper is intended to help synchronize the various transition models that have been developed in recent years in a comprehensive maturity model for a BPM team's level of self-organization.

# 3 Method

This research in progress paper aims to outline the idea of a multi-criteria maturity model. Its basic research question is: *How can a team's level for self-organization in BPM be measured?* To answer the question, the research design follows the approach by [23] as described in Fig. 1: First, a list of relevant categories that are critical to self-organization in a team will be collected. Within each area, concrete factors are then to be recorded and weighted. Next, each factor will be reviewed for indicators, which in turn will be used for a questionnaire. The questionnaire-based assessment on scaled is intended to assess a team's level of self-organization. Finally, the model will be implemented in a tool for guiding teams and for overall evaluation.

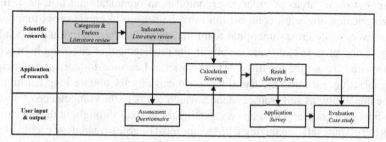

**Fig. 1.** Full research design towards the maturity model [23]

The components highlighted in gray in the figure have already been conducted and will be presented as an overview in this first contribution to this research project: Both the selection of the categories/factors to as well as the indicators to be assessed were conducted strictly according to the methodology of [24]. That is, (i) first, the research question was translated into search queries (e.g., "self-organizing team," "autonomous team," or "self-managing team"). In contrast to many well-known studies from the BPM environment (see the section before), this article focuses on a consolidation and transfer of findings from classic business management and organization design publications. This is intended to enrich the many valuable publications on the various facets of social BPM and provide new insights for the self-organization of BPM teams. (ii) IEEExplore, EbscoHost, Science Direct, ACM, Springerlink und Google Scholar databases were used to identify sources. To identify categories, factors and indicators discussed in the literature, a literature search was conducted to learn the breadth of research on a topic of interest [25]. (iii) To ensure high quality in study selection and analysis, only articles published in German and English and only peer-reviewed articles and articles published by reputable publishers were considered. In total 59 papers were in the end included in the analysis.

# 4    Initial Results

## 4.1    Categories

When developing an index for self-organizing BPM teams, several dimensions must be considered for a complete and valid evaluation. A set of six critical categories was identified that enable self-organization. (1) Work in self-organizing process teams is intended to give employees as much freedom as possible to assume their responsibilities. Autonomy is described as the team's authority to define goals, define its own social identity, secure required resources and the freedom of self-organizing behaviors [26]. (2) Achieving cross-functionality is seen as an organizational-level barrier to self-management [6]. The term can be defined as the ability of individuals to work across different functional areas in order to accomplish an organizational task [27]. In self-organizing teams, the team composition must be set out to create cross-functionality [6]. However, while cross-functional team members decrease individual dependency, self-organizing process teams are usually in the predicament of choosing between specialization and cross-functionality. (3) [28] classifies Learning-to-learn as a principle of self-organization, meaning the team requires a capacity for double-loop learning. [29] describe this ability as self-transcendence, which refers to the competence of a team to establish its own goals and to keep on elevating these goals throughout the development process [29]. Thus, self-organizing BPM teams must be able to reanalyze problems, reappraise the best work method and reconsider the required output [30]. (4) [31] describe Team Leadership as a core competency of teamwork and refer to it as the ability among others to direct and coordinate the activities of other team members, assess team performance and assign tasks. In self-organization, team leadership needs to be diffused [28] and decision making is shared rather than carried out alone. (5) Team Orientation or collective orientation is also a core competence of teamwork. It is described as the propensity to take others' behavior into account and to give priority to team goals over individual goals. [31] claim that high team orientation improves the overall team performance in self-managing groups like process teams. The category also refers to the attitudes that team members have towards one another, the acceptance of team norms and the level of group cohesiveness [32]. (6) In agile process teams, communication and collaboration were found to be major components for building a self-organizing team. Additionally, [33] state that one of the main characteristics of self-organizing agile teams is displaying high levels of collaboration within the team. A high maturity level of the category Communication and Collaboration indicates self-organization.

## 4.2    Factors

The 31 factors for the index were accumulated through a literature review of the characteristics and practices of autonomous process teams necessary to become effective, self-organizing work teams. Table 1 shows a compilation of all factors with a short description sorted by category.

The described factors specify the categories described above, which mostly describe only general dimensions. For example, the category "autonomy" can, beyond others, be divided into individual autonomy, which refers to the team members' control over the

**Table 1.** Factors indicating a team's level self-organization

| Category | Factor | Category | Factor | Category | Factor |
|---|---|---|---|---|---|
| Autonomy | F1: Minimum Critical Specification | Learning and development | F11: Knowledge Sharing | Team orientation | F20: Participatory Goal Setting |
| | F2: Decision-Making Authority | | F12: Continuous Feedback | | F21: Shared Vision |
| | F3: Self-Assignment | | F13: Team Reflection | | F22: Mutual Trust |
| | F4: Management Support | | F14: Agile Training | | F23: Crystallized Team Norms |
| | F5: Team Capability | | F15: Commitment to Change | | F24: Agile Planning |
| | F6: Informal Org.Structures | Team leadership | F16: Collective Responsibility | Collaboration and communication | F25: Effective Communication |
| Cross-functionality | F7: Team Size | | F17: Shared Leadership | | F26: Task-related Communication |
| | F8: Skill Variety | | F18: Clear Roles and Responsibilities | | F27: Porous Communication |
| | F9: Redundancy | | F19: Adoption of Informal Roles | | F28: Conflict Management |
| | F10: Team Flexibility | | | | F29: Member Personality |
| | | | | | F30: Customer Collaboration |
| | | | | | F31: Team Distribution |

planning and execution of their own tasks [34], internal autonomy, which refers to the degree of joint decision-making authority of all team members, and external autonomy, which refers to the influence of management and others within the overall organization on the team's activities [35].

## 4.3 Indicators

As the section on Related Work shows, in order to evaluate the self-organization index, a list of assessable factors must be available for use in business practice. For this purpose, the factors were converted into 80 practicable indicators for which a concrete statement is possible in the evaluation of BPM teams (see Table 2). Having again a look at the indicators resulting from the category "autonomy", for example, one can see that the factors mentioned ("Minimum Critical Specification") now become more precise ("Management does not interfere in day-to-day activities") and are finally made assessable. For this reason, based on the literature research, this step provides a set of indicators that can now be used to set up the further model artifacts.

**Table 2.** Indicators for measuring self-organization of BPM teams

| Factor | Indicator | Indicator |
|--------|-----------|-----------|
| F1 | F1I1 | Management only specifies minimum project/process criteria [36] |
|  | F1I2 | Management does not interfere in day-to-day activities [29] |
| F2 | F2I1 | The team must refer back to several stakeholders (management, client, other teams) before making a decision [16, 37] |
|  | F2I2 | The team was involved in the project/process planning from the beginning [6] |
| F3 | F3I1 | Team members control the scheduling and implementation of their tasks [16, 37] |
|  | F3I2 | Tasks are clearly outlined [16, 37] |
| F4 | F4I1 | Management provides sufficient infrastructure and resource support for effective functioning [33] |
|  | F4I2 | Management supports the team when the schedule needs to be bent [11] |
| F5 | F5I1 | Team members have the skills and expertise to accomplish the tasks [38] |
|  | F5I2 | Team members can handle the workload [11] |
|  | F5I3 | The team does not lose resources to other projects/processes [33] |
|  | F5I4 | The team feels it has the ability to self-organize |
| F6 | F6I1 | The organization has informal structures [33] |
|  | F6I2 | Management is directly accessible by all employees and maintains an open-door policy [33] |
|  | F6I3 | Team members are free to voice their opinions and raise concerns [33] |
| F7 | F7I1 | Teams have no more than 5–9 members |
|  | F7I2 | Teams have enough members to accomplish a task |
| F8 | F8I1 | Team members come from different training and backgrounds [6] |
|  | F8I2 | Team members accumulate knowledge in other areas than their own [36] |
| F9 | F9I1 | It is easy for a team member to complete someone else's task [39] |
|  | F9I2 | It is easy to shift workload among team members [31] |
| F10 | F10I1 | Team members are easily added removed [40] |
|  | F10I2 | The team can organize itself according to the current challenges [41] |
| F11 | F11I1 | Information is shared with the whole organization [42] |
|  | F11I2 | Teams set aside exclusive time for learning [36] |

(*continued*)

**Table 2.** (*continued*)

| Factor | Indicator | Indicator |
|--------|-----------|-----------|
|        | F11I3     | Team members accumulate knowledge in other areas than their own [36] |
|        | F11I4     | The team has daily meetings [43] |
| F12    | F12I1     | Team members regularly give feedback on a co-worker's work [40] |
|        | F12I2     | Team members ask for input and suggestions on their work [40] |
| F13    | F13I1     | The team regularly contemplates what they are doing and how they are working together [44] |
|        | F13I2     | Team members can question given concepts and organizational processes [45] |
| F14    | F14I1     | The team can apply agile methods [11] |
|        | F14I2     | The team is encouraged to use agile methods and self-organizing practices [33] |
| F15    | F15I1     | The team introduces changes in their work to help the organization achieve its change goals [47] |
|        | F15I2     | Change is intensively and transparently communicated throughout the whole organization [11] |
|        | F15I3     | Team members provide recognition when they see people implementing new ways of doing things [46] |
| F16    | F16I1     | The accountability for the whole project/process is shared among team members [47] |
| F17    | F17I1     | Every team member is involved in the decision-making process [35] |
|        | F17I2     | Leadership is rotated to the person with the knowledge, skills and abilities for the issues at the time [6] |
|        | F17I3     | Team members listen to the concerns of other team members [6] |
|        | F17I4     | Team members explain to other team members what is needed from them [6] |
| F18    | F18I1     | Every team member has clear roles and responsibilities [48] |
|        | F18I2     | Team members seek out new responsibilities [48] |
| F19    | F19I1     | The team identifies members who jeopardize the productiveness and initiates their removal [33] |
|        | F19I2     | The team has a member that understands both business language and technical terms [33] |
|        | F19I3     | The team has a representative of the agile cause that advertises agile methods with the clients and management [33] |

(*continued*)

**Table 2.** (*continued*)

| Factor | Indicator | Indicator |
|--------|-----------|-----------|
| | F19I4 | The team has a representative that manages clients' expectations and guides the collaboration of the client and the team [33] |
| F20 | F20I1 | The team has clear and common team goals [16, 37] |
| | F20I2 | Team members actively participated in the identifying and setting of the team's goals [6] |
| | F20I3 | The team values and considers alternative suggestions in team discussions [32] |
| F21 | F21I1 | The team has a shared vision [32, 37, 49] |
| | F21I2 | Team members are committed to the vision [32, 37, 49] |
| F22 | F22I1 | Team members believe that every member will perform their role [31] |
| | F22I2 | Team members can admit to mistakes [31] |
| | F22I3 | Team members feel respected by others [31] |
| | F22I4 | Communication mostly happens face-to-face [49] |
| F23 | F23I1 | The team approves or disapproves of behaviors |
| | F23I2 | Team members adapt their behavior to the team's behavior |
| F24 | F24I1 | The team is involved in the planning process [32] |
| | F24I2 | The team has a product delivery strategy and continuously delivers the product within small releases [38] |
| | F24I3 | The team has daily meetings [50] |
| | F24I4 | The team is proud of its agile prioritization and planning procedure [51] |
| F25 | F25I1 | Communication and negotiation in the project/process mostly happen face-to-face [49] |
| | F25I2 | The team works in an open workspace [50] |
| | F25I3 | The current project status and project/process requirements are visualized [50] |
| | F25I4 | Information is shared daily [50] |
| F26 | F26I1 | Team members know what other team members are currently working on [48] |
| F27 | F27I1 | Team members know what other teams in the project/process are currently working on [52] |
| F28 | F28I1 | The team knows what to do when conflicts between team members arise [53] |
| | F28I2 | The team can avoid the negative aspects of conflict before they occur [53] |

(*continued*)

Table 2. (*continued*)

| Factor | Indicator | Indicator |
|---|---|---|
| F29 | F29I1 | Most of the team members are very conscientious |
| | F29I2 | Most of the team members are very agreeable |
| | F29I3 | Most of the team members are motivated |
| F30 | F30I1 | The customer considers themselves responsible for elements of the project/process [33] |
| | F30I2 | The customer provides feedback regularly [33] |
| | F30I3 | The team has a product delivery strategy and continuously delivers the product within small releases [38] |
| F31 | F31I1 | The team is geographically closely located [38] |
| | F31I2 | The team is dedicated to a single project/process |
| | F31I3 | The team works in an open workspace [11] |
| | F31I4 | The team loses resources to other projects/processes [33] |

## 5 Summary and Outlook

In this paper, a systematic literature review was used to develop a factor list for assessing level of self-organization of BPM teams. This ability of teams is in line with the agile values, but a desire and at the same time a challenge of many modern companies. For the decision to use agile techniques in self-organized teams for BPM, it is not decisive whether the processes are known, but rather whether the processes concerned are not mature or are rather unstable. In further research steps, the factors derived from the fundamental categories for self-organization should lead to a maturity model. To achieve this, the authors will continue to follow the steps outlined in Fig. 1. In the next steps, suggestions for quantifying the factors will be identified and then an evaluation model will be developed. As a result, the assessment of the factors described in this work-in-progress paper will result into maturity levels for self-organized teams. The maturity model must then be evaluated and finally provides valuable development paths for BPM teams. Initial evaluations with a prototypically implemented assessment questionnaire in a German IT company shows in a proof of concept that the factors provide good information about the level of self-organization. In addition, quick implications for teams could be identified. These steps will be the part of further publications.

## References

1. Thamhain, H.J.: Can we manage agile in traditional project environments? In: Proceedings of the Portland International Conference on Management of Engineering and Technology, pp. 2497–2505 (2014)
2. Mafakheri, F., Nasiri, F., Mousavi, M.: Project agility assessment: an integrated decision analysis approach. Prod. Plan. Control **19**(6), 567–576 (2008)

3. Kosieradzka, A., Rostek, K.: The multifaceted character of process management in organizations. In: Kosieradzka, A., Rostek, K. (eds.) Process Management and Organizational Process Maturity, pp. 1–33. Palgrave Macmillan, Cham (2021)
4. Badakhshan, P., Conboy, K., Grisold, T., vom Brocke, J.: Agile business process management. Bus. Process Manag. J. **26**(6), 1505–1523 (2019)
5. Franz, P., Kirchmer, M.: Value-Driven Business Process Management: The Value-Switch for Lasting Competitive Advantage. McGraw-Hill, New York (2012)
6. Moe, N.B., Dingsøyr, T., Røyrvik, E.A.: Putting agile teamwork to the test – an preliminary instrument for empirically assessing and improving agile software development. In: Abrahamsson, P., Marchesi, M., Maurer, F. (eds.) XP 2009. LNBIP, vol. 31, pp. 114–123. Springer, Heidelberg (2009). https://doi.org/10.1007/978-3-642-01853-4_14
7. Högl, M., Gemuenden, H.G.: Teamwork quality and the success of innovative projects: a theoretical concept and empirical evidence. Organ. Sci. **12**, 435–449 (2001)
8. Gebhart, M., Mevius, M., Wiedmann, P.: Business process evaluation in agile business process management using quality models. Int. J. Adv. Life Sci. **6**(3/4), 279–290 (2014)
9. Bernstein, E., Bunch, J., Canner, N., Lee, M.: Beyond the Holacracy hype. Harv. Bus. Rev. **94**(7), 38–49 (2009)
10. Qumer, A., Henderson-Sellers, B.: A framework to support the evaluation, adoption and improvement of agile methods in practice. J. Syst. Softw. **81**(11), 1899–1919 (2008)
11. Dikert, K., Paasivaara, M., Lassenius, C.: Challenges and success factors for large-scale agile transformations: a systematic literature review. J. Syst. Softw. **119**, 87–108 (2016)
12. Guzzo, R.A., Dickson, M.W.: Teams in organizations: recent research on performance and effectiveness. Annu. Rev. Psychol. **47**, 307–338 (1996)
13. Lederer, M., Schott, P., Knapp, J.: The digital future has many names - how business process management drives the digital transformation. In: Proceedings of the 6th International Conference on Industrial Technology and Management, pp. 22–26 (2017)
14. Sidky, A., Arthur, J., Bohner, S.: A disciplined approach to adopting agile practices: the agile adoption framework. Innov. Syst. Softw. Eng. **3**(3), 203–216 (2007). https://doi.org/10.1007/s11334-007-0026-z
15. Rohunen, A., Rodriguez, P., Kuvaja, P., Krzanik, L., Markkula, J.: Approaches to agile adoption in large settings: a comparison of the results from a literature analysis and an industrial inventory. In: Ali Babar, M., Vierimaa, M., Oivo, M. (eds.) PROFES 2010. LNCS, vol. 6156, pp. 77–91. Springer, Heidelberg (2010). https://doi.org/10.1007/978-3-642-13792-1_8
16. Hoda, R., Noble, J.: Becoming agile - a grounded theory of agile transitions in practice. In: Proceedings of the 39th International Conference on Software Engineering, pp. 141–151 (2017)
17. Culha, D., Dogru, A.: Towards an agile methodology for business process development. In: Proceedings of the International Conference on Subject-Oriented Business Process Management, pp. 133–142 (2014)
18. Schmitt, A., Hörner, A.: Systematic literature review – improving business processes by implementing agile. Bus. Process Manag. J. **27**(3), 868–882 (2021)
19. Pflanzl, N., Vossen, G.: Human-oriented challenges of social BPM: an overview. In: Jung, R., Reichert, M. (eds.) Enterprise Modelling and Information Systems Architectures, pp. 163–176. Gesellschaft für Informatik, Bonn (2013)
20. Imgrund, F., Janiesch, C.: Understanding the need for new perspectives on BPM in the digital age: an empirical analysis. In: Di Francescomarino, C., Dijkman, R., Zdun, U. (eds.) BPM 2019. LNBIP, vol. 362, pp. 288–300. Springer, Cham (2019). https://doi.org/10.1007/978-3-030-37453-2_24
21. Kajan, E., Faci, N., Maamar, Z., Loo, A., Pljaskovic, A., Sheng, Q.Z.: The network-based business process. IEEE Internet Comput. **18**(2), 63–69 (2014)

22. Fleischmann, A., Schmidt, W., Stary, C.: Subject-oriented BPM = socially executable BP. In: Proceedings of the IEEE International Conference on Business Informatics, pp. 15–18 (2013)
23. Lederer, M., Meier, J., Heider, L.: A multidimensional indicator system for quantifying business process interface problems. Int. J. Manag. Pract. **13**(3), 295–320 (2020)
24. Mayring, P.: Qualitative Inhaltsanalyse. Beltz, Weinheim (2010)
25. Okoli, C., Schabram, K.: Guide to conducting a systematic literature review of information systems research. Inf. Syst. **10**(26), 1–39 (2010)
26. Gemünden, H.G., Salomo, S., Krieger, A.: The influence of project autonomy on project success. Int. J. Proj. Manag. **23**(5), 366–373 (2005)
27. Pinto, M.B., Pinto, J.K.: Project team communication and cross-functional cooperation in new program development. J. Prod. Innov. Manag. **7**(3), 200–212 (1990)
28. Morgan, G.: Images of Organization. Sage, Beverly Hills (1986)
29. Takeuchi, H., Nonaka, I.: The new product development game. Harv. Bus. Rev. **64**(1), 137–146 (1986)
30. Hut, J., Molleman, E.: Empowerment and team development. Team Perform. Manag. **4**(2), 53–66 (1998)
31. Salas, E., Sims, D.E., Burke, C.S.: Is there a 'big five' in teamwork? Small Group Res. **36**(1), 555–599 (2005)
32. Gulliksen Stray, V., Moe, N.B., Dingsøyr, T.: Challenges to teamwork: a multiple case study of two agile teams. In: Sillitti, A., Hazzan, O., Bache, E., Albaladejo, X. (eds.) XP 2011. LNBIP, vol. 77, pp. 146–161. Springer, Heidelberg (2011). https://doi.org/10.1007/978-3-642-20677-1_11
33. Hoda, R.: Self-organizing agile teams: a grounded theory. Victoria University, Wellington (2011)
34. Langfred, C.W.: The paradox of self-management, individual and group autonomy in work groups. J. Organ. Behav. **21**(5), 563–585 (2000)
35. Högl, M., Parboteeah, K.P.: Autonomy and teamwork in innovative projects. Hum. Resour. Manag. **45**(1), 67–79 (2006)
36. Hoda, R., Noble, J., Marshall, S.: Self-organizing roles on agile software development teams. IEEE Trans. Softw. Eng. **39**(3), 422–444 (2013)
37. Stray, V., Moe, N.B., Hoda, R.: Autonomous agile teams: challenges and future directions for research. In: Proceedings of the 19th International Conference on Agile Software Development, pp. 1–5 (2018)
38. Chow, T., Cao, D.: A survey study of critical success factors in agile software projects. J. Syst. Softw. **81**, 961–971 (2008)
39. Marks, M.A., Mathieu, J.E., Zaccaro, S.J.: A temporally based framework and taxonomy of team processes. Acad. Manage. Rev. **26**(3), 356–376 (2001)
40. Ancona, D., Bresman, H., Caldwell, D.: The X-factor: six steps to leading high-performing X-teams. Organ. Dyn. **38**, 217–224 (2009)
41. Cockburn, A., Highsmith, J.: Agile software development: the people factor. Computer **34**(11), 131–133 (2001)
42. Babb, J.S., Hoda, R., Nørbjerg, J.: Embedding reflection and learning into agile software development. IEEE Softw. **31**(4), 51–57 (2014)
43. Qureshi, M.R.J., Abass, Z.: Long term learning of agile teams. Int. J. Softw. Eng. Appl. **8**(6), 1–18 (2017)
44. Lamoreux, M.: Improving agile team learning by improving team reflections. In: Proceedings of the Agile Development Conference, pp. 1–6 (2005)
45. Kröll, M.: Innovations, agile management methods and personnel development. In: Proceedings of the International Conference on Applied Human Factors and Ergonomics, pp. 299–309 (2020)

46. Cinite, I., Duxbury, L.E.: Measuring the behavioral properties of commitment and resistance to organizational change. J. Appl. Behav. Sci. **54**(2), 113–139 (2018)
47. Thorgren, S., Caiman, E.: The role of psychological safety in implementing agile methods across cultures. Res. Technol. Manag. **62**(2), 31–39 (2019)
48. Schell, S., Bischof, N.: Change the way of working. Ways into self-organization with the use of Holacracy: an empirical investigation. Eur. Manag. Rev. **21**(5), 1–15 (2021)
49. Fowler, M., Highsmith, J.: The agile manifesto. Softw. Dev. **9**(8), 28–34 (2001)
50. Karhatsu, H., Ikonen, M., Kettunen, P., Fagerholm, F., Abrahamsso, P.: Building blocks for self-organizing software development teams: a framework model and empirical pilot study. In: 2nd Software Technology and Engineering (2010)
51. Whitworth, E., Biddle, R.: Motivation and cohesion in agile teams. In: Proceedings of the Agile Processes in Software Engineering and Extreme Programming International Conference, pp. 62–69 (2007)
52. Keller, R.T.: Cross-functional project groups in research and new product development: diversity, communications, job stress, and outcomes. Acad. Manag. J. **44**(3), 547–555 (2001)
53. Gren, L.: The links between agile practices, interpersonal conflict, and perceived productivity. In: Proceedings of the 21st International Conference on Evaluation and Assessment in Software Engineering, pp. 292–297 (2017)

# Are BPM Practitioners and Researchers Friends? Current Questions of Process Professionals and the Impact of Science

Matthias Lederer[1](✉), Stefanie Betz[2,3], Werner Schmidt[4], and Matthes Elstermann[5]

[1] Technical University of Applied Sciences Amberg-Weiden, Hetzenrichter Weg 15, 92637 Weiden, Germany
ma.lederer@oth-aw.de

[2] University of Applied Sciences Furtwangen, Robert-Gerwig-Platz 1, 78120 Furtwangen, Germany

[3] Lappeenranta-Lahti University of Technology LUT, Yliopistonkatu 34, 53850 Lappeenranta, Finland

[4] Technical University of Applied Sciences Ingolstadt, Esplanade 10, 85049 Ingolstadt, Germany

[5] Karlsruhe Institute of Technology, Kaiserstraße 12, 76131 Karlsruhe, Germany

**Abstract.** The well-known discussion of what kind of research is relevant (brings value to the companies) and rigorous (brings value to the researchers) and thus should be conducted in the discipline of business informatics in general and in the field of business process management (BPM) in particular is ongoing. In this paper, the authors contrast current rigor BPM research trends with relevant practical trends. The practical trends a collected based on a survey of process practitioners. It turns out that many data-driven research topics have not (yet) a huge relevance in companies; rather, management topics play an important role. Questions concerning the modeling of processes are particularly frequent in science and practice.

**Keywords:** Business process management · Trend analysis · Research discourses · BPM body of knowledge

## 1 Introduction

The debate about the tension between rigor and relevance of scientific research has been going on for decades [1, 2]. Especially in the field of information systems – to which business process management (BPM) will be assigned in a simplified way in this paper – the special value of application-oriented research is often emphasized [3–6]. This is demonstrated, for example, by the widespread use of the Design Science approach, which explicitly provides for the evaluation of results (artifacts) [7]. However, many participants in the BPM community will agree on the fact that contributions in journals and at scientific conferences do not always live up to this claim of applied research. Think, for example, of the (perceived) millionth BPMN extension that was never put into

© The Author(s), under exclusive license to Springer Nature Switzerland AG 2022
M. Elstermann et al. (Eds.): S-BPM ONE 2022, CCIS 1632, pp. 165–173, 2022.
https://doi.org/10.1007/978-3-031-19704-8_11

productive use, or the (far too) many meta-studies that, in the context of the digitization hype, describe existing academic results in new structures over and over again.

Nevertheless, the simple confrontation of academic rigor and practical relevance does not show the full reality of information systems. From the field of innovation techniques and also from data analysis, one can find numerous reports, case studies and concepts that combine both. For example, authors use scientific methods to solve a practical challenge. This paper aims to bridge the gap between theory and practice putting the current scientific developments in the field of BPM in relation to the needs of BPM business practice. A comparison and synthesis of topics is intended to show which BPM-related issues and trends represent particularly relevant research. BPM topics that are investigated scientifically and at the same time are important for business practice (e.g., when practitioners have a need for solutions and BPM consultants run many projects in the same field, etc.) have great potential for intensive theory-practice dialog. At the same time, rigor-relevance-gaps will be described, where either it would be good for researchers to take more application orientation to heart or where practitioners currently have open questions that are not yet supported by scientific findings – a possible source for future research roadmaps [8–11]. This article is structured as follows: We first describe the methodology applied, this is followed by a discussion of the individual description how the experts rated the relevance of the individual topics and trends (Sect. 3). Next, we describe a comparison of practical relevance and rigor in the scientific community (Sect. 4). Finally, we conclude the paper with a discussion and a summary.

## 2 Methodology

The methodology of this paper follows the study by [12], that related rigor and relevance in a BPM related topic in a pragmatic way. The starting point here is an overview of scientific trends that are currently investigated in the BPM community. The authors of this paper presented such an overview in 2018 as well as in 2020 at the S-BPM ONE conference [13, 14]. Like the previous iteration, [14] shows important research trends in data-driven (e.g., process mining), management-driven (e.g., modeling), and technology-driven (e.g., IoT) areas. The total of 11 topics emerged from a qualitative content analysis of conference proceedings from the major BPM and information systems conferences and were also quantified based on publication count (rigor) [13, 14].

Based on this, in a short survey (n = 39), process consultants, process owners, and other BPM practitioners (see Fig. 1) were asked about their assessment of the relevance of the identified topics (relevance). This web-based survey contained qualitative as well as quantitative components. First, the invited participants were asked to name up to three topics from BPM practice that were 'particularly relevant from [their] point of view'. This initial query was intended to ensure that the interpretations in this paper also use the terminology used in practice (qualitative). Next, for each of the scientifically based BPM trends, participants were asked 'how relevant the [...] topics are in current BPM practice'. The survey design was deliberately one-dimensional, with the same question asked each time: after naming the trend (e.g., 'conformance checking'), a brief explanation was then given (e.g., 'algorithms and tools that check whether models correspond to reality') to ensure understanding of the topic. Practitioners then rated the relevance on a seven-point Likert scale. All eleven topics were asked in sequence. The survey was conducted in early 2022.

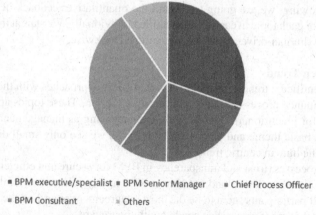

■ BPM executive/specialist  ■ BPM Senior Manager  ■ Chief Process Officer

■ BPM Consultant  ■ Others

**Fig. 1.** Distribution of participants (n = 39)

## 3 Relevance: BPM Trends in Business Practice

In [14], we identified a number of topics that academic BPM research was addressing at that time. We have assigned them to the dimensions 'People', 'Data' and 'Technology' (see Fig. 2).

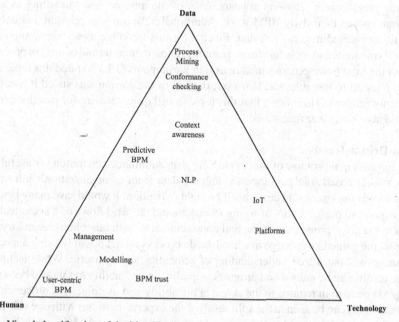

**Fig. 2.** Visual classification of the identified BPM trends into the three identified dimensions [14]

In the following, we are going to discuss the quantitative feedback of the process practitioners for each topic in each trend identified individually. We start at the left corner of the triangle (human-driven trends) and continue clockwise.

## Human-Driven Trends

In [14] we identified a trend to combine classical BPM approaches with the topic *management* to enhance process implementation and adoption. These topics appear also to be important for practitioners. This is again not surprising as management of business processes is a basic theme and part of BPM. Overall, we see only small differences in the topics of the human centric trend.

*Trust* in processes (trust and transparency in BPM for secure and efficient processes) is for all participants relevant and for almost 50% highly relevant. Overall, this is the topic where all participants seem to be the most in agreement regarding the relevance of it. This shows that more research is needed with this regard.

*User-centric* approaches (to involve stakeholders in the development and alignment of the processes) is also seen as relevant by almost all participants except one who rated the topic as 'not relevant'. However, over 50% rated it as a very relevant topic for their current BPM practice. This is the highest ('single') rating a topic got. Again, it shows how relevant the involvement of stakeholders is and that the topic should be taken into account for future research.

When looking at the answers regarding process *modelling* (manual mapping/description of processes in models) a similar still quite homogenous picture regarding the practitioners' answers appears. 65% of the answers see Modelling as a very relevant task in their daily BPM work. Additional 32% see it as relevant and only one practitioner stated it as not relevant. Finally, for this trend the topic '*managing of processes*' (methods and tools for classic planning, implementation and control of processes) shows the least homogeneous picture as four participants (10.3%) rated this topic as not at all relevant to less relevant. However, the rest of the participants stated it as relevant to highly relevant. This shows that this topic is still quite relevant for practitioners and should also be further researched.

## Data-Driven Trends

The fundamental promise of *process mining* – an automated generation of 'useful' process models based solely on inputted logging data from an organization's information systems – is intriguing and desirable if brought to fruition. It would save many laborious and expensive person hours of trying to understand the workflows of a socio-technical system via error-prone interaction and communication with other humans and trying to express the gained knowledge in a hand-made process model possibly using a modeling language without a true understanding of semantics and syntactic. While technically some results can be gained and progress in quality and reliability has indeed been made, some skepticism in regards to the actual applicability and usefulness of process mining remains. This can be seen in the split result of the experts' opinions with one side having favorable or high hopes or expectations for this trend (around 61,5%), while a second, more spread out group (38,5%), is massing around the more skeptical position towards the lower end. Which of the group has actual experience with process mining and the according result in their respective organizations is unclear.

*Conformance checking* as a sub-domain or off-shoot of process mining is conceptually concerned with making sure existing process instances conform to formally expressed rules, e.g. in form of automatically process-mined and then modified process models. This automated control mechanism is potentially equally, if not even more promising than process mining, but falls under a similar amount of skepticism and split in opinion. With a clearer application and utility scenario[1] though the skeptical sides is not as negative while the positive views are mainly not overestimated and simply evaluated as good. In numbers: Two again distinctive distribution can be seen at roughly a 48,5% to 51% split but at a higher mean value on the skeptical side with median of 3 vs. median of 2 for process mining, and only a median of 6 instead of 7 for the positive evaluation.

The uniform spread (roughly 18% for all ratings between 3 and 7) of evaluations for *context awareness*, in contrast to other of in this study, could be interpreted as an indicator for the hypothesis that the topic itself sounds interesting but is not that well known or possibly understood. From its denomination, a simple interpretation of the topic is about the idea that BPM activities, in general, and participants during the executions of an organizations processes, in particular, should at all-time consider a brought range of potential impact factors for their work and what impact their work will have on others. This is a good thing and important if applicable to everyday work. At the very least it is a natural goal to strive for. The research in regards to this topic covers meta-models as well as tools to support the complexity challenge that comes with implementing the required technologies (e.g. Internet of Things).

**Technology-Driven Trends**

In the field of technology, '*Platforms*', '*Internet of Things (IoT)*' and '*Natural Language Processing (NLP)*' crystallized as important objects of research.

Only about one quarter of the respondents attached little or no importance at all to *platforms*. In contrast, more than 60% rated it as relevant in practice from very high to high, while the rest answered neutrally. The advancing digital transformation not only drives digital business models in the form of platforms, but also process digitalization. The expansion of platforms into extensive ecosystems means that processes are increasingly being executed in the platform context. This applies not only to the consumer area, but also to B2B portals. Finally, the pandemic has also accelerated this development, so that the answers from practitioners here are not surprising.

The practical relevance of the *Internet of Things* as a topic is rated at 60%, which is similar to that of the platforms. Neutral statements only amount to around 5%, so that the rate for the assessments of little to no relevance is higher at around 35% and balanced out by a large amount of relevant ratings. The comparatively wider spread could be because a larger proportion of the respondents come from service sectors, for example, in which there are no physical devices that interact with each other in the course of processes and that would require handling technology that falls under the IoT term.

With *Natural Language Processing* (NLP), the picture is more balanced. While 41% state little or no practical relevance, 44% take the opposite position and approximately

---

[1] 'What are automatically mined process models good for?' vs. 'The system can tell me when rules are not followed'.

15% take a neutral view. Here, too, the opposing views can probably be explained by the professional context of the respondents. For people who want to use chatbots for customer interactions in service process automation, for example, NLP is likely to be of high importance, unlike for someone who primarily automate processes with Robotic Process Automation (RPA).

## 4   Rigor and Relevance: Trend Mapping

In addition to assessing relevance, the survey participants also had the opportunity to give open feedback on topics that they consider to be particularly relevant. These responses are included in the interpretation of the portfolio (Fig. 3), in which academic Rigor and Relevance are related to each other [12, 14].

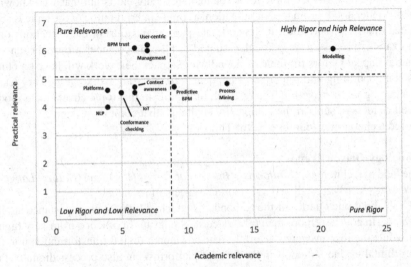

**Fig. 3.** BPM trends in the Rigor-Relevance-Portfolio [12, 14]

With their answers in the 'Pure Relevance' quadrant, the BPM practitioners emphasized that operational, human-driven and pragmatic questions often dominate. Questions about how people can work together on BPM projects, how process orientation can be achieved in general, and also how integration into other frameworks of the company can be organized (e.g., agile development, prototyping) are found in this field. Whether processes can be trusted and how people can participate in processes also is and remains an important question. In summary, this field shows that the management of the classic BPM lifecycle in the narrower sense (e.g., continuous improvement) and the governance of processes as a part of socio-technical systems is a core of BPM. Moreover, practitioners also subsume under the term *management* new tasks that are pending in companies and for which processes can provide a good basis (e.g., trends towards sustainability, digitization initiatives in general, cooperation beyond company boundaries, testing business rules, etc.).

A total of five trends can be found in quadrants of '*Low Rigor and Low Relevance*'. It can be seen that both very technical (e.g. NLP, platforms, IoT) and very business-oriented (e.g. context-awareness) issues appear here. The below-average relevance is perhaps due to the fact, that practitioners and researchers (e.g., technical faculties vs. business schools) may see BPM issues from separate perspectives and therefore the absolute numbers are lower. The open responses show that BPM is still a discipline that is in between two domains: Some mentions go much deeper into technical details with RPA and cloud orchestration. The same applies when management-oriented answers ask how continuous transformation of processes or agile change projects are to be realized.

In the '*High Rigor and high Relevance*' quadrant, only one trend is mentioned. The modeling of processes has a particularly high relevance for BPM practitioners and at the same time has the most scientific publications. Models have always had a special significance in BPM, because they often represent the starting point for any further consideration or optimization. Not only in training courses on BPM and in BPM books, but also in process consulting literature in general, models are mentioned as the common language of various disciplines and team members. Many other concepts that pursue technology penetration (e.g., automation, NLP), and also in the direction of human-driven innovation need a common basis for initiatives. In this respect, it is generally evident that the question of complete and syntactically correct models, which is also historically significant (think of ARIS or the beginnings of programming), continues to be of particular importance. In particular, however, this insight can be the starting point for further research because general questions about the quality or the creation process of models seem to be state of the art (established and known). Specific questions of BPM practitioners go towards using the models for very special concerns. These are primarily issues of correctness (e.g., synchronization, timeliness, and governance), reduction of effort (e.g., modeling on the fly, reuse of model parts), and comprehension (e.g., understandability). Many practitioners' comments also relate to the governance of process models, which inevitably arise as more and more complex processes are modeled in an enterprise. In summary, this means that modeling as the first and often particularly central task in the BPM lifecycle continues to have special significance and the need for good process models continue to increase. Modeling is to be caught between standardization (mentioned in the open responses) and the desire for an individually perfect notation (mentioned with many different facets).

The data-driven topics predictive BPM lightly and process mining in particular - appear in the '*Pure Rigor*' quadrant. Many scientists are particularly concerned with these two topics, but BPM practitioners do not see a particularly high demand for them. There are two fundamental reasons for this: On the one hand, the necessary raw data may not (yet) be available for advanced statistical methods, especially for existing processes in established companies. On the other hand, in the countertrend, research on data-based issues (e.g., data science, analytics, etc.) is a particularly important direction, especially within the hype on artificial intelligence. In the open feedback, practitioners used scientifically rather old terms such as 'simulation', 'benchmarking' or 'continuous improvement', which should also be organized in a data-based way. In summary, one can see in this short study that the belief in higher data-based practices has probably not yet arrived in business practice. Exceptions in repetitive processes (e.g. mass production) are present, but practitioners seem already to be helped by well-known frameworks (e.g. TQM, Six Sigma, etc.) in these cases.

Summarizing the interpretation, we find that modeling is the essential foundation and starting point for BPM and any kind of digitization. Therefore, it is still relevant for industry and academia. As an implication, it can be concluded that modeling should be taught and trained intensively and that there must be more ways to easily transform different models. Moreover, there seems to be a gap between management and IT regarding BPM in many areas. One reason why data-driven topics, for example, are currently comparatively unimportant in practice could be that while they provide important objective diagnostic information such as bottlenecks or unnecessary process variants, experienced practitioners often tend to trust their gut feeling. Additionally, the meaningful interpretation of the obtained analysis information and the design of optimization measures still requires human creativity and the personal experience background (e.g. of the process owner). Therefore, viable methods and tools that provide a bridge between IT and management are still needed.

Overall, it seems that - simply speaking - academia focuses on modern and sometimes fancy topics, while industry, however, has pragmatic and sometimes long-known problems. This provides an indication that more empirical research (e.g., in the form of action research) would be useful.

## 5   Discussion and Summary

In this paper we presented a short study about current relevant topics in daily BPM practices and relate the results to our older studies regarding BPM research in order to compare academic rigor and practical relevance. This said, we have to admit that the practitioner study could, of course, not go as deep as the academic study went. Due to the fact that we did not want to stress the time of the process practitioners, we could not go into details regarding each topic and the actual implementation of it in the daily BPM practices, e.g. how is trust in process handled in companies, why is it an important topic, what a BPM approaches they use etc. This remains future work. Moreover, as our study has quite a small number of only German speaking participants we cannot generalize our findings. However, this is not our intention. We only want to emphasize that both are important, relevance and rigor and we want to show current trends in both areas.

To summarize, providing an overall interpretation, we might state that relevance and rigor are both quite diverse and already focusing on many small-scale or advanced issues. However, the BPM core, namely, to organize the recording, optimization and implementation of good cross-functional processes remains relevant and at the focus of practitioners in Germany.

## References

1. Sidor, J.: Debate over rigor and relevance in scientific study of management. Manag. Bus. Adm. **23**(3), 32–46 (2015)
2. Daft, R.L., Lewin, A.Y.: Can organization studies begin to break out of the normal science straitjacket? Organ. Sci. **1**(1), 1–9 (1990)

3. Hidding, G.J.: Information systems as a professional discipline: focus on the management of information technology. J. Organ. Comput. Electron. Commer. **22**(4), 347–360 (2012)

4. Drechsler, A.: Design science as design of social systems - implications for information systems research. J. Inf. Technol. Theory Appl. **14**(4), 5–26 (2014)

5. Nunamaker, J.F., Briggs, R.O., Derrick, D.C., Schwabe, G.: The last research mile: achieving both rigor and relevance in information systems research. J. Manag. Inf. Syst. **32**(3), 10–47 (2015)

6. Palvia, P., Mao, E., Salam, A.F., Soliman, K.: Management information systems research: what's there in a methodology? Commun. Assoc. Inf. Syst. **11**, 289–309 (2003)

7. Hevner, A., March, S., Park, J., Ram, S.: Design science in information systems research. MIS Q. **21**(8), 75–105 (2004)

8. Leyer, M., Vogel, L., Moormann, J.: Twenty years research on lean management in services: results from a meta-review. Int. J. Serv. Oper. Manag. **21**(4), 389–419 (2015)

9. Ahmad, T., Van Looy, A.: Business process management and digital innovations: a systematic literature review. Sustainability **12**(17), 6827 (2020)

10. Lederer, M.: What's going to happen to business process management? Current status and future of a discipline. In: Proceedings of the S-BPM ONE 2019. CEUR, Sevilla (2019)

11. Lederer, M., Schott, P., Knapp, J.: The digital future has many names - how business process management drives the digital transformation. In: Proceedings of the 6th International Conference on Industrial Technology and Management. IEEE, Cambridge (2017)

12. Quitt, A., Groher, E., Lederer, M.: Rigour versus relevance for purchasing trends and processes: an analysis of how research trends and business needs are in line. J. Supply Chain Manag. Logist. Procure. **3**(3), 294–306 (2021)

13. Lederer, M., Betz, S., Schmidt, W.: Digital transformation, smart factories, and virtual design - contributions of subject orientation. In: Proceedings of the S-BPM ONE 2018. ACM, New York (2018)

14. Lederer, M., Elstermann, M., Betz, S., Schmidt, W.: Technology-, human-, and data-driven developments in business process management: a literature analysis. In: Freitag, M., Kinra, A., Kotzab, H., Kreowski, H.-J., Thoben, K.-D. (eds.) S-BPM ONE 2020. CCIS, vol. 1278, pp. 217–231. Springer, Cham (2020). https://doi.org/10.1007/978-3-030-64351-5_15

# Author Index

Printed in the United States
by Baker & Taylor Publisher Services

Printed in the United States
by Baker & Taylor Publisher Services